Vote and Voice

Wendy B. Sharer

VOTE AND VOICE

Women's Organizations and

Political Literacy, 1915–1930

Southern Illinois University Press

Carbondale

Publication partially supported by the Office of Research, Economic Development, and
Community Engagement at East Carolina University.

Library of Congress Cataloging-in-Publication Data
Sharer, Wendy B.
Vote and voice : women's organizations and political literacy, 1915–1930 / Wendy B. Sharer.
p. cm. — (Studies in rhetorics and feminisms)
Includes bibliographical references and index.
1. Women in politics—United States. 2. Women's International League for Peace and
Freedom. 3. League of Women Voters (U.S.) I. Title. II. Series.
HQ1236.5.U6S468 2004
305.42'0973—dc22
ISBN 0-8093-2588-8 (cloth : alk. paper)   2004004853

Printed on recycled paper. ♻

For my mother and my grandmother

Contents

Illustrations

Acknowledgments

It is impossible for me to think of this text as "my" book because I have drawn extensively on the resources of others. I can only attempt to thank most of them here.

First, I am deeply indebted to my mentor and friend Cheryl Glenn, who provided constant support and insightful feedback through many earlier versions of this manuscript. Heartfelt thanks also go to Don Bialostosky, Steve Browne, Sharon Crowley, and Jack Selzer for stimulating my thinking and keeping me on track while I worked on this project at Penn State University. It has been a true privilege to work with each of them. I was also fortunate enough to work with some wonderful people at Syracuse University. I am especially grateful to Louise Wetherbee Phelps, who introduced me to a fascinating field, and to Catherine Smith, who continues to share her brilliant ideas with me.

This project would not have been possible without the financial support I received from several sources. My archival work at the Schlesinger Library, the Library of Congress, and the Swarthmore College Peace Collection was supported by funds from the Research and Graduate Studies Office and the Institute for Arts and Humanistic Studies at Penn State University. A fellowship from the Spencer Foundation for Research in Education allowed me to focus on writing for an entire academic year—a luxury I appreciate beyond words. I am also indebted to the many wonderful people at the Spencer Foundation for putting me in contact with Linda Brodkey, who has also provided valuable feedback on my work. Additional research on Julia Grace Wales and time for final revisions of this manuscript were enabled by a Summer Research/Creative Activity Award from the College of Arts and Science at East Carolina University. I would like also to thank Keats Sparrow, Dean of East Carolina University's Harriot College of Arts and Sciences, for a teaching release that allowed for writing time, and Thomas Feldbush, Vice Chancellor for Research, Economic Development, and Community Engagement at East Carolina University, for his office's financial support of this project.

Thanks are due to the many people who have helped me find my way in the archives. Archival records—notes, typescripts, clippings, photos, etc.—are at the heart of this project, and I am grateful to those who helped me locate and use them. Thanks to Ellen Shea and the staff of the Schlesinger

Library on the History of Women; Wendy Chmielewski and the staff at the Swarthmore College Peace Collection; Patrick Kerwin and the staff of the Manuscript Division at the Library of Congress; Lyndsey Farrington, Shirley Ponomareff, and Gretchen Knell at the League of Women Voters of the United States; Stacey Patricoski at the League of Women Voters of Illinois; the staff of Photoduplication Services at the National Archives of Canada; and Patricia Bakunas at the University of Chicago Library, Special Collections Department.

Thanks are also due to Studies in Rhetorics and Feminisms series editor Shirley Wilson Logan for her useful suggestions as I revised this book and to Karl Kageff, executive editor at Southern Illinois University Press, for his tremendous patience and helpful responses to all of my questions.

Of course I would never have finished this book without the assistance of my family and friends. Many wonderful colleagues in the Department of English at East Carolina University have helped me complete this project with their useful feedback and an occasional shoulder to cry on. Invaluable encouragement also came from my dear friends Laura Sitterley, Amelia Devin Freedman, and Erica Rosen. Many thanks to my brother, Brian, whose humor kept my spirits up and to my mother, Carolyn, whose unwavering confidence in me has kept me going. Finally, loving thanks are due to my wonderful husband, Brent Henze, whose intellectual and emotional support amaze and sustain me.

Vote and Voice

Introduction

Boyfriend's Lament
(To the tune of "The Man on the Flying Trapeze")

Once I was happy but now I'm forlorn
O how I wish I had never been born
Left all alone for to weep and to mourn
Betrayed by the girl that I love,

I plead for her love and I beg her to wed,
She joins a new club down at central instead.
They call her a leader, I call her misled,
Alas and alack—and alas
Now some weekends are sacred to cupid, say some
But not to this viper in skirts.
She goes to a conference stupid and dumb
And when I protest she says "nerts"—O—
She floats through the "Y" with the greatest of ease
She helps raise the budget because they say "please"
She won't give me dates though I beg her on my knees
That "Y" has blighted her love.
                    —Song from the Volunteer Training Program,
                    YWCA Y-Dames, Bethlehem, Pennsylvania

The lyrics of this comical song for new members of the Y-Dames club in Bethlehem, Pennsylvania, suggest that the women who sang the tune realized the challenges they posed to popular expectations about women's behavior. Not afraid to ridicule those expectations, the Dames used the song to express their satisfaction with the educational and leadership opportunities the club afforded—opportunities to intervene in traditional patterns of courtship and to explore alternative outlets for women's energies. I begin with the song from the Y-Dames in order to explain the direct, and some might say personal, connection between this project and my life.

As many historians have argued, writing history is not merely an exercise in the objective recording of factual information. Rather, it entails the careful selection and arrangement of historical traces from among an infinite number of possibilities. JoAnn Campbell has remarked that the writer of a historical account "is never a disinterested, objective observer of fact but always a selector of objects and interpreter of tales, [and therefore] the writing of history requires recognizing the location of the teller, the impetus of her investigation, and her vested interest in the tale" (305). The "vested interest" that propels historical investigation often involves feelings of admiration:

> There is love here between writer, reader, and historical subject, and that love fuels the search for historical predecessors. As we articulate our individual relationships with the dead, we challenge writing conventions that would compartmentalize the history and historian, the text, and the love that produced and discovered the text. (308)

In a similar vein, Patricia Bizzell has suggested that "we perhaps need more discussion of the part played in the setting of scholarly agendas and the constructing of scholarly arguments by our emotions about research topics" (12). By explaining my vested interests in the telling of this tale here, at its beginning, I resist compartmentalizing the elements of this history and effacing the emotions that helped me to engage with this project.

Naomi Steward, my maternal grandmother, was a longtime member of the Y-Dames of Bethlehem. My brother and I knew that Grandma frequently got together with her friends and ladies from her church—her "old cronies" as we jokingly referred to them—and we assumed that these meetings involved teas, shopping outings, crafts, and other social activities. When Grandma came over, as she regularly did, for dinner and a game of Yahtzee, she never said much about what the Dames did, and we never thought to ask because we assumed we already knew. During my early years in graduate school, Grandma passed away, and my family faced the difficult task of going through her years of collected memories. Among many scrapbooks, postcards, and photos, she had also saved programs, letters, and yearbooks from the Dames and several other women's organizations she had been active in throughout her lifetime. To my great surprise, the materials included records of meetings and collaborative projects that were devoted to, among other things, reforming international affairs, studying political history, and advancing career opportunities for women. There were social activities of course, but these were not, as I had mistakenly believed, the organizations' exclusive or even primary business.

My surprise upon discovering these materials was followed by sharp disappointment. I had not learned about these organizations in my many years of education, and I had missed the chance to talk with my grandmother about how she and so many other women used collective rhetorical practices to participate in active citizenship. Too late I realized that my understanding of "citizenship" and "politics" was severely limited and, as a result, so was my knowledge of women's discursive practices of civic and political engagement. The prominent citizens and preeminent debaters of American and international politics in my history courses had been mostly men and, almost exclusively, individuals. In these classes, politics referred primarily to the "official" institutions and offices of the government or to partisan electoral activities. A similarly limited conception of "citizenship" in my education typically referred to formal rights or to an abstract, often militaristic "duty to country." These constructions of politics and citizenship, and the models of civic discourse and political activism they informed, excluded much of the collaborative, nongovernmental, extrapartisan political work done by organized women.

When women's contributions to civic or political discourse were addressed, the decades between 1920 and 1960 had been presented as a rather silent period—a period of still water between two "waves" of American women's activism. Because the historical accounts I had learned in school focused largely on individual, male actors within governmental forums and on large, highly visible movements in a "wave model" of American women's history, my education obscured the rhetorical activities and politically involved projects that had been central to my grandmother's life. The history I tell here is a response to the painful gaps in my education, gaps that, I fear, are still being perpetuated though the political and rhetorical histories that are taught in American schools today.

Spurred on by the gaps in my education, I began to investigate women's participation in collaborative rhetorical practices of civic engagement after the passage of the Nineteenth Amendment. While the Nineteenth Amendment was indeed a significant achievement in American women's political activism, it did not mark the ascent of women to prominent positions of political influence. Post-suffrage American women did not possess power within critical deliberative and administrative structures of diplomacy or partisan politics. Gender continued to play an important role in political participation as male partisans and diplomats relied on gender-based exclusions to keep women from holding positions of responsibility within political parties and official governmental bodies. Newly enfranchised women possessed what Anna L. Harvey has called "votes without leverage." As a result, many politically minded American women in the 1920s continued to rely on their previous organizational tactics of civic engagement, extending and transforming the rhetorical practices of suffrage agitation and other Progressive Era reform movements. The "wave model" of American women's history, with its attention to the suffrage movement, has had the effect of distracting attention from the ways women continued to use these rhetorical practices in their political work. As historian Lori Ginzberg has suggested,

> both before and after the advent of the woman suffrage movement, women . . . lobbied for new laws, sought appropriations for their organizations, and argued for changes in their own status—in short, they worked hard to influence the leadership of local, state, and national governments. The historical focus on the radical demand for the vote as women's only significant political act, however, has had the effect of both foreshortening and distorting the history of women's participation in the political process. (69)

This book attempts to change popular perceptions of women's participation in political discourse in the decade after suffrage through an investigation of the extensive, collective literate practices large groups of women used to create widespread pressure for reform even *after* they were granted official status as voters.[1]

Although I discovered several post-suffrage women's organizations that merit attention during my preliminary research, I focus here on two visible and active groups organized by prominent former suffragists: the League of Women Voters (LWV), founded by the last president of the National American Woman Suffrage Association, Carrie Chapman Catt; and the Women's International League for Peace and Freedom (WILPF), cofounded by leading suffragist and progressive reformer Jane Addams.[2] Both organizations relied on collective, widespread rhetorical practices to pressure for reform from their location outside of partisan electoral politics and traditional diplomacy. This book explores the rhetorical practices through which these organizations entered into and challenged existing structures of political discourse in the decade after suffrage. These practices have not received full attention in histories of rhetoric for a variety of reasons, and this text is my attempt to bring them to the light they deserve.

Beyond drawing recognition to the rhetorical work of these two groups, I also intend the historical traces I have gathered here to raise questions about what counts as historically significant rhetorical practice. My goal is to extend the work of recent scholarship in rhetoric and composition that questions how scholars have traditionally understood key terms in the field and that challenges how those understandings have limited historical narratives, particularly along gender lines. Joy Ritchie and Kate Ronald nicely summarize the questions that have driven historical projects that, similar to my own, seek to reinterpret rhetorical history through lenses that do not obscure women's participation:

> Since the language and conceptual constructs most available to women in the discussion of women's rhetoric have been the product of a western, male tradition, the process of recovery almost immediately demands resistance. It demands as least that women ask, Do these terms that have been accepted as givens work for women in talking about women's writing? Or are other terms needed? If this is the only paradigm available for talking about women's rhetoric, what is left out? What is marginalized? ("Riding" 230)

With the publication of several edited collections and scholarly studies, feminist historians of rhetoric have well begun the processes of addressing these questions and expanding the boundaries of and terms of inclusion in "The Rhetorical Tradition."[3]

These studies argue for the inclusion of work by women in histories of rhetoric in part by challenging traditional configurations of the rhetor that have informed previous historical work. Within traditional histories, women have been at a considerable disadvantage. As Cheryl Glenn notes,

> For the past twenty-five hundred years in Western culture, the ideal woman has been disciplined by cultural codes that require a closed mouth (silence), a closed body (chastity), and an enclosed life (domestic confinement). . . . Men have acted in the *polis*, in the public light of rhetorical discourse. (1)

Work by Glenn and others disrupts assumptions that women have not participated in the "public light" of rhetorical activity by chronicling the many contributions, long buried in archives, personal papers, and individual memories, women have made to the practice and theory of rhetoric.

I see my research expanding on this substantial body of work by considering not only how predominantly male constructions of the rhetor have obscured women's participation in "the public light of rhetorical discourse," but also how assumptions about what counts as a significant textual form have effaced the efforts of women in historical accounts of rhetoric. The occlusion of women's work from histories of rhetoric derives in part from the types of literate activity that are commonly identified as worthy of record in historical studies. This identification is often strongly influenced by a long-dominant hierarchy that privileges individual authorship and thus obscures collaborative rhetorical efforts. A focus on individual authors in the rhetorical tradition has been particularly detrimental to the place afforded women in the history of rhetoric. Women's collaborative rhetorical work, Barbara Biesecker argues, has been largely excluded by the paradigm of the individual rhetor: "The exaltation of individual rhetorical action is secured by way of the devaluing of collective rhetorical practices which, one cannot fail to note, have been the most common form of women's intervention in the public sphere" (144). In an attempt to revalue collaborative rhetorical work by women, scholars such as Anne Ruggles Gere, Shirley Wilson Logan, Carol Mattingly, and Jacqueline Jones Royster have begun to document the vast rhetorical history of American women's organizations.

That the work of such organizations has only recently entered histories of rhetoric and composition is also attributable to the trend within previous histories of focusing on academic contexts. In his preface to *The Origins of Composition Studies in the American College, 1875–1925,* John Brereton acknowledges the limits of institutional histories of writing instruction, explaining that the selection of documents for composition histories from academic institutions "ignores important trends in writing instruction by women" (xvi). Standards for inclusion in histories of rhetoric and composition have also distanced those histories from important literate practices outside of the academy. Responding to such distancing, Thomas Miller has called for research into "community literacies," or practices of information access and use enacted in specific locales beyond the university (*Formation* 283). This project responds to calls for research in community literacies by exploring the rhetorical goals and the literate practices central to American women's political activity after suffrage.

Traditional histories of rhetoric have also been limited by evaluative schemes that locate originality and prompt impact at the pinnacle of rhetorical success. Historical examples of rhetoric thus typically do not include the persistent persuasive practices that sustain movements in unfavorable times and that slowly, sometimes repetitiously, cultivate broad receptivity to innovative arguments. While the texts that generate notable public response and that have widespread impact when they are produced or delivered certainly deserve a place in histories of rhetoric, it is also important to remember the preceding rhetorical practices that cultivated a responsive audience for those texts. Notable texts—literate practices that are openly visible in the history of rhetoric because of the impact they had or reception they received—are notable largely because their writers drew upon the rhetorical resources supplied by previous rhetors. As Christian Weisser notes, "successful discourse in any community recognizes the types of conversations that have preceded it, the style in which arguments are presented, how interlocutors are evaluated, and what can and cannot be said in this community" (xii). Focusing on celebrated essays, speeches, and treatises diverts attention from the cumulative rhetorical power of everyday micropractices of rhetoric and the rhetorical skills needed to use them most effectively. Just as the "wave model" of American feminism can obscure the work of politically active women between suffrage and the 1960s, paying primary attention to "seminal" literate practices in our histories of rhetoric can remove a great deal of important, if not immediately effective, rhetorical activity from our collective view.

Yet gradual, multifaceted literate practices are extremely significant because they are often used to confront complex problems over long periods of time, and they have been central to the social activist initiatives of marginalized groups who face the difficult task of cultivating a kairotic moment for their arguments. By way of studying the literate practices used by such groups to increase receptivity to their aims, we can witness how potentially liberating forces remain alive despite oppressive climates. For example, as Diane Helene Miller has described, white married women relied on such practices to gain property rights in New York state in the mid-nineteenth century. When Elizabeth Cady Stanton addressed the New York state legislature in 1854, she urged them to amend property rights in marriage so that women might enjoy full rights independent of their husbands'. When the legislature failed to pass the amendment, Stanton and other supporters of reform in property laws "recognized the need to create a social context in which the arguments for women's rights could be heard and . . . acted upon by those with political power" (162).

In response to this need, Stanton and other supporters campaigned to raise public favor for married women's property rights. The campaign involved extensive publicity practices, as leaders of the property rights movement canvassed the state, delivering speeches and conducting door-to-door petition drives. Thanks largely to these efforts, the legislature responded positively to Stanton's arguments in favor of altering property ownership laws for married women in 1860. Miller suggests that Stanton's "opportunity to be heard, as well as the attitudes of her listeners, were shaped in part by the groundwork that had been laid before she even began to speak by many women activists working to publicize the need for the amendment" (154). Stanton's success relied on the extensive persuasive practices of organized women who collaborated to create a receptive environment for amending the law.

Another goal of the tale told here is to challenge existing understandings of politics and citizenship that have effaced the rhetorical traditions of organizations such as those in which my grandmother participated. In the pages that follow, I use the term "politics" in a manner similar to Paula Baker in her groundbreaking historical study of American women and political organization. Baker posits that, to encompass political activity beyond formal institutions, the term "politics" must be understood "in a relatively broad sense to include any action, formal or informal, taken to affect the course or behavior of government or the community" (622). Politics, according to this understanding, involves both the actions of officeholders and the persuasive work of individuals and organizations that influence the actions of officeholders. My understanding of politics also grows out of the work of scholars who have argued that a definition of politics must address power relations. Jacqueline Jones, for example, defines politics "as the system by which power, wealth, and justice are distributed within a given society" (110). In this definition, individual actors are not as important as the organizational networks in which they move and the larger effects those networks produce. With the focus of politics shifted from individuals to organizations, systems, and networks, collaborative work gains visibility, and the rhetorical activities of political organizations gain value in historical accounts of political discourse.

The historical materials presented here promote an ideal of "citizenship" as an active, collaborative endeavor based upon communication. Democratic citizenship, John Dewey argues, is "primarily a mode of associated living, of co-joint communicated experience" (*Democracy and Education* 212). Citizenship, in this communicative view, relies not only on the possession of certain rights (although these are important) but also on the dynamic circulation and discussion of issues of public importance. As I will examine in the following chapters, such a discursive understanding of citizenship informed the LWV's challenges to political parties and prompted the WILPF to question traditional methods of international relations. Both groups also considered active, collaborative participation a central component of democracy. The LWV and WILPF upheld a construction of citizenship similar to that recently articulated by Rian Voet. According to Voet, citizenship means

> having a political subjectivity, knowing how to play political roles, and being capable of political judgment. It means showing in your actions that you are not a subject, but a citizen; that you are not an obedient slave, but someone who is capable of determining, together with others, the future of public affairs. (138)

Promoting this kind of politically empowered citizenship was a central concern for women in both organizations.

My ultimate hope is that the story I tell will enrich histories of rhetoric and provide insights for those who wish to teach rhetoric and composition in a way that enables public participation. When I discovered my grandmother's materials, I was teaching my first undergraduate composition course and feeling that what I was teaching was inadequate for the kinds of writing I hoped my students would do. The lessons in argument, analysis, and grammar that I provided for my students were meaningful, but I doubted that I was teaching them the many rhetorical skills they would need to be active citizens in national and international contexts. In exploring the archival materials of the LWV and the WILPF, I found strategies and lessons that seemed to point in the direction I wanted my teaching to go. The LWV's early programs promoted what they called "political literacy": methods of analyzing, assessing, arguing, and changing the American political system. At the same time, the WILPF was busy teaching its members how to promote internationalism and how to communicate across national boundaries in ways that countered the traditionally antagonistic rhetorical methods of diplomacy. Both groups provided their members with rhetorical education for political involvement and both, I believe, can provide contemporary educators with useful ideas for engaging students in public discourse and for preparing them in the literacies of citizenship.

Here, and elsewhere in this text, I understand the term literacy as Royster explains it in her study of literacy and social change among African American women. According to Royster, literacy "is the ability to gain access to information and to use this information variously to articulate lives and experiences and also to identify, think through, refine, and solve problems, sometimes complex problems, over time" (45). Royster's definition of literacy is similar to what Catherine Hobbs calls "effective literacy," or "a level of literacy that enables the user to act to effect change, in her own life and in society" (1). In both of these constructions of literacy, the descriptor "literate" refers not only to the ability to read and write, but to the rhetorical savvy to participate actively in larger, more complex processes of information access and use. This is the kind of rhetorical savvy I was hoping to teach in my composition courses when I stumbled across the materials in my grandmother's house.

By way of archival research into the collections of both the WILPF and the LWV, in addition to the collected papers of several leaders of each organization, I have identified examples of literate practices these organizations used to challenge structures of political discourse in the decade after suffrage. Documents providing insight into these practices include, but are not limited to, organizational plays, study kits, handbooks and pamphlets, convention reports, and minutes of meetings where rhetorical tactics were discussed. I also study public responses to these practices as reported in letters, memos, and popular press coverage.

While I do include detailed rhetorical analysis of an occasional text, I am here most concerned with exploring the overall rhetorical assault perpetrated by these organizations. My goal is not to unearth exemplary essays. Rather, I examine larger processes of persuasion, consisting of a myriad of types of texts all working to effect a change in public sentiment, such as the change Diane Miller observed in her study of Stanton's address to the New York state legislature. With the hope that future studies will contribute more in-depth studies of particular genres overviewed here, I intend this work to provide a broad view of the types of literate practices the organizations used to influence the worlds around them.

Throughout this history, I consider how the literate practices of the organizations are situated in larger cultural contexts that determine their meanings. Thinking of literacy as situated discursive practice, Linda Brodkey explains, enables the linking of specific, localized literacy practices "to more remote and less visible but critical historical and sometimes even historic circumstances, . . . which also determine the social, economic, and political meaning and value of literacy" (6). To fully explore the situatedness of the literacy practices that form the core of this history, I have drawn on the idea of "rhetorical sequencing," a research heuristic articulated by Richard Enos. According to Enos, rhetorical sequencing involves four types of scholarly activity beyond the initial identification of historical materials to be studied. In the first layer of research, the historian identifies "the political structure, the social patterns, and cultural hierarchies of values" operative at the time of the historical materials' origin (75). The second task for the researcher in rhetorical sequencing is the recreation of the specific rhetorical situation(s) to which the material responded. In recreating the rhetorical situation, the historian "isolat[es] the exigencies, audience and constraints [in order to] reconstruct the context within the social dynamics of the culture" (75). The third task is analytical, involving close study of the text(s) in relationship to these social dynamics. The final step in rhetorical sequencing is presentation, or the historian's attempt to display the historical material meaningfully and engagingly in what Enos identifies as the "dynamic interaction" of texts and contexts.

My approach to the archival materials is also informed by my understanding of the members and leaders of the WILPF and LWV as participants in large, diverse, and gradual movements that were struggling on many fronts against contemporary social and political conditions. In approaching the historical documents, I consider the members of the WILPF and the LWV as participants in social movements aimed at changing restrictive practices of political communication. According to Robert Cathcart, a "social movement can be said to emerge when the languaging strategies of a change-seeking collective clash with the languaging strategies of the establishment and thereby produce the perception of a group's operating outside the established social hierarchy" (269). What Cathcart refers to as "languaging strategies," I explore as literate practices that established shared political goals among members of the organizations and that aimed to effect change in the traditional functioning of American and international political communication.

I also examine both organizations as examples of what Nancy Fraser has called "counterpublics." According to Fraser, there has never been one, unified public sphere; rather, there is always a "plurality of competing publics," each with distinct concerns and diverse discursive practices ("Rethinking" 61). Counterpublics, she explains, can be distinguished along several lines, including ideology, "stratification principles like gender . . . and class," profession, and "central mobilizing issue." Publics can also be differentiated according to the power each holds. The most powerful publics are "large, authoritative, and able to set the terms of debate for many of the rest." These "leading publics," Fraser notes, "usually have a heavy hand in defining what is political. . . . They can politicize an issue simply by entertaining contestation about it" (*Unruly Practices* 167). Or they can depoliticize something by ignoring or minimizing it.

Against these powerful leading publics stand what Fraser calls "subaltern counterpublics"—

> parallel discursive arenas where members of subordinated social groups [such as women, workers, and peoples of color] invent and circulate counterdiscourses, which in turn permit them to formulate oppositional interpretations of their identities, interests, and needs. ("Rethinking" 67)

These different publics "challenge, modify and/or displace hegemonic elements of the means of interpretation and communication" particularly as those elements affect what gets widespread acknowledgement as politically important (*Unruly Practices* 171). As groups of women seeking voice and power within the male-controlled "leading publics" of partisan electoral politics and traditional diplomacy, the LWV and WILPF functioned as such competing publics, challenging the exclusionary rhetorical traditions of international and domestic politics. Both groups performed the two key functions Fraser identifies for counterpublics: 1) to provide communities in which the members can support one another in endeavors to change dominant power relations; and 2) to "function as bases and training grounds for agitational activities directed toward wider publics" ("Rethinking" 68). I do not mean to suggest that the predominantly white, middle-class women who made up the bulk of membership within these organizations constitute a "subaltern counterpublic" on all levels. Certainly, many were bourgeois by race and class affiliation. Despite these "hegemonic" attributes, women in the two groups remained subordinated and marginal to structures, procedures, and discourses of political parties and international relations as a result of exclusionary, gendered norms.

Several lines of inquiry inform my exploration of the LWV and WILPF as examples of "subaltern counterpublics." First, I address the rhetorical strategies that the groups used to create a sense of common purpose by exploring questions such as those posed by Thomas Miller in his call for scholars to reinvent rhetorical traditions: "How does rhetoric help to create group identity and transform shared values into practical action toward common goals? And how is the formation of social groups shaped by broader hegemonic forces, including existing economic conditions, political relations, and dominant ideologies?" ("Reinventing" 33–34). Second, I consider the rhetorical goals to which the groups aspired and the changes in political discourse that they hoped would result from their persuasive work. Third, I detail the ways in which both groups trained members in agitational literate practices. Both organizations expended much effort to educate their members in the literate practices of political influence.

While I firmly believe these organizations are worthy of historical investigation, I have attempted to resist presenting them as wholly liberatory or free of oppressions of their own. Thus I also examine the limitations of the organizations' rhetorical practices. The leadership of these organizations, for instance, primarily included white, middle-class women—a fact that, as I explore at several points throughout this study, limited the appeal of the groups to a large segment of women. Not only did these groups struggle at times to engage women, they also found it constantly difficult to negotiate their positions vis-à-vis official political organs. While many of the literate practices women used to challenge partisan politics and traditional diplomacy were quite novel, those practices were often complexly intertwined with the literate practices of traditional electoral politics and international relations that the organizations were trying to change. Mikhail Bakhtin's work is helpful in understanding the kind of tension involved in the challenges these organizations posed to political discourse at the time. Language use, Bakhtin suggests, contains the push for novel meanings and uses as well as the pull of already established meanings and uses. Any spoken or written text, he explains, "is addressed not only to its own object, but also to others' speech about it; . . . it cannot be broken off from the preceding links that determine it both from within and from without, giving rise within it to unmediated responsive reactions and dialogic reverberations" (94). In other words, the challenges the LWV and the WILPF posed to male-dominated political discourses inevitably engaged those very discourses, sometimes relying on those discourses in the process of opposing them.

For me, the practice of pulling rhetorical traces together in a historical account is intended, as Royster explains, "not to romanticize the experiences of forebears but to observe and document behavior and to contextualize that behavior within meaningful frameworks" (228). Throughout this study, I have tried to maintain a balance between valuing and critiquing the practices I have discovered in the archives, always keeping in mind that critique is often a form of valuation. As bell hooks argues, "critical interrogation is not the same as dismissal" (49). Rather, critical interrogation demonstrates scholarly interest in and engagement with that which is critiqued. I hope that this project achieves a goal similar to that elaborated by Jane Greer in her study of socialist-feminist rhetor and educator Marian Wharton. Like Greer, I aim "to develop a rich, historically-situated conception of how the rhetorical activities of women and other marginalized people are a complex interweaving of alliance and antagonism, of free choice and restricted options, of accomplishments and failure" (249).

I have organized this project into five chapters. Because rhetorical practices do not originate in a void, I examine the history of literate practices among American women's political organizations in chapter 1. What traditions informed the rhetorical tactics embraced by the LWV and the WILPF in their challenges to the status quo? What previous collective work— through abolition and racial uplift organizations, temperance societies, suffrage organizations, women's clubs, and settlement houses—weighed most heavily in the educational and persuasive practices employed by the two organizations? My aim in setting up these traditions of women's collective rhetorical activity is not to suggest that women have an inherent proclivity for collective practice. In fact, both organizations used practices familiar to organizations of men and often collaborated with other groups, both of men and of mixed membership. I wish instead to do as Royster has in her study of literacy and social change among nineteenth-century African American women: to

> identify and to contextualize general patterns of literate behavior, . . . to document and account for what was accomplished by elite . . . women as a cadre of educated professional women, and to suggest how their activities might connect . . . to the practices of others both before and after them in the making of various traditions. (8)

Following this historical overview, I dedicate two chapters each to the WILPF and the LWV. In the first chapter about each organization, chapters 2 and 4, I examine the formation of each organization and the rhetorical reforms each wished to enact within political structures. Chapter 2 examines the WILPF's goals to incorporate women's voices into international relations and to expand opportunities for collaboration and negotiation in diplomatic arenas. Chapter 4 focuses on the rhetorical changes the LWV hoped to promote in American politics, particularly through the establishment of nonpartisan channels of political information and through extensive educational campaigns promoting "political literacy."

In the second chapter about each organization, chapters 3 and 5, I examine the rhetorical tactics each organization used to promote these reforms, paying particular attention to how those practices both challenged and reinforced traditional models of political discourse. I conclude by considering how the rhetorical practices of political engagement used by the WILPF and LWV might inform current pedagogy in composition and rhetoric. It is my hope that this history might contribute to twenty-first-century efforts to help students emerge from courses in composition and rhetoric not only able to write for school and work but also able to use writing and rhetoric to intervene in their communities.

Before Suffrage
Rhetorical Practices
of Civic Engagement

1

> Aristotle, 2300; Augustine, 1600; Ramus, 430; Blair, 200. The figures
> here represent roughly the number of years scholars have focused on
> these canonical icons. . . . By contrast, feminist scholars have spent a few
> decades recovering information about women's rhetoric. Even this short
> time has allowed for a recognition and esteem for women rhetors and
> their rhetorical distinctions that validates women and gives credence to
> beliefs that women were active participants in a tradition long conceded
> to men.
>
> —Carol Mattingly, "Telling Evidence:
> Rethinking What Counts in Rhetoric"

Scholars have recently begun to pay a good deal of attention to the reading, writing, and speaking practices of American women's organizations, particularly as those practices developed before suffrage. Prior to the Nineteenth Amendment, scholars have suggested, women formed extensive networks to explore political issues such as slavery, suffrage, temperance, and the conditions of labor in industry.[1] Through these organizations, women entered wider conversations about political affairs by publicizing issues that received insufficient attention from politicians and the popular press. Drawing on Carroll Smith-Rosenberg's study of women's political participation in the nineteenth and early twentieth centuries, Vicki Ricks notes that these women's organizations "were 'effective manipulators of public opinion' and soon became 'expert' at social change" (67).

Cultivating widespread political influence—what Ricks refers to as manipulating public opinion—served as American women's primary method of political intervention prior to their enfranchisement. While some of the more elite nineteenth-century female benevolent organizations had access to political influence through husbands or other male family members, most women lacked power within important arenas of politics. As I will explain in greater detail in chapters to follow, women discovered that enfranchisement did not grant them power within established institutions of government. Many newly enfranchised women thus continued to rely on pre-suffrage rhetorical practices of collaborative, widespread persuasion. As they struggled to make a difference in and through political structures that had been constructed around their exclusion, women in post-suffrage organizations such as the LWV and the WILPF adapted publicizing tactics familiar to them through their previous organizational work. What rhetorical practices, drawn from previous organizational work, were of particular importance for post-suffrage organizations like the WILPF and the LWV as they struggled for power in arenas of political decision making? In this chapter, I consider some of the rhetorical traditions within which the WILPF and the LWV developed.[2]

Traditions of Influence Before 1920

While women's work in American political organizations dates back to colonial times and involves an immense array of objectives and campaigns, my purpose here is to identify some of the most influential groups through which the women who would lead the WILPF and the LWV developed their rhetorical practices of political influence.[3] With this purpose in mind, I consider the rhetorical tactics developed within several sites of women's organizational activity in nineteenth- and early-twentieth-century America: women's benevolent societies and abolitionist groups, women's clubs, settlement houses, missionary societies, and suffrage and temperance organizations. Although these organizations are not the only channels through which women learned rhetorical tactics of political influence—several leaders of the WILPF and LWV received formal instruction in rhetoric at female seminaries and other institutions of higher education then just opening to women[4]— they represent the kinds of movements through which large numbers of women practiced and honed their persuasive skills. Participants in these organizations could practice and revise rhetorical tactics based on their successes and failures, all within an environment that supported their rhetorical endeavors.[5]

Benevolent Societies and Abolitionist Organizations

Female benevolent societies were an important site of persuasive activity for early American women who wished to intervene in social and political matters. Benevolent societies aimed to eradicate poverty and "vice" among the poor by eliminating prostitution, unemployment, and various other forms of "moral degradation." The names of early benevolent organizations reflect their purposes and the rather paternalistic approach many of them took toward their work: the Female Association for the Relief of Women and Children in Reduced Circumstances; the Female Association for the Sick Poor; the Widows' Society; the Female Society for Relief of Indigent Women and Children; and the New York Female Moral Reform Society, an organization that sought to reform prostitutes (A. Scott 14–16).

Nineteenth-century abolitionist societies also influenced the rhetorical practices of women who would lead post-suffrage groups. LWV historian Louise Young explains the powerful influence of women's experiences in antislavery work on that organization's tactics of political influence: "The rise of antislavery agitation in the 1820s provided women with the initial issue on which they were to have significant political impact, while stimulating the emergence of the formative generation of feminist political leaders" (35). Women's abolitionist societies gave American women some of their earliest occasions to learn and employ rhetorical tactics of public opinion formation.

To support their work in abolitionist and benevolent associations, women developed careful arguments to bolster their ethos, often relying on popular beliefs about women's domestic natures. Religious justifications were also particularly useful for constructing gender-based defenses of women's intervention in political and economic issues. As Anne Firor Scott explains, "benevolence [was] a quality good Christians were expected to exhibit, especially those whom God had favored with health, wealth, and standing in the community" (12). Leaders of women's abolitionist and benevolent organizations also argued that women had a particular responsibility to ameliorate the social ills of prostitution, poverty, and slavery because those ills threatened the family, woman's chief concern and her area of expertise. Women could thus defend their support of antislavery measures by pointing out that slavery separated mothers from their children. Antislavery and charitable work, in other words, simply extended women's home duties, in effect providing them with extra practice toward domestic perfection (Ginzberg 14–16). The practice of justifying political activism by linking it to protection of the home was a common rhetorical tactic for women's political groups throughout the nineteenth century, and even after suffrage both the LWV and the WILPF would rely on this ethos-building strategy.

Women's organizations also strengthened women's presence in political affairs through appeals to widely held beliefs that women were by nature more compassionate and morally pure than men. To avoid censure from political officials, women argued that the causes around which they organized were not political but moral and thus within women's purview. By separating moral reform from political participation or partisan advocacy, women enabled themselves to transgress traditional boundaries of rhetorical activity.

The Female Anti-Slavery Society of Lynn, Massachusetts, for example, suggested during its first annual meeting that women had an important role to
play in abolitionism because "its brightest and most distinctive aspect is a
moral and a benevolent one, and in this sphere it is not denied that women
may operate with propriety and efficiency" (qtd. in A. Scott 49). Socially
sanctioned stereotypes of women thus enabled women's abolitionist and
benevolent work to continue throughout much of the nineteenth century.
Remarking on women's participation in political rhetoric, Karlyn Kohrs
Campbell notes that "women have been unable to challenge social values
overtly; they have had to find ways to reinterpret tradition[s] such that they
support women's agency or an enlarged sphere of influence" ("Consciousness-Raising" 60). This situation did not change with formal enfranchisement, and claims about gender difference and women's moral nature would
be used by various women's groups to justify their entry into domains of
political control in the post-suffrage era.

    In addition to helping women establish justifications for their political
work, benevolent societies and abolitionist groups enabled women to develop and practice rhetorical methods of political influence. The New York
Female Moral Reform Society (NYFMRS), for example, distributed pamphlets to women throughout the community in order to generate new members and to persuade prostitutes to abandon their trade. NYFMRS members
chastised male patrons of prostitutes by recording the names of men they
saw going into brothels and publishing them in their paper, the *Advocate of
Moral Reform* (A. Scott 39). Many women discovered through antislavery
and benevolent work that publicity could also be a powerful tool in the legislative arena. The NYFMRS, for example, moved from publishing the
names of brothel patrons to lobbying the state legislature in support of a law
against seduction—a law that, although practically unenforceable, passed the
legislature in 1848 (A. Scott 40). Abolitionist women also became adept at
orchestrating massive petition drives that helped educate the general public through the face-to-face work of acquiring signatures and that displayed
powerful public sentiment to lawmakers across the nation.

    Other organizations developed important literate practices that exploited
the rhetorical power of statistics and social science research. Smith-Rosenberg
remarks of the growing use of quantitative research in the NYFMRS:

> by the 1860's . . . instead of filling its publications with exhortations to moral and
> spiritual perfection, it now published analyses of city inspectors' reports on health
> and housing, articles concerning milk adulteration, and discussion of the proper diet
> for the working poor. (41)

Detailed studies of urban conditions formed evidence from which female benevolent organizations could argue for the reform of local, state, and national law. Quantitative surveys of living conditions, as several scholars have noted (e.g., Black, Muncy, Kirschner, Silverberg, Fitzpatrick, Trolander), would become central forms of evidence in support of the political initiatives of various women's organizations later in the nineteenth and early twentieth centuries.

Organizational work, particularly for abolition, also revealed to women the importance of controlling communicative channels through which to articulate political viewpoints. Strong opposition to abolition meant that popular media channels often resisted abolition arguments, particularly if those arguments were made by women. Remarking on the mob-burning of a meeting hall used by the Female Anti-Slavery Society in Philadelphia, Anne Firor Scott notes, "Although all antislavery activity aroused opposition, women, defying popular opinion both by calling for an end to slavery and by speaking out in public, seem to have aroused particular violence" (47). As might be expected, many popular news organs were not willing to publish women's views against slavery. Women also struggled against sexism in order to gain authority for their writings within abolitionist presses. While women were regular contributors to popular antislavery publications such as William Lloyd Garrison's *Liberator,* their voices often occupied marginal or segregated positions within "Ladies Sections" of those publications.

In an effort to exert greater control over publications, women established their own organizations and published their own papers. Largely in response to the exclusionary policies of male antislavery societies, the Philadelphia Society merged with several similar female antislavery groups to found the Anti-Slavery Convention of American Women in 1837 (L. Young 9). From 1836 to 1837 alone, the number of female-only abolitionist organizations rose from approximately fifty to seventy-seven, reflecting women's increasing belief in their abilities to effect change without the assistance (or perhaps the interference) of men (A. Scott 47). Women's abolitionist papers included Lydia Marie Child's *National Antislavery Standard* (1841), Julia Ward Howe's *The Commonwealth* (1851), and Mrs. C. C. Bentley's *Concord Free Press* (1851) (Jerry 20).[6] Not only did women's exclusion from male-dominated abolitionist societies encourage the development of alternative publications, it also contributed to the formation of the first women's rights convention at Seneca Falls, New York, in 1848. The idea for the convention originated when five female delegates from the United States were denied seating at the 1840 World Anti-Slavery Convention. LWV historian Louise Young explains that the Seneca Falls meeting induced the transformation of local antislavery societies into local suffrage groups: "The Seneca Falls meeting occasioned others, and a number of women's rights groups sprang up, modeled on the female antislavery societies" (10–11). The organizational tactics and writing skills women developed through their antislavery work, combined with their awareness of male reformers' general opposition to their equal participation in reform efforts, would have a tremendous impact on the post-suffrage organizations I examine here.

Women's Clubs

Women's traditions of collective rhetorical practice also emerged within nineteenth-century women's clubs. National club organizations active at the beginning of the twentieth century included the General Federation of Women's Clubs (founded in 1898); the National Association of Colored Women's Clubs (1896); the National League of Women Workers (1899); the Young Women's Christian Association (1858); and the National Council of Jewish Women (1893). There are of course many others. Between 1890 and 1910, membership in these organizations flourished, increasing from an estimated 139,000 to an estimated 800,000 members (T. Martin 17). Many women, Royster explains, used clubdom as

> a means by which (1) to develop, enhance, and make manifest their intellectual abilities. . . ; (2) to carry forth traditions of community leadership that emerged from their own uniquely situated sociopolitical place in society; and (3) to gain an informal training ground that facilitated the use and refinement of their rhetorical abilities in public discourse. (217)

To develop cohesive networks among such a broad swath of women, women's clubs developed publications to enable the sharing of their ideas and projects with one another. As it did for women abolitionists, self-publication provided clubwomen the opportunity to counter the biases of male-dominated popular publications. Gere suggests that, for many women's clubs, "printing their own national publications and other documents enabled [them] to assume some authority in a sphere dominated and controlled by men" (29). In addition to providing channels to voice views silenced in popular media, clubwomen's publications enabled members to sustain extensive cooperative networks through which a sense of group identification could develop. As Gere explains, "Reading and writing for these publications helped individuals see themselves as part of an 'invisible community' that extended across time and space, making them seem part of an 'all-together' experience" (50).

Other scholars have demonstrated that the publication efforts of nineteenth-century African American clubwomen played a major role in involving women in the critical social issues of their day:

> The black women's club movement was also a site of extensive issue-oriented public discussion, as any edition of the *Women's Era* demonstrates. The pages of this periodical, published by the Women's Era Club of Boston, from 1894 to 1897, were filled with reports from the various black women's clubs around the country raising their public presence in current affairs. (Logan, *"We Are Coming"* 2)

As they had for white clubwomen, self-sponsored publications provided a vehicle through which African American women could challenge dominant sociopolitical power structures: "Newspapers and magazines helped the community articulate its own problems, deliberate its own needs, celebrate its own achievements, and identify strategies capable of effecting change in the larger sociopolitical context" (Royster 218).

Future WILPF founder Jane Addams clearly appreciated the extensive networks enabled by the rhetorical practices of women's clubs. In an address to the General Federation of Women's Clubs, she asserted that "the great function of the women's clubs throughout those earlier years [was] to create community of feeling and thought about the world and the way it works ... which is so essential in any effort toward concerted action" ("Women's Clubs" 28). Club rhetorical practices, Addams suggested, created a shared basis for discussion of important political issues and for influencing public opinion about those issues.[7]

Clubwomen also became adept at the rhetorical practices of circulating their texts to broader audiences. Work in women's clubs helped members develop more than the ability to write about political issues—it moved them toward what Hobbs calls "effective literacy"—literacy that "in its broadest sense denotes not only the technical skills of reading and writing, but the tactical—or rhetorical—knowledge of how to employ those skills in the context of one or more communities" (1). For clubwomen, effective literacy included the means of strategically distributing texts. The processes by which club texts were circulated, in fact, cannot be separated from their rhetorical force. The GFWC, the National League of Women Workers, the National Council of Jewish Women, and the National Association of Colored Women all maintained central offices to coordinate text-circulation and to serve as repositories for club texts that might be borrowed by club branches. Clubs also often developed methods of circulating texts through local institutions, particularly through public libraries. Members regularly worked with library staff to acquire texts and establish special shelves of materials relating to topics of interest to club members. Women's organizations, in fact, are credited with beginning seventy-five percent of U.S. libraries (Hobbs 17). For areas where free public libraries were not available, clubs organized traveling libraries or reading rooms that could be brought to the people they hoped to reach (Haarsager 156). Post-suffrage organizations would continue to rely on public libraries to help distribute materials to influence public opinion on matters deemed unimportant in traditional political channels.

To combat urban problems, clubwomen made forays into the legislative arena and, in the process, honed their lobbying abilities. For example, in 1913 the Woman's Club of Orange, New Jersey, collaborated with the state Department of Health to study milk safety. The club's secretary used state laboratories to test six hundred samples of milk from commercial sources. The club's published results revealed extensive contamination and recommended that an ordinance be issued requiring municipal inspection of milk. The club drafted the ordinance, lobbied for it in the state legislature, and succeeded in having it adopted. In a similar effort to discover and resolve community troubles, Atlanta's Neighborhood Union researched the impact of school segregation on African American children. Lugenia Hope, leader of the Neighborhood Union, believed strongly in the detrimental effects of segregated education on African American children and, in order to demonstrate these detrimental conditions, conducted studies of public schools. The dismal results of these studies led the union to present a petition, bolstered with evidence from their research, to the Atlanta Board of Education. Through the union's efforts, African American women gained experience in using print to "make their reasoning about the Atlanta schools public" (Gere and Robbins 668).

Clubs also served as sites for women to increase their familiarity with the literate practices of legislative activity. Many large club organizations relied on parliamentary procedure and followed *Robert's Rules of Order* at their meetings. Several women actually earned a living by providing instruction in parliamentary procedure to clubwomen. A particularly noteworthy example is Emma Fox, one-time honorary vice president and recording secretary of the General Federation of Women's Clubs. Fox's guide to parliamentary usage for women's clubs went through four editions between 1902 and 1963, with each edition reaching upwards of five printings. Following the rules of parliamentary procedure, clubs elected officers, composed constitutions and by-laws, and established committee agendas. Adhering to parliamentary procedure provided a means for women to write their organizations into "official" discursive forms, while also familiarizing them with the kinds of discourse they would encounter in working for legislative reform. Clubs helped large numbers of women to understand the formal rhetorical conventions of governmental institutions while at the same time preparing them to intervene in those institutions through club-authored petitions, resolutions, and testimony.

One of the most effective ways to convince legislators and policy makers to adopt a certain policy, clubwomen believed, was to create a widespread public demand for it. Thus, while numerous clubwomen focused their energies on learning legislative procedure and on persuading policy makers directly, many others explored rhetorical practices of public opinion formation. One such practice involved aesthetic and dramatic appeals to heighten awareness of particular social issues. Pageants—typically elaborate productions that mixed music, dance, and theatre—were often funded, directed, and acted by women's clubs in the nineteenth century. These pageants included performances such as

> the working women's national convention pageant detailing the history of women's work, the Mormon Mother's Day pageants, Mary Church Terrell's [of the National Association of Colored Women] Phyllis Wheatley pageant, the Minneapolis pageant for the Jewish War Relief fund, and the peace pageant sponsored by the Woman's Club of Sioux City, Iowa. (Gere 127)

Through theatrical performances, clubwomen involved others, even if only vicariously, in political issues that received little or only biased attention through other channels.

The pre-suffrage work of clubwomen encouraged leaders of post-suffrage organizations to believe that collaborative literate practices could lead to material and social change. Speaking at the Twelfth Biennial Convention of the General Federation of Women's Clubs in 1914, Jane Addams asserted the critical role of clubwomen's rhetorical practices in the push for progressive reform. Because they had devoted extensive time to the study of social and economic problems affecting metropolitan areas, clubwomen were able to advocate effectively for urban reform once the need for such reform became the subject of legislative attention:

> When . . . there [was] inquiry into the facts and tendencies of city life, it was again important that women everywhere had been taught the value of inspecting milk and foods, the needlessness of tuberculosis, the necessity of good factory conditions. . . . What a difference it made in the discussion and understanding of all these public policies that a million women all over the nation were already conversant with them and constantly disseminating information! ("Women's Clubs" 28)

Mission Societies and Temperance Work

Particularly after the Civil War, women gained experience in the rhetorical practices of political persuasion through several religious-affiliated organizations, perhaps most notably through the Women's Christian Temperance Union and home and foreign mission societies. Women in foreign mission societies in many ways paved the way for women who would form the WILPF by expanding women's involvement in global politics and economics. Under the auspices of religious service, American women in foreign mission societies "fought for the right of single women to serve abroad [and] tried to promote intercultural understanding" (A. Scott 86). These goals were advanced through carefully structured self-education programs in which women "studied geography and history, listened to returned missionaries, and made extraordinary efforts to understand cultures different from their own" (A. Scott 87).

Similarly, home mission societies served as places where women could expand their understanding of social, cultural, and economic issues in America. Women's home mission societies helped establish schools and conducted poverty relief work in the post–Civil War South. The American Missionary Association and the American Baptist Home Mission Society, in conjunction with the Freedman's Bureau, strongly supported educational work by women among free blacks (Logan, "To Get an Education"). African American female missionary societies were especially active in these educational endeavors. In the black Baptist church, female mission societies provided black women with forums for discussing and ultimately acting to confront socioeconomic conditions that oppressed their race. Women in these Baptist mission societies opened opportunities for other black women to study and discuss social and political issues and to learn skills for employment. These opportunities often took the form of new educational institutions such as Spelman College and the National Training School for Women and Girls. Mission societies, both at home and abroad, witnessed women studying and discussing the possibilities of new social and political formations.[8]

Her experiences in mission societies led Jennie Willing, a college professor and a veteran of the Women's Foreign Mission Society of the Methodist Church, to help establish the WCTU in November 1874. For the next five years, leaders of the organization devoted their time to speaking tours, letter writing, organizing local unions, and setting up state and national administrative structures. By 1879, when Frances Willard assumed leadership of the WCTU, the national organization could boast a membership of twenty-six thousand with one thousand local unions (A. Scott 96). Willard's work with the WCTU, Louise Young explains, had a direct impact on the methods later adopted by the LWV and the WILPF. According to Young, Willard "fashioned . . . an instrument through which feminist activism could be professionalized and techniques of public persuasion refined . . . and thus prepared the way for Carrie Chapman Catt and Jane Addams," the leaders of the LWV and the WILPF (12). Among the many active members of the WILPF and LWV who received training in political influence through membership in the WCTU were Mary Garret Hay, first chair of the New York LWV; Mary McDowell, second chair of the National LWV's Committee on Women in Industry; and Carrie Chapman Catt herself.

In many ways, the WCTU consciously planned for the rhetorical education of its members. It provided diverse occasions and venues for women to address their messages to multiple audiences, including Chautauqua classes, church congregations, labor groups, and prison inmates (Mattingly, *Well-Tempered* 62). Other attempts to train women in rhetorical tactics of civic engagement came through WCTU-sponsored "Training Schools," "School of Methods" and "Schools of Methods and Parliamentary Usage" (Mattingly, *Well-Tempered* 62). Through such educational forums, the WCTU provided instruction in parliamentary usage, press relations, public speaking, and special topics such as the "Best Methods of Influencing Public Opinion" (Mattingly 63). These practices of rhetorical education undoubtedly influenced the WILPF's international summer schools and the LWV's citizenship schools, both of which I explore later.

WCTU-sponsored rhetorical education also involved publications that taught women how to conduct successful meetings. As Carol Mattingly suggests, "leaders of the Women's Christian Temperance Union systematically encouraged and instructed vast numbers of nineteenth-century women in rhetorical, organizational, and parliamentary techniques" (*Well-Tempered* 6). Perfecting meeting techniques was not easy for many women, but, as one WCTU member remarked, the process of learning these procedures was often richly rewarding:

> How the women of our town loved [the WCTU]. . . . With what pure and single-minded ardor they gave themselves to learn to serve it, [to learn] legal technicalities, . . . *Robert's Rules of Order,* [and] the whole ritual of public procedure. . . . During those first years there was scarcely a meeting in which they did not more or less go to grief over parliamentary procedure. . . . And then they would hold hands and sing a hymn and begin all over again with the result that for precision and directness in the conduct of public meetings, American women finally reduced our Senate and House of Representatives to shame. (qtd. in A. Scott 101)

Learning discursive conventions of parliamentary procedure in preparation for these meetings provided members of the WCTU with a level of expertise in political discourse and negotiation, both of which were particularly important to their dealings with legislatures as they lobbied for temperance measures.

Work in the WCTU also taught women activists to regard the popular press with a very critical eye and to develop alternative sources to distribute their information. As Mattingly notes in her discussion of newspaper accounts of nineteenth-century temperance reformers,

> early critics often noted women's becoming "unsexed" by taking on public personas and concentrated on speakers' masculine or feminine appearances. . . . [E]ven favorable reports often focused far more on women's physical appearance and dress, and on their backgrounds and values, than on their words or on temperance reform. (*Well-Tempered* 97)

In response, WCTU members developed expertise in creating their own communication channels and building extensive networks of diverse women. Through its Signal Press, the WCTU produced and distributed a variety of educational books, pamphlets, and posters (Mattingly, *Well-Tempered* 4). Members also wrote and distributed WCTU periodicals to disseminate temperance arguments and to link temperance supporters across the country. The most widely circulated WCTU publication, the *Union Signal,* "linked women from many parts of the country and many walks of life, and helped build the movement" (A. Scott 96). The organization supplemented its publication network with county, state, and national temperance conventions. Through such meetings, women met new contacts, developed wider networks, and coordinated reform activity. Convention delegates often composed detailed convention reports which, when published and circulated through WCTU networks, helped even the most remote local union member feel like part of a widespread effort at social change.

Experience in the WCTU also furthered women's abilities to deploy gendered arguments about their unique ethos for political life—the same kinds of arguments that would inform pacifist women's arguments in the WILPF. WCTU leaders often couched their arguments for a prohibition amendment in terms of the benefits that would accrue to suffering women and children. These victims of alcohol abuse could claim a unique perspective on the sufferings it caused and thus were credible witnesses in legal battles over it. Women were both pure as a result of their distance from saloons and credible as a result of their victimization—two factors that served as sources of their rhetorical authority. The link between women's traditional, protective roles in the home and the eradication of vices that threatened the home became a powerful source of ethos for female political rhetors. As Estelle Freedman suggests, "the WCTU appealed to late nineteenth-century women because it was grounded in the private sphere—the home—and attempted to correct the private abuses against women" (517). Leaders of the WILPF would rely on similar arguments about women's unique perspective on military conflict in the years after suffrage.

Suffrage Organizations

In the latter half of the nineteenth century, suffrage organizations provided women with extensive opportunities to develop rhetorical practices of political activism. Like other women's organizations mentioned here, suffrage groups offered activists arenas to practice rhetorical tactics of creating what Kenneth Burke calls "identification" among diverse, and sometimes divisive, groups of women.[9] While the suffrage movement was long fragmented by issues of race, class, and tactics, the National American Woman Suffrage Association, under the leadership of Catt in the early twentieth century, established "formidable organizational sinews" (L. Young 14)—sinews that would enable the formation of the LWV and the WILPF.

During her time in the NAWSA, Catt learned the organizational skills she would bring to the LWV. A particularly important effort was her "plan of work" for the suffrage organization in 1895. The plan, according to Louise Young, "underlined the suffrage movement's shortcomings and called for a revolution in organizational structure and methods of work" (15). In other words, Catt analyzed the tenor of the movement and constructed methods to make its rhetorical impact greater. Her plan called for increased cooperation and coordination of activities among the seven hundred autonomous auxiliaries that made up the NAWSA. This goal, she argued, could be accomplished through extensive speaking tours, frequent conventions, active publications, and coordinated work among local, state, and national offices. Through these efforts, Young asserts, Catt "rose quickly to prominence, providing a moulding influence over the suffrage movement down through the ultimate achievement of the Nineteenth Amendment in 1920, and guiding its resurrection as the League of Women Voters" (14).

The WILPF also owed much of its original structure to the suffrage movement, particularly to the International Woman Suffrage Association (IWSA). In fact, the inaugural meeting of the WILPF was enabled by the mechanisms of the IWSA. This first meeting resulted largely from the cancellation of the annual planned meeting of the IWSA. Dutch suffragist Aletta

Jacobs, determined to gather women leaders from around the world in spite of international hostilities, arranged for a meeting of suffrage leaders to discuss possibilities for peace. Founding WILPF member Emily Hobhouse notes in her preface to the report of this first meeting that the gathering brought together women who were determined to prove that "the International Suffrage Alliance had not in vain been training women for years from all parts of the world to know and work with each other" (x).

Suffrage work also provided many avenues of rhetorical education for women, particularly in journalism and periodical publishing. Suffragists, Martha Solomon explains, "recognized the vital importance of . . . the periodical edited and published by sympathizers. Through this channel, the movement could reach, educate, and inspire scores of women who could not be tapped by other means" ("Role" 3). In all, no fewer than thirty-three suffrage publications appeared between 1870 and 1890 (Jerry 24). Not only did suffrage publications allow for the expansion of suffrage networks, they also enabled suffrage supporters to spread positive and encouraging words about their movement on the local, state, and national levels—an important ability given the largely negative coverage afforded the suffrage campaign in the popular press.

One of the best-known suffrage publications was the *Woman's Journal,* which ran from 1870 to 1920 before changing its name to the *Woman Citizen* and becoming the post-suffrage channel through which Catt and fellow LWV founders established the post-suffrage configuration of the NAWSA. Catt's belief in the importance of this national publication in coordinating and strengthening the suffrage movement is reflected in her assertion that "the *Woman's Journal* has always been the organ of the suffrage movement, and no suffragist, private or official, can be well informed unless she is a constant reader of it" (qtd. in Solomon, *Voice* 87). By 1915, the *Journal* circulated to forty-eight states and thirty-nine countries (Huxman 91). Information in the *Journal* provided for an extensive network of suffrage activism, even for suffragists unable to attend conventions or public debates about the issue. The *Journal* brought details of suffrage events to a widespread audience and thus helped maintain a sense of political involvement among suffragists across the country.

On the national level, the NAWSA strengthened its publication power in 1915 by developing a suffrage publishing company, headed by Mrs. Cyrus W. Field and Esther Ogden. By its third year, the company reported a three-percent dividend and produced both extensive and diverse textual forms of pro-suffrage publicity. In 1916 alone, the suffrage publishing company issued approximately five million fliers and, through a news service, sent press releases to six thousand newspapers throughout the country. Ultimately, the lessons learned from suffrage publication work—that "journals provided ways to keep members informed, to offer them arguments to use in their own work, and to reinforce their sense of purpose and progress" (Solomon, "Role' 15)—would be remembered by those who led post-suffrage groups.

The NAWSA served as a training ground for many other tactics of political influence as well. According to the *New York Times* in 1917, the organization set up a series of suffrage schools across the country and staffed them with trained suffrage professionals. These itinerant faculty members traveled across the United States, providing instruction to other women in "four essential points for suffrage workers: How to organize women; how to do press work; how to canvass voters; how to be ready with quotations from suffrage history and with suffrage arguments" (qtd. in Jerry 27). Through this rhetorical training, women could promote the suffrage cause. The idea of holding schools to teach women strategies of public influence would take root in the later work of both the LWV and the WILPF. The suffrage movement, particularly in the 1910s, also educated many women in literate practices of mass advertising and commercial appeal. As Margaret Finnegan explains, suffragists in the 1910s "incorporated modern methods of advertising, publicity, mass merchandising, and mass entertainment into their fight for voting rights" (2). Many suffragists learned how to integrate the appeal of consumerism into their persuasive tactics, selling goods and fashions that promoted suffrage and developing extravagant pageants, elaborate window displays, and star-powered moving pictures to interest the curious consumer in the suffrage cause.

The Settlement House Movement

Other women trained for post-suffrage political work through the settlement house movement in the late nineteenth and early twentieth centuries. A brief sampling of settlement workers who contributed their experience to the LWV and the WILPF includes Jane Addams, founder of Chicago's Hull House and first International President of the WILPF; Emily Greene Balch, head social worker at Boston's Denison House and cofounder of the U.S. WILPF; and Mary E. McDowell, director of the University Settlement in Chicago and second chairwoman of the national LWV Committee on Women in Industry. In addition, WILPF officers Florence Allen and Julia Lathrop lived and worked at Hull House, and original WILPF member Mable Kittredge resided for many years at New York's Henry Street Settlement.

Women's participation in the settlement house movement resulted largely from the increasing number of college-educated women at the turn of the century. This increase in graduates meant an increasing number of women were looking for professional outlets for their knowledge and talents. As Dorothy Ross notes of women's enrollment in graduate study in the last decade of the nineteenth century: "Between 1890 and 1900, the number of women taking graduate courses in all fields nearly doubled, to 30 percent" (158). Despite rising academic achievement, women who earned advanced degrees by and large struggled to move from academic study to a profession. The difficulty of this transition, Robyn Muncy explains in her study of women in social reform in the early twentieth century, resulted from "prescriptions for female behavior [and] lingering nineteenth-century feminine ideals [that] urged women toward passivity, humility, and self-sacrifice" (xiii). While a few women earning advanced degrees might take positions in the academy, choices were limited, and pay was not commensurate to work or qualifications, particularly at co-educational institutions. The struggle women faced in finding careers in social science, despite extensive preparation and education, is illustrated by the predicament of the first nine women who earned doctorates in sociology, political science, and political economy at the University of Chicago between 1892 and 1907: None of these women were able to get a regular faculty appointment at a co-educational university while two-thirds of their male counterparts secured such appointments (Fitzpatrick 72).

In response to these limited professional opportunities, women established new outlets for their social science expertise. The settlement house movement became one such outlet, providing institutions that served "as incubator[s] for new female-dominated professions and a peculiarly female professional culture that held public service to be its supreme value" (Muncy xii). The "settlement house movement," Judith Trolander explains, "refers to [the] practice of well-to-do outsiders 'settling' or residing in" buildings within inner city areas in an attempt to provide both daily services and larger organizing work for economic and social reform.[10] While both men and women participated in the movement, the independent living and career development provided through settlement work, Trolander suggests, was particularly appealing to women because it was acceptable under contemporary gender configurations: "since the stated purpose was to help the poor, young women who eschewed family obligations to be settlement residents could hardly be accused of selfishness" or impropriety (13). When restricted from participating in the established, male-controlled engines of social science, women found alternative networks that enabled their participation in debates about social and economic issues.

Through their experiences in inner-city neighborhoods, women active in the settlement movement developed rhetorical abilities in the promotion of progressive legislation. Settlement houses, in fact, often became centers of trade union activism for women because they provided a space for discussion of labor issues and an important safe haven from the economic weapons of exploitative factory owners. In 1891, after witnessing working girls teetering on the edge of survival, Jane Addams and others at Hull House formed the Jane Club, a cooperative women's residence where poor working girls could live without fear of eviction during strikes. Hull House also provided meeting space for wage-worker unions such as the Shirt Maker's Union, the Women's Book Binders Union, the Men and Women's Cloak Maker's Union, and the strike committees of the Garment Worker's Union (Kenney 22). The discussion of labor conditions and the organization of groups to address those conditions influenced several prominent settlement women to assist in the founding of the Women's Trade Union League in 1903. In fact, the Chicago branch of the organization originated at Hull House. Such settlement house experiences strengthened women's interests in labor and childcare issues and their abilities to advocate for legislative reforms in these areas—abilities that would play a central role in the WILPF and the LWV's strong support for the Sheppard-Towner Maternity and Infancy Protection Act in the 1920s.[11]

The settlement experience also provided many women with new perspectives on literature, theater, music, and artwork as rhetorical practices of political activism. More specifically, teaching in settlement houses led many women to see the potential of connecting artistic and real-life experience in order to promote political involvement. While the early years of Hull House saw cofounder Ellen Gates Starr hosting readings of George Eliot's *Romola* and Hawthorne's short stories, English classes slowly shifted to the study of literature that addressed concerns of the working students. Similarly, study of theater began at Hull House with a rather elitist mission—to teach immigrants to appreciate the "classics" of Ancient Greece and Elizabethan England. This elite study of "masterpieces of drama" was rather quickly replaced by participatory instruction in drama through the production of plays related to contemporary workers' lives. Participatory instruction culminated in the founding of the Hull House Players in 1900. According to a report in *Theatre Magazine,* the Players acted out "high ideals of life and society" through their presentation of "plays that deal with the serious moral and social problems of the day" (Weil 94). Similarly, performances by the Henry Street Settlement's Neighborhood Playhouse Theatre included politically controversial plays such as *Rachel,* an anti-lynching drama by Angelina Weld Grimke, grandniece of abolitionists Sarah and Angelina Grimke (Coss 12).

In addition to their educational projects, settlement leaders, particularly Addams and her associates at Hull House, promoted the development of new communication channels that might expand dialogue among various economic groups and, in the process, advance labor legislation. As Trolander explains, "The settlement workers saw themselves as bridging class lines by interpreting the poor to the rich and using their influence among the rich to better the lives of the poor" (15). Women at Hull House used their abilities in research and writing to publish numerous articles and books on the activities of the house and on the conditions of surrounding neighborhoods. Addams alone produced a best-selling text, *Twenty Years at Hull House*, and published numerous articles in well-known journals such as the *Survey*, the *Forum*, and the *Atlantic Monthly*. Trolander reports that a study of fourteen settlement house leaders in the early twentieth century reveals that, as a group, those leaders had published a total of at least forty-five books (15). One prolific leader, Catheryne Cooke Gilman of Minneapolis's Northeast Neighborhood House, reported composing over two hundred pamphlets and articles.[12]

Often, these publications reported observations and studies of working-class communities in an effort to procure legislation. Such labor advocacy provided women with experience in the power of detailed statistical study to influence public opinion and policy. Through work at places like Hull House, a class of professional women became familiar with rhetorical tactics of social scientific writing and its use in legislative influence. The work of scientific investigation for Addams and her settlement colleagues never meant merely the accumulation of objective data. Instead, as Catherine Peaden has suggested, Addams "use[d] science to better 'picture' the problems around her, all the while rejecting the increasingly atomistic, objectivist epistemology of science" by employing scientific methodology in the interest of social amelioration.[13]

Of particular importance in this development was Florence Kelley, who joined Hull House in 1889. Kelley was instrumental in initiating an extensive demographic survey of the neighborhoods surrounding the settlement—a project that would become the well-known volume *Hull House Maps and Papers*. Data from this demographic study was used by Hull House workers to argue for legislation regarding fair wages, working hours regulations, state factory safety and compliance inspections, and industrial homework restrictions (Kelley 26). Other collaborative investigations and reports undertaken at Hull House covered topics such as infant mortality, children's reading habits, cocaine use by youth, and the causes and prevention of truancy.[14] Through such collaborative writing activities, Muncy argues, settlements served "as a place where women struggled to find a public voice" (xv).

Through this struggle, Jane Addams developed several attitudes toward social reform that would be instrumental in her work as first president of the WILPF. First, she came to believe that a local focus, such as she had initially taken at Hull House, could do little in the long run to change the conditions that created poverty and unrest in the United States and internationally. While at Hull House, Addams learned, in her own words, not to believe in "geographical salvation," but instead to approach change on a much broader scale—the kind of scale on which the WILPF would attempt to operate. Additionally, Addams's experiences at Hull House convinced her of the centrality of communication to true democracy. John Dewey, a member of the Hull House Board of Trustees, wrote approvingly of Addams's attempts to improve the discursive conditions of the Hull House neighborhood:

> In these days of criticism of democracy as a political institution, Miss Addams has reminded us that democracy is not a form but a way of living together and working together. I doubt if any other one agency can be found which has taught so many people and brought to them a conception of the real meaning of the spirit of common life. (qtd. in Kellogg 191)

After Suffrage: Continuing Rhetorical Traditions

At first glance, low voter turnout among women and the continuing paucity of women officeholders during the 1920s seem to indicate that, despite all their agitation for the vote, women were not overwhelmingly interested in politics. The anticipated "woman's bloc" never materialized at the polls, suggesting to several observers then, and to a few historians since, that American women did not relish enfranchisement. Disappointing voter turnouts in the years following the Nineteenth Amendment, however, should not be interpreted automatically as evidence of women's indifference about political affairs or their reluctance to be political agitators. Viewing the Nineteenth Amendment as a turning point in women's political participation, as Nancy Cott points out, overlooks significant non-electoral activity by women: "The Nineteenth Amendment is the most obvious benchmark in the history of women in politics in the United States, but it is a problematic one for the viewer who intends to include more than electoral events in the category of politics" ("Across" 153). Naomi Black has similarly argued that notions of political participation that focus only on the electoral realm "provide no room for a definition [of politics] that focuses on educational, pressure, and, above all, nonpartisan activities" (243).

Understanding these low voter turnouts requires contextualizing newly enfranchised women within the rhetorical traditions of women's collective civic engagement. That women did not abandon these traditions and pick up the rhetorical tools of electoral politics is hardly surprising. Nonpartisan, non-electoral arenas of political participation remained extremely important for newly enfranchised women who faced what Baker has called "a period of party government and strong partisan loyalties [in which] party identifications and the idea of partisanship passed from father to son" (627). Parties in the early twentieth century served as sites for the festive affirmation and perpetuation of patriarchal (and racist) power structures, perhaps more than they did as places for political discussion: "Parties and electoral politics united all white men, regardless of class or other differences, and provided entertainment, a definition of manhood, and the basis for a male ritual" (Baker 628). In this male-dominated and transmitted system, women found little opportunity for agency and influence.

Carrie Chapman Catt's analysis of the women who assembled at the first meeting of the LWV holds true for both of the organizations I examine in the following chapters:

> When suffragists were marching upward, on the last lap of their century old campaign, they spied Old Age coming down the path to meet them. . . . Glancing over their shoulders, they saw an army plodding upward behind them, younger, healthier, stronger, much handsomer, and beaming with patriotism. The Old Ones spoke softly to the Young Ones, saying 'Hear ye, we are dropping an incomplete task that we can no longer carry. Come, take hold and finish it.' The answer "Aye Aye," unanimous and confident, came in quick response. The army picked up the dropped tools and went to work. (Address 1)

The literate practices of the organizations I discuss in the following chapters reflect this picking up of "the dropped tools." Although it proved impossible to maintain the immense coalition of women who had united under the suffrage banner after the passage of the Nineteenth Amendment, and although women had been granted formal access to electoral politics, women did not cease working together in political organizations. Indeed, the conditions that had initially encouraged them to work in separate, gender-specific organizations were far from eradicated.

The Women's International League for Peace and Freedom

Rhetorical Practices of a New Internationalism

2

> There is something in the international politics of today, which are
> managed by men only, which causes war.
> —Louise Keilhau, WILPF founding member,
> from report of the 1915 Congress

When Dutch suffragist Aletta Jacobs learned of the cancellation of the annual International Woman Suffrage Association (IWSA) convention due to the difficulty of travel in wartime, she summoned various international women, including prominent American activists Jane Addams and Emily Greene Balch, to the Hague to discuss possibilities for ending male-run wars that interrupted progress toward international, universal suffrage.[1] The women who gathered at the Hague in 1915 as the International Congress of Women for Permanent Peace (ICWPP)—renamed the Women's International League for Peace and Freedom in 1919—expressed dismay about the antagonistic atmosphere of male-dominated international relations. Many representatives at the meeting, including Addams and several American women who accompanied her, were in the midst of heated struggles for suffrage in their own countries and were deeply troubled by the disruption of international structures of suffrage support that resulted from the outbreak of war. Open international communication, Jacobs asserted in her call announcing the meeting at the Hague, enabled suffragists around the globe to maximize their persuasive efforts. Wars created by statesmen thus not only disrupted economic and social life, they also halted the progress of women's rights by shutting down channels of international communication.

Beginning with their first meeting in 1915, the founders of the WILPF sought to correct what they saw as fundamental flaws in traditional methods of international communication—flaws that led to militant nationalism, antagonistic diplomacy, and violence. The women of the WILPF wished to infuse rhetorical structures of international relations with literate practices of cooperation, practices that they believed were particularly well-suited to women. To this end, they initiated a campaign to alter radically the rhetorical practices of traditional, male-dominated international relations. In this chapter, I consider the rhetorical reforms the WILPF wished to enact within international politics during the 1920s, focusing particularly on the role American women played in defining and promoting these reforms. These reforms include increasing the presence of women in diplomatic spheres; restructuring traditional diplomatic bodies; revising conventional diplomatic procedures of negotiation; and transforming the role of the press within and across national boundaries. In the next chapter, I examine in greater detail the rhetorical practices the organization used to create widespread support for these international reforms. Throughout my analysis in this chapter and the next, I also consider the difficulties the organization encountered as it endeavored to present itself as a unified, global force of reform-oriented women.

Reconfiguring Gender Difference in International Relations

Chief among the WILPF's critiques of traditional diplomatic communication was the membership's belief that the exclusion of women perverted international politics. To advance their critique of traditional diplomatic procedures and to develop an ethos from which to argue for reform that would include women in the rhetorical structures of international relations, organizers of the WILPF strategically employed gendered social expectations to undermine men's exclusive claims to power in international politics. Drawing on the arguments of the previous century's activist women, the vanguard of the WILPF suggested that women derived their ethos for international intervention from their role as mothers.[2] The organization approached reform in international relations from what Mary Dietz calls a "maternal feminist" perspective—a perspective that "claim[s] that women's experience as mothers in the private realm endows them with a special capacity and a 'moral imperative' for countering both the male liberal individualist world view and its masculinist notions of citizenship" (387).[3] The strength of this perspective among women at the Hague is reflected in the description of the origins of the congress as published in the meeting report. In this report, British member Emily Hobhouse explains the origin of the WILPF through a metaphor of immaculate conception:

> From the moment of the declaration of War . . . the hearts of women leapt to their sister women, and the germ of the idea, nameless and unformed, that the women of the world must come to that world's aid, was silently and spontaneously conceived and lay in embryo in the hearts of many. (iii)

In a seemingly biological response, women became the mothers of peace, conceiving—in the absence of men—a plan to end war.

The WILPF also critiqued the exclusion of women from international negotiations with a related argument that, because they have devoted their lives to nurturing human life, women are more attuned to the human costs of war. Delegates at the Hague undermined the gendered divide that excluded women from international politics by arguing that men's historical development had damaged their ability to reconcile international disputes in a humane way. In her welcome address to the congress, Jacobs asserted that

> we women judge wars differently from men. Men consider in the first place, its economic results. What it costs in money, its loss or its gain to national commerce and industries, the extension of power and so forth. But what is material loss to us women, in comparison to the number of fathers, brothers, husbands and sons who march out to war never to return? We women consider above all the damage to the race resulting from war, and the grief, the pain, and misery it entails. (WILPF, *Report of the International Congress* 6)

Because women's work typically contributes to the initiation and preservation of the human race, the leaders of the new organization argued, women's presence in international bodies of political debate might counterbalance aggressive male voices. The leaders of the new organization believed that new rhetorics of negotiation, based on women's impulses to preserve life, must supplant masculine, rational paradigms of international relations.

The founding members of the WILPF thus argued in favor of what scholars have called a "feminist standpoint"—a privileged location for women's voices—based on an essentialist understanding of "women's work" as mothering and nurturing. While in many ways challenging exclusionary constructions of "women," leaders of the WILPF also relied on traditional understandings of this identity to signify a shared attitude toward pacifism and a collective, powerful ethos in the international arena. In her discussion of the use of such strategies by women, Nancy Hartsock explains how such a standpoint can enable women to enter conversations about sociopolitical conditions. The "standpoint" of women's lives, Hartsock writes, "make[s] available a particular and privileged vantage point on male supremacy, a vantage point that can ground a powerful critique of the phallocratic institutions" (231). Sara Ruddick, elaborating on Hartsock's theory, suggests that this standpoint derives from women's traditional roles as providers of "caring labor," including "birthing labor and lactation; production and preparation of food; mothering; kin work; housework; nursing; many kinds of teaching;

U.S. delegation to the International Congress of Women for Permanent Peace, held at the Hague, Netherlands, 1915. Courtesy of the Records of the Women's International League for Peace and Freedom, U.S. Section, Swarthmore College Peace Collection.

and care of the frail and elderly" (130). According to the WILPF, women's caring labor credentialed them for leadership in international relations.

WILPF founders also employed historical evidence to critique the exclusion of women's voices from diplomatic arenas. Leaders of the organization argued that, rather than hindering women, prior exclusion from forums of international negotiation actually empowered women to provide a much-needed perspective in international relations. Addams, in fact, justified the formation of a women-only peace organization by arguing that men's historical participation in military endeavors had damaged their ability to reconcile international disputes in ways that do not rely on force. Strategically employing Darwinian theories of evolution, Addams claimed that past impulses to military prowess remained in present man, ill-fitting him to address international disputes through negotiation and peaceful methods:

> There is one thing which the theory of evolution has given to us. It is very hard for us to detach ourselves from the past. . . . [As a result] it may always be harder for a body of men . . . to reform than it will be for women. [Men] are not quite free from the fighting instinct yet. (Address 253)

Addams concluded that women are better equipped by their evolutionary course to design and execute peaceful methods of conflict resolution among nations.

Since they are not hindered by a fighting instinct, Addams argued, women orators and writers are uniquely qualified to participate in diplomatic relations, particularly through conversations with other women who are uniquely responsive to appeals based on the sacredness of human life. Addams maintained that women belong in international relations because they have the rhetorical ability to "discover and substitute ideas, to let loose other emotions, to find incentives which shall seem as strenuous, as heroic, as noble and as well worthwhile as those which [have] sustained this long struggle of warfare" ("New Ideals" 107). Other founders of the WILPF certainly agreed. Edith Waterworth, a delegate to the Hague meeting, placed responsibility for the development and proliferation of these peaceful ideas on women rhetors: "Women writers and women speakers may do a great deal by dropping the seed of thought into women's minds, and making the fact that they are the natural defenders of the young, a permanent and active thought" (WILPF, *Report of the International Congress* 90). The texts the WILPF produced to announce its purposes reflect this belief in the importance of women speaking and writing to spread the idea of peace. The "Preamble and Resolutions Adopted" at the Hague Congress begin with an assertive articulation of the beneficent rhetorical power that WILPF members believed women might bring to international relations:

> We women, of many nations, in International Congress assembled, . . . come together both from the warring and the neutral countries, . . . bound together by the beliefs that women must share in the common responsibility of government and that international relations must be determined not by force but by friendship and justice, we pledge ourselves to resist every tendency to rancour and revenge, to promote mutual understanding and good-will between the nations and to work for the reconciliation of the peoples. (WILPF, *Report of the International Congress* 35)

Where men had failed, women might succeed, thanks in large part to the benefits of evolution. Throughout their constructions of gender, leaders of the WILPF established the term "women" as a universal marker of all that is opposed to male militarism.[4]

Challenges to Maternal Thinking

While maternalist thinking enabled many of the WILPF women to unite behind an image of a mother figure who would contribute an ethical corrective to male-dominated political structures, the approach had several drawbacks. Most importantly, it masked critical differences among women by ignoring how gender is constituted differently through class and race. Maternalist thinking "threaten[ed] to turn historically distinctive women into ahistorical, universalized entities" (Dietz 389). The identity that WILPF leaders asked members to assume in constructing women's authority as international rhetors was predominantly white, western, and middle-class. Indeed, a Eurocentric, middle-class bias was visible in the physical presence of the women who attended the Hague meeting.[5] What British delegate Emmeline Pethick Lawrence asserted as a virtue of the Hague Congress— that "there was nothing in general appearance to distinguish one nationality from another" (143)—can also been seen as a dangerous shortcoming. The observation reveals that, while the organization was "international," it was not tremendously diverse.

Appeals to maternalism failed to address the different constructions of women across and within the national boundaries the organization sought to transcend. Political theorist Nira Yuval Davis notes that "constructions of nationhood usually involve specific notions of both 'manhood' and 'womanhood'" (1). WILPF leaders did not fully consider that the subject position "woman" could vary based on different national climates.[6] Because of these oversights, the WILPF had difficulty employing what Gayatri Spivak calls "strategic essentialism"—the temporary suspension of difference for purposes of amassing power against oppression. The suspension of difference among international women was so fundamental to the WILPF's formative arguments that its leaders sometimes failed to see that suspension as temporary and strategic.

The erasing of difference among women was embodied at the Hague Congress. Mary Church Terrell, founder of the National Association of Colored Women and delegate to the Hague Congress, critically noted the whiteness of the meeting: "women from all over the white world were present, for there was not a single solitary delegate from Japan, or China or India or from any other country whose inhabitants were not white. In fact, I was the only delegate who gave any color to the occasion at all" (qtd. in Schott 134). In many ways, the white tint of this first meeting derived from the racism that troubled the international suffrage movement, particularly the powerful American contingent of that movement. As historian Lori Ginzberg has explained, the question of separating and elevating gender over race had led to a prolonged split in the American suffrage movement:

> activists had by 1870 divided over whether to support black male suffrage . . . or to work only for truly universal suffrage. Those willing to postpone woman suffrage

in order to work for black male suffrage formed the American Woman Suffrage Association. Women who insisted on immediate universal—and therefore woman's—suffrage joined . . . the smaller National Woman Suffrage Association. (183)

This latter organization even employed racist rationales in support of suffrage in order to gain the backing of wealthy southern women. The historical presence of racism within suffrage organizations surely lessened the appeal of any related organization to diverse women. WILPF leaders reflected this racist background, particularly through their expressed belief in the "backwardness" and ignorance of "foreigners." Throughout the resolutions adopted by the WILPF in its first decade, one finds numerous references to protecting or helping "the backward races." Despite their good intentions, many members maintained a view of nonwhite populations as naive and inferior in political understanding.[7]

The class privilege of founding WILPF members was also evident at the Hague Congress. The very fact that these women were able to afford the meeting—to cover the expenses of the trip and to expend the time of traveling and attending the conference—reveals their economic advantages. The published report of the congress also reveals the classed nature of the female identity that WILPF founders constructed and promoted. Debating a resolution that protested the violent measures used by some worker-revolutionaries, delegate Catherine Fuller stressed that the wording of the resolution needed to convey sympathy with workers, rather than strictly condemning them, because "a group like ours, in counseling against violence, must recognize that the only way in which violence can be avoided is for the possessing classes to give up their possessions and consent to the new order without resistance." Therefore, Fuller continued, "I suggest that the chief function of women like ourselves [read: not workers] is to prepare the minds of the wealthy and possessing classes to persuade them to yield without hesitation, and thus save bloodshed" (WILPF, *Report of the International Congress* 123–24). Fuller's caution to her fellow delegates reveals a gap between the new organization and the working class—the group is not itself representative of the working class; rather, it is in a position to display sympathy for them and to advocate on their behalf. Like middle-class settlement workers, WILPF leaders envisioned themselves "bridging class lines by interpreting the poor to the rich and using their influence among the rich to better the lives of the poor" (Trolander 15). The middle-class privileges of the organization remained visible throughout the first decade, particularly in the U.S. WILPF, whose newsletters often include details about teas, socials, and meetings at members' "vacation homes" (WILPF, *Proposals as to Policy* 1).

This class bias of the new organization derived in many respects from the class-based nature of previous women's organizational work. From the early nineteenth century, women's philanthropic work and the gendered arguments that supported it "served a powerful conservative function; . . . the ideology sought to mute real differences among women, especially the class privileges of its middle-class proponents" (Ginzberg 25). These gendered arguments ignored the fact that, while members of benevolent organizations perhaps shared a standard of home life, other women certainly did not. As Ginzberg explains, "For women involved in building charitable organizations, the rhetoric of female benevolence concealed authority that they wielded in the distribution of resources and services in their communities" (35). Concealing class differences meant concealing considerable power differences among women.

The WILPF's construction of women's authority could also be challenged in terms of the assumption that women were uniquely qualified to find peaceful resolutions for international conflict. Congress delegate Amy Lillingston issued this challenge when she pointed out that many women, in fact, did not desire peace:

> I beg to say that for every hundred women that were willing to come to this Congress, a thousand women are ready to go to France and fight. . . . We have been hearing a good deal about the influence of women on the destiny of humanity, but we know that most of the women are quite as ready to fight as men. (WILPF, *Report of the International Congress* 128–29)

Lillingston's argument, however accurate it may have been, was greeted with hissing from other delegates and was ruled "out of order" by Addams, who served as the presiding officer. Despite this initial silencing, Addams would acknowledge the truth of Lillingston's critique in a published reflection on the conference. "The belief that a woman is against the war simply because she is a woman and not a man," Addams wrote shortly after the Congress, "cannot of course be substantiated. In every country there are women who believe that war is inevitable and righteous" (Addams, Balch, and Hamilton 128).

Lillingston's challenge to the WILPF's construction of women as inherently peaceful is similar to Sara Ruddick's critique of gender-specific constructions of "maternal thinking." As a basis for peace, Ruddick has argued,

> women's peacefulness is at least as mythical as men's violence. Women have never absented themselves from war. Wherever battles are fought and justified, whether in the vilest or noblest of causes, women on both sides of the battle lines support the military engagements of their sons, lovers, friends, and mates. (154)

Ruddick suggests that arguments about the foundations of a peaceful world must be based not on gender essentialism but on types of behavior and priorities, such as those underlying good mothering, whether that mothering is practiced by men or women. For the WILPF's founding members, however, such a perspective on the gender-neutrality of mothering practices would have significantly reduced the ethos they were trying to build for women in international politics. For better or worse, WILPF leaders elected to omit from their formative arguments the possibilities that the nurturing perspectives they attributed to women were not, in fact, embraced by all women and that those perspectives were not the exclusive business of women.

While there is much to critique in the WILPF's arguments of gender solidarity, it is important to remember, as WILPF historian Linda Schott suggests, that "however inaccurately this conception of gender roles may have described the lives of real women and men, and however limited it may seem today, it was used by some women to expand their opportunities" (11). Delegates at the Hague clearly recognized the strategic benefits of gender-exclusivity in their new pacifist organization. Such exclusivity was necessitated by women's exclusion from positions of power within male-controlled peace organizations. WILPF secretary Lucia Ames Mead reported in her account of the Hague meeting that "those who questioned why women should form a new society and not unite with men and women in the old organizations were shown that women held very few offices in the old societies and had some fresh methods of their own which they wanted to employ" (42). The organization used gender-based separatist arguments to create leadership possibilities that did not exist in mixed pacifist groups.

Furthermore, the essentialized construction of "women" forwarded at the Hague Congress resonated with contemporary popular opinion. As Burke reminds us, the skilled rhetor "will seek to display the appropriate 'signs' of character to earn the audience's good will. True, the rhetorician may have to change an audience's opinion in one respect; but he can succeed only insofar as he yields to the audience's opinions in other respects" (56). By suggesting that women's biological and social experiences provide them with a particularly strong ethos in international relations, the WILPF employed the kind of rhetorical strategy Burke describes. The argument responded to opinions held by much of the audience that the founding members wished to persuade, and it used common understandings of the term "woman" to resist the limitations the term often implied.[8]

woman = peace-loving
≠ assumption held by
audience

New Organizations of Diplomacy

In addition to promoting women's voices in international discourse, the WILPF aimed to "make it clear that bodies of people can act together without [the] fight spirit, without the spirit of competition, without the spirit of rivalry" (Addams, Address 253). In other words, the organization worked to establish the literate practices of cooperation, discussion, and negotiation that men had failed to develop. A first step toward these practices involved developing and promoting a new understanding of nations and their relationships to one another. Early-twentieth-century understandings of what constitutes a "nation," American WILPF member Emily Balch argued, were antithetical to cooperation. According to Balch, "perfectly artificial national boundaries are made to signify collective greeds and hatreds," which ultimately lead to violent confrontation (Addams, Balch, and Hamilton 21). Similarly, Addams critiqued the antagonistic spirit of patriotism that often accompanied the concept of the nation. Addams argued that a "tribal emotion" of patriotism bound a nation's people together and, through a regressive appeal, set them in opposition to the people of other nations.

As an alternative to traditional antagonistic versions of nations, the organization proposed a "New Internationalism," which might unite diverse populations in global interactivity and sympathy. Working from a Kantian ideal of "cosmopolitan" human interaction and influenced by international socialism, Addams urged communities, regardless of geography, to help one another adjust to new modes of life in an increasingly industrialized world. Social legislation and economic reform might fuel this process as different classes looked out for one another and as women led the movement for global cooperation. This rise in cooperative life, Addams maintained, would be accompanied by a decline in "war virtue"—or the nationalistic sentiments that fostered militant patriotism. "New Internationalism" would foster a phenomenon Addams called "Cosmic patriotism," a feeling of pride in belonging to the world community rather than a militaristic sense of allegiance to an artificially bounded geographic area. Under Addams's leadership, the women of the WILPF used the term *international* to signify more than the diverse national backgrounds of their membership; they hoped the word would come to signify the transcendence of the possessive idea of the "nation" as a distinct entity. Ideally, a global force of pacifist women would unite to eradicate the national boundaries that led to economic conflict, to nationalistic hatred, and ultimately to war.[9]

As part of their challenge to the negotiating tactics of conventional diplomacy, the WILPF also questioned traditional notions of political authority, particularly the use of threats as instruments of international relations. Leaders of the new organization questioned constructions of authority that see it as what Kathleen Jones has recently described as "a relationship occupying a discursive space somewhere beyond persuasion, only slightly short of force" (75). Authority, Jones elaborates, has traditionally been associated with maleness and rhetorical practices culturally coded as male—"descriptions of those who act as public authorities—public spokespeople—and of the norms and rules that they articulate." These associations, she continues, "generally have excluded characteristics culturally coded as 'feminine,'" such as listening and joint inquiry (78). In opposition to such characterizations, the WILPF asserted that authority should not derive from the ability to frighten or force but from one's ability to negotiate solutions and to persuade others of the viability of those solutions. Balch, for example, was highly critical of the confrontational bent of much international communication, even within existing channels of peaceful communication. Writing of Gandhi's decision to issue an ultimatum to the British in 1930, Balch objects:

> An *ultimatum* is in essence a war method and issues from a war mentality. One never presents an ultimatum to a friend and if Gandhi does not consider the British as friends—however wrong and however wicked—then he has surrendered something more precious than the non-violent principle—the good will principle. (qtd. in Schott 102)

Ultimately, the WILPF held, "Nations—people as well as governments—must be animated by good will and acquire the habit of working together. Their cooperation must be positive and active, and there must be a truly international authority" (Cahier Committee 5).

Balch and other WILPF leaders objected to what Sonja Foss and Cindy Griffin call "conquest rhetoric" as a model of argument in international relations. According to Foss and Griffin, the object of interaction in conquest rhetoric

> is to secure an idea, claim, or argument as the best, strongest, and most powerful among competing positions.... Such interactions produce winners and losers.... The goal of conquest rhetoric, then, is to win an argument more than to affect listeners or to change their image of a subject in some significant way. (10)

The WILPF sought to expand the argumentative strategies typically used in international relations so that conquest became subordinate to peace as the goal of rhetorical interaction. Addams suggested to delegates at the Hague that "appeals for the organization of the world upon peaceful lines have been made too exclusively to man's reason and sense of justice" (WILPF, *Report of the International Congress* 21). Other types of appeals must arise in order to cultivate favorable public opinion for international peace. Reason, Addams explained, "is only a part of human endowment." Other appeals—of which "women were the earliest custodians," according to Addams—must combine with rational arguments to convince people of the desirability of peace:

> Emotion and deep-set radical impulses must be utilized; . . . those primitive human urgings to foster life and to protect the helpless must be given opportunities to expand and the most highly trained intellects must serve them rather than the techniques of war and diplomacy. (WILPF, *Report of the International Congress* 21)

Faulty techniques of diplomacy, in other words, must be supplanted by techniques of discussion and integration based on emotional impulses to preserve and improve life, impulses that the WILPF argued are unique to women. Anticipating Ruth Lister's recent feminist critique of traditional citizenship, the WILPF "illuminat[ed] the way in which the civic-republican conception of the citizen *was* 'aggressively male,' so that the exclusion of the female, far from being an aberration, was integral to the theory and practice of citizenship" (Lister 68).

The organization also promoted reform related to language differences in international relations. More specifically, the WILPF advocated the development of an international language for global diplomacy. This concern for language difference in international relations developed in part from difficulties the organization faced in its own attempts to facilitate international discussion. Despite the fact that programs, resolutions, and speeches at the 1915 Hague Congress were translated into three languages, difficulties arose due to the time required to complete translations. At one point in the meeting, French delegates protested that the translations they received seemed much shorter than the ones provided to the German delegates (WILPF, *Report of the International Congress* 106). At another point, British delegate K. D. Courtney expressed concern that resolutions under consideration had not been translated into yet more languages so that representative women from countries that did not speak English, French, or German could easily contribute to discussion (WILPF, *Report of the International Congress* 150).

After having witnessed the exclusionary power of language difference, the 1921 WILPF Congress passed a resolution urging that

> National Sections ask their respective governments and the League of Nations to appoint National Committees of experts, representing labour and science, to examine

existing auxiliary languages and to select from them the one best fitted to furthering international intercourse between peoples. (*Report of the Third Congress* 48)

Reflecting similar concerns about the advantages granted certain nations through the privileging of some languages over others in international communication, the Dutch national section of the WILPF passed a resolution "in favor of Esperanto or Ido as a Universal Language, an auxiliary language carrying in it more educational power towards Internationalism for all than a living [language], besides not giving supremacy to any nation" (WILPF, *Report of the Third Congress* 236). Only an international language could provide equal communicative footing in the discussion and resolution of international disputes. Furthermore, the Dutch section's actions suggest, a truly international language needed to develop separately from existing languages because existing languages were entangled in national borders and mired in national power. The organization recognized that, as Bruce Horner and John Trimbur have recently explained, "the territorialization of languages according to national boundaries puts into place a reification of social identity in terms of language use: one's social identity is defined in terms of nationality, which itself is defined in terms of a single language" (596). An auxiliary language, one that had not undergone this process of territorialization, might enable diplomatic leaders to transcend the national.

To support their advocacy of a more just international order, the WILPF argued for the immediate establishment of forums for international discussion and mediation. According to Balch, the first condition for successful international discussion is "the possibility of rapid and universal discourse" ("Hopes" 17). Communication technologies thus are critical to improving international relations; however, their existence alone is not a guarantee of improvement. Technologies, she argued, can be beneficial or detrimental depending on the ends to which they are employed: "the effect of the shrinkage of time and space [through expanding channels of communication] depends on what use we make of our opportunities and may increase friction rather than friendship." Therefore, Balch suggested, two more conditions are necessary for the construction of functional structures of international negotiation. First, the world must be made to desire peace. Second, "orderly methods of doing what is now done by war, that is, settling clashes between nations, must be organized." Defective, antagonistic methods of resolving disputes among nations should be replaced by forums for negotiation such as "a world court, an association of nations preventing aggression at once by world opinion and by providing non-violent methods of securing fair demand," for "these are parts of the necessary machinery of world peace" ("Hopes" 17).[10]

The Wales Plan

The kind of rhetorical machinery the WILPF sought to establish in the international arena received its first formal articulation in *Continuous Mediation Without Armistice,* a proposal to initiate arbitration of the First World War. The proposal, as written by U.S. WILPF member Julia Grace Wales (who was also an instructor of English at the University of Wisconsin), argues for the creation of a conference of nongovernmental experts to discuss economic, social, and scientific aspects of international relations.[11] These experts, according to the proposal, would be drawn from neutral nations and would have as their principal task the composition, international circulation, and subsequent revision of propositions for ending hostilities and for establishing a lasting peace. Following the Hague Congress, envoys from the WILPF presented the plan to various world leaders with the hope of encouraging such a conference of experts.

In addition to detailed plans for this "continuous meditation without armistice," the Wales Plan incorporates many of the WILPF's significant critiques of traditional diplomacy. In the plan, Wales argues that, because traditional diplomatic methods had failed to prevent large-scale international violence, "the situation calls for a conference cast in a new and larger mould

Julia Grace Wales. Photo courtesy of the National Archives of Canada/PA-182511.

than those of conventional diplomacy." Rather than a meeting of heads of state in which each participant would consider only the material interests of his nation, Wales proposes a meeting of "persons drawn from social, economic, and scientific fields who have genuine international experience" ("Appendix" 167). What makes international experience "genuine," according to Wales, is its basis in globally defined criteria that value not national greeds but global human livelihood. Conventional diplomats, Wales argues, are too accustomed to protecting their nation's interests to lead innovative negotiating practices or to meet in the spirit of "New Internationalism." In contrast to customary diplomatic mindsets, the conference of neutral nations should serve as a "world thinking organ," rather than as a site for competition and compromise among self-interested diplomats ("Appendix" 169).

Because the plan was to be distributed though traditional diplomatic spheres, Wales carefully constructs her arguments so that they would not alienate traditional diplomats. She strategically blends critiques of traditional diplomacy with appeals to the values that supposedly inform that diplomacy. For example, the proposal begins by praising the rational spirit of scientific progress: "Today, if our scientific spirit and intellectual development are worth anything, we should be able . . . to break through the paralysis of tradition and find a rational way out" (*Continuous* 1). When she composed the plan, Wales recognized the credence granted scientific and rational thought in traditional diplomatic circles. Despite the WILPF's larger critique of over-rationalism in diplomacy, Wales appeals to these characteristics in order to argue for the adoption of her mediation plan.

This appeal to rational values is quickly followed by a critique of the self-interested motives that lead to deception and ultimately to violence in traditional diplomacy. "Let us imagine," Wales suggests, "that all the nations now fighting were to awake tomorrow morning in their right minds, able to survey the wreck already caused." Wales proceeds to explain that being "in the right mind" means being able to understand more than the material, territorial claims at stake in warfare. It entails the capacity to "sum up the suffering, the human loss . . . to realize the futility of vengeance, the unwisdom and wrong of trying to crush or humiliate a race, the folly of continued competition" (*Continuous* 1). The "right mind," similar to the woman's mind as the WILPF constructed it, measures the impact of war in terms of the value of human life.

While the opening of the proposal details some objections women had to traditional diplomatic methods, the bulk of the proposal lays out the rhetorical methods and machinery the WILPF believed necessary for resolving the disputes at the heart of the First World War. First, Wales stresses the "advantages of co-operation . . . with utter honesty, simplicity, and courage," in opposition to secret treaties and to the complexity of diplomatic discourse. As Addams would later describe it, the Wales Plan "was founded upon the assumption that the question of peace was a question of terms" (*Peace and Bread* 8)—a question of misunderstandings that might be resolved if discursive mechanisms were available for the mutual definition and revision of disputed terms among warring countries. In presenting her plan for consideration to the women at the Hague, Wales explained the importance of developing such mechanisms:

> It is one of the customs of war, that when war has been declared, at once communication between the countries will cease. I ask why should that be the case? It is one of those customs which have grown up in earlier ages, when possibly there was some occasion for them, but which is no longer necessary. At one time communication was so difficult between nations at war, that it was practically impossible to continue communication. But now we have telegraph and cables and there is no reason why negotiations should not continue. (WILPF, *Report of the International Congress* 155)

Technologies for continued wartime communication existed, but forums and practices for the discussion of peace among belligerent nations did not. Wales suggested to the women at the Hague that it was their task to demonstrate how these forums and practices might be developed.

The Wales Plan also specifies a new discursive role for neutral countries in the mediation of international conflict. In the early years of the war, belligerent and neutral countries alike, Wales asserts, had "been paralyzed by a traditional mode of thinking." This traditional mode positioned neutral nations as silent observers, morally and ethically removed from taking part in or addressing the conflicts that fueled the war. Contrary to this traditional practice of diplomatic withdrawal, Wales proposes that neutral countries serve as the locus of international discourse during war, actively engaging warring countries in dialogue aimed at ending war before the utter destruction and surrender of one side—a situation that, Wales stresses, would only increase hostility and lead to future conflicts. Under this new construction of international discourse in wartime, leading citizens of neutral nations become the political actors "to whom the task of thinking openmindedly for the world is, for the time being, entrusted" (*Continuous* 4). It is thus their responsibility to take the initiative of developing and circulating "reasonable propositions" for the resolution of disputes. The neutral-nation-led process of mediation, as the Wales Plan describes it, depends upon processes of collaborative, continuous composition and revision among members of neutral nations.

More specifically, Wales calls for the development of a conference of neutral nations to engage in a process of collaborative writing—to "come together in conference and endeavor to frame a reasonable proposition" to resolve conflicts among belligerent nations. Leading experts from neutral nations would initiate the mediation process by circulating the proposition to belligerents, asking for feedback. With feedback from belligerents, the conference of neutrals would revise the proposition and resubmit it to the belligerents:

> If the first effort fails, [the conference of neutrals] should consult and deliberate, revise their original propositions or offer new ones, coming back again and again if necessary, in the unalterable conviction that some proposal will ultimately be found that will afford a practical basis for actual peace negotiation. ("Appendix" 167–68)

For Wales and the WILPF, "continuous mediation" meant "continuous revision."

Not only does Wales propose the methods of collaborative writing for international mediation, she provides suggestions for what the new diplomatic genres produced through that writing might look like. For the document to be effective and convincing, she stresses, the writers of the proposition for peace should "append to it all conceivable arguments for its adoption, every possible appeal to the self-interest of every warring nation" (*Continuous* 4). The document must include rebuttals to anticipated objections and must be suitably geared toward the interests of the audiences it addresses. Additionally, a written request for feedback should be part of the genre so it appears not as an order but as an attempt to negotiate. Wales even includes examples of the specific kinds of language she believed would foster further dialogue in the event that a belligerent country rejects the initial proposition. She recommends that the initial proposition include the following requests addressed to the belligerents:

> (1) If at any time while the war continues, you are willing to adopt or consider our proposition, or a modified form of our proposition, as a basis of peace provided the other warring powers will do likewise, we beg that you will notify the conference of the neutral powers.
>
> (2) In the meantime the conference of the neutral powers, WHICH WILL SIT WHILE THE WAR CONTINUES, will be grateful to receive any information which you may care to give as to your ultimate wishes—that is, as to the maximum which you desire to obtain—in order that the conference may be aided in an effort to discover at the

earliest possible moment a plan of settlement such as may appeal to all as worthy of
consideration. (*Continuous* 4–5)

The wording of this feedback request suggests a dialogue (rather than a
command) by "begging" for response and by emphasizing, through all caps,
that the conference will be an available, receptive forum for mediation as long
as the war continues.

Wales acknowledges that her plan might not lead to an immediate cessa-
tion of hostilities. But, she maintains, the process of writing propositions and
initiating international communication among nations at war would have
important implications. The composition of a proposal for peace by an international conference would have both political and psychological effects.
First, such a composition would "give a concrete expression to the inarticulate passion of all idealists in the peaceful and troubled lands. And if ever in
the world's history there was dire need of such a common expression, it is now"
(*Continuous* 6). A document that puts forth terms and arguments for peace,
even if those terms are ultimately not accepted, might foster good will among
different peoples by giving "common expression" to their perspectives on
world conflict, perspectives that otherwise tend to be censored in wartime.

Second, a visible conference of neutral nations would "present a spectacle
of profound significance" by suggesting the viability of pacifism as a political position. A "common expression" of pacifistic sentiment from a respected
international body would grant credibility to the idea of negotiation and
peaceful resolution of international conflict. As Wales asserts in her plan, the
adoption of the plan might result in "the lifting of the programme of pacifism into the realm of serious political consideration. As a proposition made
seriously from governments to governments, it would gain a hearing, it would
have a psychological effect, such as no private propaganda could ever give
it" (*Continuous* 6).

Third, a conference of neutrals and the propositions it developed would
be excellent publicity for pacifism and would counter militaristic nationalism propagated in the interest of war. The conference might establish the
precedent of international officials working together peacefully. This precedent, Wales argues, "would go far to restore the shaken faith of humanity and
enable it to set its face with new hope toward the goal of ultimate World
Federation" (*Continuous* 6). Additionally, because the propositions written
by the conference of neutrals would incorporate principles of lasting peace
rather than strategies to halt immediate hostilities, the spectacle of the conference would weaken militaristic appeals to popular fears. These fear-based
appeals, Wales explains, suggest that "defeat would mean at the least in-

creased armaments in the future, military enslavement, [and] the weakening of the democratic principle." The work of the conference of neutrals, in contrast, would put forth "an appeal yet stronger, for it would promise security not only from the aggression of a victor but from the revenge of a vanquished foe" (*Continuous* 7). Wales and women at the Hague were confident that, in the struggle to influence public opinion, a threat-based appeal to self-preservation would lose to an appeal based on the idea of productive, collaborative stability.

Fourth, the plan for continuous mediation would introduce the international rhetorical devices and attitudes necessary to achieve permanent peace without military victory in the immediate context of World War I. The only way to "straighten out the tangle" of international hostilities, leaders of the WILPF believed, was

> to adopt and persistently employ the device of placing simultaneous conditional proposals . . . before the belligerents [because] neither side can think correctly or effectively unless it has among the data of its thinking, exact knowledge as to how the enemy . . . would react to every possible proposal for settlement. (Wales, "Appendix" 168)

Without these devices of international discussion, delegate Pethick-Lawrence argued in support of the Wales Plan, the "peace" at the end of the war would be based "upon exhaustion on the battlefield of misery and despair, a peace that is founded on the victory of physical force" (WILPF, *Report of the International Congress* 156).[12]

Beyond its impact on the immediate world situation, the conference of neutrals would contribute to the development of permanent peace by altering understandings of the rhetorical process of "mediation" in international contexts. Through her plan, Wales maintains,

> the word *mediation* is . . . extended in meaning to include more than such formal mediation as implies the acquiescence of the belligerents. . . . *[T]he neutral conference would not confine itself to offers of mediation but would begin at once to frame and put forward standing proposals based on principles favorable to the establishment of a permanent peace.* (*Continuous* 5)

The mediation process, in other words, would have as its goal not merely the end of fighting but the establishment of enduring peace. Mediation, as constructed in the Wales Plan, thus means not the antagonistic process of composing a tenuous, transient treaty, but the construction of a collaborative document establishing sustainable accord on key international questions.

Finally, Wales argues that a conference of neutrals would cultivate a spirit of idealism within diplomatic relations. While practical, rational arguments had long held sway in international politics, the WILPF wished to increase the influence of ethical, emotional, and spiritual arguments. In a spirit similar to Addams's critiques of the prominence granted reason in international relations, Wales asserts that "humanity is not a shallow thing," and therefore the means of negotiating international disputes must appeal to motives other than rational or economic ones. "[T]he higher motives are incalculable," Wales stresses, and although "idealism is from the point of view of practical politics uncertain and therefore a negligible quantity, . . . it exists." These higher motives are particularly important when it comes to issues of war because in such volatile times "individuals are everywhere thinking, feeling, suffering, facing the ultimate issues of life and death" (*Continuous* 9). Despite their seeming impracticality as a basis for international negotiation, idealistic motives, involving emotional, spiritual, and ethical concerns, must be employed in the service of resolving conflict peacefully and in gaining widespread support for peace.

The WILPF attempted to model the rhetorical methods of international relations it advocated through the Wales Plan. As Lida Heymann notes in her history of the first nine years of the WILPF: "We in our League have not only preached mutual understanding and cooperation; we have tried to live up to our own principles" (44). Under Addams's guidance, the organization developed a discussion method through which disagreeing parties might arrive at an acceptable course of action. Addams explained to delegates at the Sixth International Congress of the WILPF in 1929 that dominant discussion methods based on competitive confrontation among differing parties should be replaced by discussion that makes use of the benefits of "pooled intelligence," a concept similar to dialectic. According to Addams, pooled intelligence employs productive processes of defining, addressing, and integrating differences of position. Following Addams's model of pooled intelligence, the WILPF envisioned the resolutions determined through discussion at their meetings not as watered-down compromises, but as "adjustments" or "integrations." Leaders of the WILPF encouraged members not to judge the congress's resolutions in terms of their individual aims and desires, but in terms of how well those resolutions integrated differing views so that the organization might back them with a unified voice.

Ultimately, the WILPF envisioned its rhetorical methods as a blueprint for a permanent League of Nations to arbitrate international matters even beyond the end of the Great War. When the charter for the League of Na-

tions failed to embody the rhetorical structures the WILPF believed necessary for lasting peace through mediation, Swiss WILPF member Clara Ragaz
suggested that the WILPF demonstrate for the diplomatic world how the
charter should have configured the League of Nations:

> May we succeed in creating a miniature League of Nations in which all Nations, the
> small with the great, the conquerors with the conquered, can work together on the
> same footing, and may it be the lot of the future League of Nations to meet under as
> great-hearted and kind, as clear-sighted and safe a guidance as we enjoy today.
> (WILPF, *Report of the Second International Congress* 17)

New Models of International Journalism

As the WILPF tried to change the structures of diplomacy, they also tried
to change popular acceptance of war as a method of international relations.
This acceptance, they found, was molded by the popular press. Jane Addams
spoke for many WILPF members when she expressed her frustration with
the press in 1916: "At moments I [find] myself filled with a conviction that
the next revolution against tyranny would have to be a revolution against the
unscrupulous power of the press" (Addams, Balch, and Hamilton 91). Journalists and politicians have used this power, Addams believed, to control the
scope of citizens' thinking around the globe:

> the people of the different countries [cannot] secure the material upon which they
> might formulate a sound judgment . . . because the press, with its opportunity of
> determining opinion . . . has assumed the power once exercised by the Church when
> it gave to the people only such knowledge as it deemed fit for them to have. (Addams,
> Balch, and Hamilton 91–92)

This knowledge often included embellished images of war. Under the rhetorical influence of popular wartime correspondents such as Irving Cobb
and Heywood Broun, American newspaper readers came to view frontline
warfare as the frolics of "schoolboys on a lark" who, with no seeming concern about the destruction around them, demonstrated "great pride in having been chosen for the job" (qtd. in Sproule 13).

The Press and Pacifism

The WILPF's frustration with the press only escalated as a result of the
press's refusal to provide accurate coverage of the organization's activities.
According to American members Addams, Balch, and Alice Hamilton, most
of the journalists in attendance at the First International Congress arrived

at the Hague already knowing what they would report: "Most of them apparently had been sent to get an amusing story of an international peace gathering of women—base and silly enough to try to meet in war time—breaking up in a quarrel. Day by day they went away with faces long with disappointment" (14). When the quarrel did not emerge, the journalists created one. Lies concocted to suit the expectations of journalists and the interests they served included a French journalist's fabrication of an insulting speech directed at French women (who had been unable to attend the conference due to travel difficulties) and a British correspondent's report that the congress had broken up in confusion and disorder. In response to the latter report, Addams explained that the congress had closed at mid-day on its final day and the tables were cleared, in an orderly manner, for a luncheon to follow. Not surprisingly, newspapers did not publish her explanation ("Peace and the Press" 55).

The response of the American popular press to the 1924 WILPF Congress in Washington, D.C., provides another example of the journalistic bias the organization faced. In a report chronicling the travels of the *Pax Special*—a train carrying international delegates from the main congress in Washington to various meetings around the country—U.S. WILPF secretary Amy Woods expresses her exasperation at the lack of unbiased coverage afforded the endeavor:

> Anti-peace propaganda of "one hundred percent American patriotism," based on misinformation and deliberate falsehood, preceded the *Pax Special* and was given wide publicity, not only in every city where meetings had been planned, but through the country. . . . The real facts that the President received the delegates at the White House; that they were entertained at Goucher College at a luncheon, through the invitation of President and Mrs. Guth; that they visited other universities; that a May breakfast was given in their honor in Philadelphia; that on Mothers' Day . . . they spoke in Pittsburgh at sixteen churches of different denominations, and at a large mass meeting, was not considered "fit to print." (WILPF, *Report of the Fourth Congress* 133)

The press in Detroit was particularly unfriendly to the *Pax Special*. Detroit papers, according to Woods, published "a most offensive letter by a young physician connected with the ROTC stating that the members of the 'Pax Special' should be mentally examined and placed in an insane hospital" (WILPF, *Report of the Fourth Congress* 135).

When popular newspapers and magazines could not find specific reasons to condemn the WILPF, biased publications cast a red shadow on the organization. In one widely circulated anti-WILPF pamphlet, *Peace at Any Old Price*, R. M. Whitney accuses the WILPF of censoring their own press releases in order to hide the severity of their "subversion":

> That the participants in this conference were aware of their disloyalty was evidenced by the fact that the publicity department of the conference did not give out to the newspaper the rabidly red sentences and expressions of the speakers. Every news release, covering such speeches . . . was carefully and adroitly censored so that the real sentiment of the conference was not available to newspaper correspondents. (3)

Perhaps the most infamous and damaging press event affecting American WILPF members was the wide circulation of the so-called "Spider Web Chart." The chart, prepared by Lucia Maxwell, a librarian working in the Chemical Warfare Office of the War Department, purports to diagram an extensive international conspiracy of pacifists and communists. The chart names fifteen women's organizations and twenty-nine women leaders, including Addams and Balch, as suspected communist subversives. Some verses that accompanied the publication of "The Spider Web Chart" in 1923 reveal the defensive rhetoric deployed against the WILPF:

> Miss Bolshevik has come to town
> With a Russian cap and a German gown,
> In women's clubs she's sure to be found
> For she's come to disarm America.
> She sits in judgement on Capitol Hill
> And watches appropriation bills
> And without her O.K. it passes—NIL
> For she's there to disarm America.
> (qtd. in Women's Joint Congressional Committee, "Meeting Minutes")

The chart and its accompanying verses appeared across the country in the popular press, and leaders of the WILPF were maligned as communist radicals. After extensive protests from many of the women named in the chart, Secretary of War John Weeks retracted the chart and ordered all copies destroyed. Most newspapers, however, did not cover this retraction. Nor did they issue any apologies for the stories they printed in support of the chart.

Challenges to Wartime Propaganda

Because of such misinformation, the WILPF urged its members to examine the press critically. Distorted press coverage led Addams to write an extended critique of the international press for the magazine the *Indepen-*

dent in late 1915. The article begins with Addams stressing the importance of the press as an agent of public opinion formation. Addams opens her critique by commenting on the power of the press to influence popular responses to politically controversial issues: "Public opinion must of course depend upon the data which are provided, it can be formed in no other way, and the power of the press to determine these data gives it ultimate control over the minds of the multitude who read but one type of journal" ("Peace and the Press" 55). After introducing the idea that the press has such formative power over public opinion, Addams focuses on how the press perverts international relations by favoring militarism and discrediting pacifism.

More specifically, Addams presents an extended analysis of how journalistic bias permeated the popular press's coverage of the Hague meeting. The presses of the belligerent nations presented largely negative or belittling reports of the women's efforts. Press coverage accorded the Hague meeting, Addams elaborates, "gave evidence of a spirit of journalism which is ready to create the desired news, that it is unable to procure in any other way, quite in the spirit of the *agent provocateur* who himself manufactures the conspiracy he later discovers" ("Peace and the Press" 55). In this description, the journalist, rather than the pacifists, becomes the dangerous subversive, threatening freedom and democracy. Addams further argues that journalists were both unscrupulous in their coverage and uninterested in the serious business of the meeting:

> The journalists of many nationalities . . . were united in the belief that a "row" was inevitable, both because it was a woman's congress and because of the strained international situation. They therefore waited for "the story," ill concealing their boredom during the unemotional business meetings which considered the somewhat technical resolutions. ("Peace and the Press" 55)

Addams's description suggests that the journalists, not the women, were unable to maintain interest in the real issues of the conference.

Addams directly links the work of the press at the Hague meeting to the intentions of militaristic diplomats and national officials. According to Addams, "The attitude taken by the press toward the Hague meeting was to a degree a reflection of what was conceived to be the governmental attitude." Furthermore, she claims, national presses, in the service of armies and power-hungry leaders, play an important role in prolonging hostilities:

> As the delegation of which I was a member went from one country to another [presenting the Wales Plan] we everywhere met men who felt tied hand and foot by their inability to receive any information or to express any opinion contrary to that

which the press had decided to foster as in the interests of patriotism and a speedy victory. ("Peace and the Press" 55)

The "facts" upon which the public must make their decisions, Addams asserts, are inevitably carefully monitored, if not manufactured, by governments.[13]

Censorship everywhere during a war works against peace by limiting the purview of the larger public and by prohibiting the formation of networks of like-minded peace advocates: "under the censorship of the press one man cannot tell how many men are feeling as he does. Although a man reaching similar conclusions may be living in the next street or town, he cannot be found" ("Peace and the Press" 55). When any attempt is made to express opinions against traditional diplomatic procedures, the writer "exposes himself to the most violent abuse." Addams provides the case of Ramsay MacDonald, a British member of parliament who had spoken out against war and, as a result, had a "campaign of persecution" carried out against him, with posters distributed around London calling for his execution. Throughout her analysis, Addams asserts that the popular press during wartime served as a barrier to the mobilization of public opinion for anything other than war.[14]

The slavish relationship between existing governments and the press, Addams argues, leads to political stagnation and citizens' disempowerment. Because of the size of modern society, the printed word, Addams maintains, is the only way through which public opinion can be discovered and expressed. With the press controlled by traditional, primarily militaristic diplomats, the printed word can no longer mobilize public opinion—it dictates it and works to maintain the governmental status quo. This stagnation of the press has negative impacts both nationally and internationally. As Addams points out, "if like-minded people within the borders of a warring nation cannot find each other, much less easily can the search be conducted beyond the lines of battle" ("Peace and the Press" 56).

The public's passive acceptance of the images and opinions presented to them in print compounded the danger of militaristic media. Addams and other WILPF leaders faulted the American public for the sacred attitude it took toward the press in wartime. Because the public seemed ill-prepared to read the popular press critically, the WILPF promoted and engaged in resistant readings of popular media's militaristic discourses. In this way, the WILPF's efforts prefigured the work of post-war propaganda critics Walter Lippmann, Will Irwin, and George Seldes, who, Michael Sproule has recently argued, initiated "a great body of literature generally known during the 1920s and 1930s as *propaganda analysis*" (37). As part of a campaign against the National Defense Act of 1923, for instance, the national bulletin of the U.S. WILPF included a list of suggested actions for state and local branches. The list proposes that members consider these questions: "What inducements are offered young men on posters, in local papers, movies, etc. to enlist in the Reserves; in the Regular Army and Navy?" Furthermore, the list suggests that members should investigate the extent of broad public understanding of these inducements: "Are [young men] enlisting and do they understand what enlistment means?" (Woods, "Suggestions").

The organization also made a regular practice of analyzing popular patriotic icons. In 1927, Balch critiqued the American press for its attitudes toward the American flag, suggesting that the use of the flag to stir the fight spirit in the American populace was akin to desecration. Responding to an article in the *Transcript* that accused the WILPF of unpatriotic conduct because members refused to salute the American flag, Balch argues that the organization was in fact very patriotic, but that they did not support the rhetorical work the flag was made to perform in wartime. Balch begins her letter by equating her position as a leader of the U.S. WILPF with that of Shakespeare's Cordelia: one who truly loves her "father"—in this case, her country—despite her inability to speak that love as fawningly as her sisters: "Cordelia, when she was pressed to put into words her love for her father, found it hard to do so. Any normal person has something of the same sort of inarticulate shyness as to expressing love of country."

Emily Greene Balch. Courtesy of the Papers of Emily Greene Balch, Swarthmore College Peace Collection.

Balch continues her critique of traditional patriotism by suggesting that such patriotism is more rote than real. Balch explains that the WILPF's respect for the American flag is a genuine, rather than a learned, response: "I shall never forget how the tears came into my eyes the first time that I saw our flag in a foreign country. I am not sure my feeling would have been as fresh, real and first hand if I had been trained to daily salutes." In other words, Balch suggests, the WILPF's hesitation to salute the flag should be met with praise for the organization's critical yet true loyalty to the ideals for which America and its flag supposedly stand.

Balch proceeds to assert the importance of training the public how to respond to symbols and icons, particularly as those are circulated in popular media. To guard against unthinking allegiance to patriotic symbols, nations should carefully consider the methods through which people learn how to read and respond to those symbols. Balch argues that, in much the same way that "Literature classes often make children hate literature" and "Sunday school classes . . . dull the religious sense and breed irreverence," instruction in attitudes toward patriotic symbols can teach students to resist careful reading of those symbols. The danger of such instruction derives from the fact that symbols are transferable. They can be used by multiple parties for radically different purposes: "Especially do symbols have their dangers," Balch cautions. "Traitors and fools can wave a flag as readily as anyone else and interested persons may seek to identify disastrous purposes with its poignant appeal." Automatic or unthinking allegiance to a symbol, Balch argues (rather presciently in light of Hitler's rise to power in the following decade), might bring catastrophic consequences:

> The more we standardize emotion, the more, by ingrained habit from childhood, we set up a mechanical association between the flag and unquestioning acceptance of whatever is advanced in connection with it, the more is the danger of the desecration of the flag by misuse. (Letter)

Critical reading of popular symbols and careful presentation of them in popular media, Balch hoped, would guard against the deployment of those symbols in deceptive, destructive arguments.

Readers of popular publications, WILPF leaders believed, also needed to learn critical resistance to the corrupting force of oft-printed patriotic slogans. In a critique of war slogans, Addams suggests that these "stirring formulae" were so frequently reiterated in the media of the Allied countries that they "took on the abstract characteristics of general principles" with the effect that the goals of democracy became inextricably linked to victory in battle. Slogans such as "this is a war to end war and a war to safeguard the world for democracy" became so ingrained in Allied countries that, Addams explains, those who carried on the war "firmly believed that the aims of the war could be accomplished only through a victory of the Allies." After hearing these slogans again and again, large populations of the Allied powers "would not brook this separation of the aims from the method." In other words, repetition of the slogans prevented widespread consideration of the possibility that means other than warfare might work to prevent future war. Indeed, as Addams soberly remarks, "Apparently the fighting had become an integral part of the slogan itself" (*Peace and Bread* 98). Addams's belief in the power of slogans to deaden critical thinking was echoed in the resolutions adopted by the WILPF international congress in 1924. The second resolution adopted at the congress reads:

> Although an effort is made in every specific war to disguise it as something holy or humanitarian—such as a war to end wars, a war to make the world safe for democracy, a war in defense of the rights of small nations—it is today invariably nothing but the death grapple in a competitive struggle among different groups of moneyed interests for domination of the earth's natural resources, and more particularly, for economic control of the less developed parts of the earth. (WILPF, *Report of the Fourth Congress* 210)

Through their critiques of popular icons of patriotism and war slogans, Addams, Balch, and the WILPF pursued what Paulo Freire several decades later called "a truly liberating course of action, which, by presenting the oppressors' slogans as a problem, helps the oppressed to 'eject' those slogans from within themselves" (*Pedagogy* 76). By shaking the widespread, automatic acceptance of symbols and slogans, the WILPF hoped to open discussion of pacific means of conflict resolution.

Throughout the course of its first decade, the WILPF, in spite of a hostile press, did much to cultivate a climate for the discussion of pacifism and reform in international relations. As I explore in the next chapter, these efforts ranged from top-down approaches involving direct appeals to traditional diplomats, to bottom-up approaches that aimed to alter educational curricula so that children might be educated for pacifism.

"We Must Make Enormous Propaganda"
The WILPF and Public Opinion for Peace

3

We must make enormous propaganda all over the world. We must awaken
women to their responsibilities, and to the influence they can have in
creating the New Psychological Order of the world.
  —WILPF member Lillian Holby at the
  Fourth International Congress of the WILPF

The significance of the WILPF involves not only their challenges to traditional
rhetorical functioning of international politics but also the collaborative, widely
dispersed persuasive activities they engaged in to mobilize support for those
challenges. Due to the militaristic bent of traditional international relations
and the popular press, the pacifist ideas the WILPF wished to promote remained largely outside of public discussion. Yet the women who met at the
Hague in 1915 believed that they might, through the power of public opinion, effect substantial change in the rhetorical traditions of diplomacy.
Women's aversion to war, founding member Louise Keilhau argued to fellow delegates, was not a new phenomenon; the historical moment, however,
presented women with new opportunities to publicize their arguments for
peace. According to Keilhau,

> In all countries and at all times, women have regretted war, but they have been
> obliged to agree with it. But now a great change is taking place. Public opinion all
> over the civilised world is now created by women as well as by men and therefore
> war or rather the impossibility of war in [the] future must be influenced by women
> also. (WILPF, *Report of the International Congress* 79).

The kairotic moment for the rhetorical activity of the WILPF was at hand.
    In this chapter, I examine some of the tactics the WILPF used to publi-
cize their arguments to broad, international audiences and to powerful diplomats whose practices of international communication they wished to
change. Of central importance to their endeavors were rhetorical practices

familiar to them through club, suffrage, and social betterment work, particularly "educational" tactics that involved the creation and dissemination of publicity materials to familiarize the public with reasons and options for peace. The WILPF advocated the critical involvement of all citizens in the conduct of international discourse. Balch argued that the WILPF's methods of studying and discussing international matters should become widespread, everyday practice: "Study clubs and peace forums and subscriptions and keeping oneself informed are humdrum matters, yet they too are hitched to a star, the star of hope in human destiny beyond the war clouds" (Addams, Balch, and Hamilton 20). In hopes of rising above the war clouds, the organization dedicated much of its first decade of work to creating widespread interest in international affairs through lobbying, education, publication, and the arts.

WILPF members Jane Addams and Mary McDowell. Courtesy of the Jane Addams Memorial Collection (JAMC neg. 64), Special Collections, the University Library, University of Illinois at Chicago.

Strategic Positioning

Cultivating an environment receptive to changes in diplomatic discourse required WILPF members to address the diplomats whose discourse they hoped to change. When the WILPF first organized at the Hague in 1915, most of its members came from countries—including the United States—in which women did not have access to the ballot. Even as more women gained the vote, they remained largely excluded from positions of power in international politics. Because official channels of international relations tended to exclude women, the WILPF attempted to position their arguments in locations where they might be seen, read, and heard by the men who held official diplomatic status—a tactic I refer to here as "strategic positioning." An early attempt at such strategic positioning developed at the end of the Hague meeting when delegates decided to convene "an international meeting of women [to be] held in the same place and at the same time as the Conference of the Powers which shall frame the terms of the peace settlement after the war" (*Report of the International Congress* 41). From a nearby location, the organization might monitor negotiations and pressure statesmen to define terms of peace that would prevent future conflicts. Members were hopeful that they might influence the terms of the peace settlement through the pressure of proximity.

More specifically, women in the organization believed that their proximity to the site of peace treaty negotiations might bring to light options that were beyond the scope of traditional diplomatic discourse. The recalcitrance of traditional diplomats to discuss serious economic and social problems or to propose innovative solutions to those problems, Addams asserts in her book *Peace and Bread in Time of War*, meant that other parties would need to intervene in the war settlement. Addams accuses statesmen of falling behind social progress and modern thought:

> Because in every country [diplomats] are seldom representative of modern social thought and the least responsive to changing ideas, it was considered supremely important that when the conference of diplomats should come together, other groups should convene in order to urge the importance of certain interests which have hitherto been inarticulate in international affairs. (153)

The inflexibility of traditional diplomatic discourse extended even to the individual words employed by its adherents. The antiquated, ornate vocabulary of traditional diplomacy prevented innovations that, Addams believed, were necessary for lasting peace. Traditional phrases used in established forms of diplomacy, Addams contends, are outdated, "18th century phrases" rather than "plain economic terms fitted to the matter in hand" (*Peace and Bread* 210). As if demonstrating their antipathy to innovation, the statesmen who convened peace proceedings in 1919 prevented the WILPF from holding a proximal conference. Because WILPF delegates from the Central powers were not permitted to enter Paris, the organization was forced to convene in Zurich.

A second plan devised at the 1915 Hague conference also reflected the WILPF's desire to place their arguments physically near the agents of traditional international politics. In order to "urge the Governments of the world to put an end to [World War I] and to establish a lasting peace," the WILPF delegated "envoys to carry the message expressed in the Congress Resolutions to the rulers of the belligerent and neutral nations of Europe and to the President of the United States" (*Report of the International Congress* 41). In-person delivery of resolutions avoided the dangers of massive wartime disruptions and censorship in postal service and made it much more difficult for diplomats to ignore the message. Following the congress, two delegations visited governments in seven belligerent nations and five neutral nations, presenting to leaders the resolutions from the meeting and the Wales Plan for continuous mediation.[1]

The WILPF also relied heavily on the strategic deployment of messengers and texts within national sections. From their legislative headquarters on Capitol Hill, the U.S. WILPF regularly dispatched lobbyists to legislators and government officials. At their 1920 meeting, the U.S. section "voted to send Mrs. Florence Kelley and Miss Jeanette Rankin to Washington as our representatives for protest and appeal to the state department" (U.S. WILPF, "Minutes" 3). Similarly, in conjunction with the 1923 annual meeting of the U.S. section, several envoys visited with "official heads of Federal Departments," including Secretary of State Hughes, Secretary of Commerce Hoover, and the head of the Department of Justice, urging an international conference on disarmament (U.S. WILPF, "Envoys"). Lobbying became a staple of the organization's activity, particularly after the 1924 appointment of Dorothy Detzer as executive secretary. Detzer held the position for over twenty years and developed a national reputation as a hard-nosed lobbyist for the organization.[2]

In addition to positioning members in strategic locations, the WILPF positioned texts strategically within administrative structures, particularly within the League of Nations following the First World War. The secretariat of the League of Nations served as a critical channel of influence in the assembly of that organization. Although the members of the secretariat did not make policy, they were responsible for the circulation of information among League of Nations policy makers. As WILPF member Catherine Marshall explained to delegates at the 1921 international congress, "if an important letter is sent for presentation to the Assembly, it is the duty of the Secretariat to see that it gets on to the Agenda to be discussed and to see that the people doing the work are provided with the necessary facts" (*Report of the Third International Congress* 67). The secretariat, in other words, determined what was discussed and on the basis of what evidence. The WILPF thus often lobbied the secretariat to put specific measures on the agenda and to supply members of the assembly with certain "facts."

Due to limited financial resources for travel, the WILPF regularly used mass mailings to place their arguments before elected officials. A major campaign for the U.S. WILPF during the middle of the 1920s supported the passage of a constitutional amendment outlawing war. In the organization's "Plans for 1924–5," the national board instructs chapters of the WILPF to "see that every candidate, federal, state, and local, on the ballot in your state is informed of the growing public demand that war shall be made legally a crime." To spread the word, members are encouraged to organize mass memo-writing campaigns: "Work in your own state to have the legislature, the state, councils, churches, newspapers, organizations, and persons memorialize Congress to take such action. Instruct your Congressmen and Senators to represent the growing sentiment in their constituency."[3]

The petition, a tactic with deep roots in reform work, further enabled the WILPF to place their concerns within traditional diplomatic structures. A petition drive often involved members in extensive speaking tours and door-to-door campaigning as they tried to procure support through face-to-face appeals. During 1920–21, the WILPF circulated petitions regarding the Russo-Polish war and the blockade of Russia; the "reform of the passport regime," which they felt hampered international discussion; cheap international postage; and the appointment of women as delegates to the League of Nations assembly (*Report of the Third International Congress* 198). Perhaps the most successful petition work came as part of the disarmament campaign in 1930–31. The strong roots of petition work in women's organizations is reflected in the extensive coalition of women's groups that participated along with the WILPF in the international drive to secure millions of signatures on a petition calling for universal and total disarmament. The petition drive, which resulted in over eight million signatures, was the work of a disarmament committee composed of representatives from fifteen international women's organizations.[4]

Educational Publications

While much of the WILPF's early work involved critical analysis of existing diplomatic structures and the articulation of what members saw as peaceful reconfigurations of these structures, the organization recognized that change in methods of international negotiation had to originate from a much broader base. Thus, efforts to write and distribute a myriad of documents promoting peace heavily informed the WILPF's agenda throughout its first decade. While I cannot discuss every kind of document the organization produced, I will provide an overview of its approach to publicity, accompanied by close examination of a few specific examples in order to illustrate how the organization provided an education in the rhetorical practices of peace.

The WILPF developed their genres of publicity in a process similar to that described by Charles Bazerman, who explains that the development of a genre occurs when "over a period of time individuals perceive homologies in circumstances that encourage them to see these as occasions for similar kinds of utterances" (82). More specifically, the WILPF developed specialized genres for different situations and stages in their publicizing efforts. The leaflet, for example, was used to rally broad interest and served as an important first step in the international changes the women envisioned. The pamphlet often followed the leaflet, providing more detailed arguments and "facts" to support the WILPF's position. The Committee on Disarmament at the 1921 Vienna Congress, for example, recommended the following publicity steps to create popular pressure for complete disarmament:

a) that the National Sections publish leaflets incorporating the [WILPF] manifesto [for total disarmament].
b) that a pamphlet with a summary of facts and references be printed. (*Report of the Third International Congress* 121)

The lengthier genre of the pamphlet also allowed for substantial rebuttal to arguments and accusations against the WILPF. One of the earliest publications distributed from the international WILPF office was a "propaganda pamphlet," entitled "What Is This League?" This pamphlet was distributed in an attempt to counter rumors about the WILPF spread widely by the popular press (*Report of the Third International Congress* 196). Similar to the leaflet, this publicity genre derived its persuasive force not only from its content, but also from its ease of distribution and its independence from mainstream publications.[5]

Throughout the records of the WILPF's first decade, one encounters other methods through which the organization created portable and widely accessible texts to promote peace. State and local branches of the U.S. WILPF developed many ingenious textual forms in order to make their "delivery" more effective. For instance, in conjunction with the WILPF's "Law-Not-War" day in 1923, the Minnesota branch spread the message of peace through "billboards, posters, moving-picture films, speakers at meetings, parades, and by radio messages." However, the most intriguing method of spreading the peace message involved the branch's work with the Franklin Cooperative Creamery, which "delivered their milk bottles . . . wrapped in Law-Not-War posters" (Stockwell).

The WILPF also developed specialized texts to address potentially sympathetic women's organizations, a strategy encouraged by the fact that many of the WILPF women were also members of other organizations, such as the YWCA, WCTU, the Women's Trade Union League, and the General Federation of Women's Clubs. Reflecting the importance of these audiences to their endeavors, the WILPF included in its administrative structure "a federated committee, including representatives of Leagues of Women Voters, labour leaders, teachers, churches, and club and social workers" (*Report of the Third International Congress* 247). The extent of the organization's efforts to publicize through existing women's groups can be seen in the April 1920 decision of the executive board to form the Committee on Propaganda with subcommittees focusing on work with churches, schools, women's labor unions, women's clubs, social workers, and the League of Women Voters. The formation of new branches of the WILPF, in fact, often arose through work with existing women's organizations in a particular area. As a first step in the development of a new WILPF branch, U.S. Field Secretary Sarah Cristy suggested that organizers "attend club meetings, church, any open meeting where women are in action" (7). Studying and working through other organizations provided invaluable resources for fostering women's interest in pacifism.

The national office of the WILPF regularly composed and distributed special circulars for other women's groups. "A Call to Club Women for Reconstructive Work," written by the U.S. section for distribution at the General Federation of Women's Clubs' conventions, takes only one page to urge clubwomen to support efforts for peace in the aftermath of the war. The circular begins by praising the social good that clubwomen had already done: "Women's clubs have spread their influence for good against evil from the small select social group to the neighborhood, the city, the town, the state and the nation." The text then acknowledges the power of war slogans and praises the lofty motives of the many clubwomen who supported the war in the belief that it would "make the world safe for democracy." Yet, the document continues, the slogan must now be seen for the deception it is. Clubwomen, the circular stresses, must now "make a democracy that shall be safe for the world, a democracy in legal, political, economic, education and social concerns in which all men and women shall be able to live out their better selves."

To reach this true state of democracy, clubwomen were urged to join the WILPF's efforts to change traditional structures and practices of international relations. Club work had been moving in the right direction, the circular assured readers, but now a change was due. "There must be devotion not only to all the things to which the Club-women are now committed," the document proclaims, "but one thing more, namely, a devotion ardent and enlightened toward establishing some world-mechanism that shall substitute law for war in the settlement of disputes among nations." To further encourage clubwomen's support of the WILPF mission, the writer likens war to evils the GFWC had already taken a strong stand against: "War, like slavery and the subjection of women, must pass into the area of abolished social evils."

In addition to writing and distributing texts that publicized peace, the WILPF intervened in international media channels to encourage activities for peace and to counter the powerful influence of militaristic journalism. Leaders relied heavily on suffrage journals in particular to promote pacifist sentiments among women. Emily Hobhouse, first secretary of the WILPF, explains this reliance in her report of the organization's first year of work. According to Hobhouse, "aided by '*Jus Suffragii*,' the '*Labour Leader*,' '*Vorwaerts*,' [the Dutch suffrage journal] and a few kindred publications, [women] found means to communicate with the women of hostile lands" even during the Great War (x). Other publications geared toward women also served as channels for the WILPF to spread its pacifist vision. The U.S. WILPF passed a resolution appealing "especially to the editors and owners of the powerful women's magazines, including particularly the Women's News Service, the *Pictorial Review, The Ladies Home Journal, The Women's Home Companion, McCall's Magazine, Good Housekeeping, The Delineator,* and also the many smaller journals for women" to publish articles promoting pacifism and the work of the organization ("Minutes" 4).

To complement these initiatives directed at women, the WILPF supported the development of a peace press service that would provide popular media organs with ready-made articles reporting peaceful efforts and refuting lies about pacifist groups. In 1924, Rosika Schwimmer proposed a resolution calling for the election of "three (or five) experts" from the members of the WILPF "to formulate concrete proposals for the establishment of a Worldwide Press Service, for pacifist activities. The function of this press service shall be to furnish pacifist news to the press of the world, and to correct errors and misstatements in the press" (*Report of the Fourth International Congress* 25). The WILPF hoped to convert media from organs that solidify nationalist interests to conduits of international good will.

In other cases, the WILPF produced book-length commentary on traditional practices of international relations. For example, the literature committee of the WILPF, in conjunction with the Fellowship of Reconciliation, the American Friends Service Committee, and the NAACP, sent Balch and a committee of investigators to Haiti to conduct research for a publication on the military occupation of the island nation. After investigating the situation, Balch and WILPF members Addie Hunton and Charlotte Atwood contributed to the writing of *Occupied Haiti,* a 1927 report that exposed the injustice of U.S. military occupation. The recommendations in this report closely resemble those put forth in the 1930 report of President Hoover's investigative commission on Haiti (Pois 301). WILPF women, in collaboration with other women's and peace organizations, remained one step ahead of the government.

To build the foundations of widespread publicity for peace, the WILPF also mounted an international effort to distribute publications about pacifism and peaceful methods of international relations. The WILPF used collections of pacifist reading material to make a public argument for peace. In fact, the mere existence of such collections acknowledged peace and pacifism as legitimate topics for widespread discussion. The international office of the WILPF at the Hague served as a global peace library, actively engaging in "the collection of peace material from all countries . . . so arranged that it was easy to look it over and make use of it" (*Report of the Second International Congress* 48–49). By 1921, the library included over 450 volumes in addition to 130 papers and periodicals received regularly (*Report of the Third International Congress* 196). To increase access to these materials, the office maintained a catalogue of all items and made them available for borrowing by mail. Throughout the organization's first decade, the WILPF did not hesitate to direct its financial resources to collections development. According to the minutes of a 1922 Executive Committee meeting, the head of the WILPF peace library "was authorized to purchase whatever was necessary to maintain . . . stocks of literature for distribution" (WILPF, "Minutes of the Annual Meeting").

Efforts to educate the public about peace spread beyond the organization itself as the WILPF established local reading rooms or worked through public libraries to secure pacifist materials in their collections. In 1920, for example, the Australian section opened an "International Library and Reading Room," which loaned material to interested parties and hosted weekly study circles on various peace-related topics. That same year, the Pennsylvania branch of the U.S. WILPF began work on "a model peace library" that would provide both high school and university students opportunities for research (U.S. WILPF, "Work of 1923"). In other locations where separate libraries or reading rooms could not be constructed, women worked through local public libraries to ensure that patrons had access to peace-related materials. Through its advocacy of reading spaces and repositories of information, the WILPF ensured the physical availability of material to promote their pacific vision.

Art as Argument for Peace

Education via the printed word was only one way the WILPF encouraged broad support for peace. In keeping with their belief that emotional impulses had to complement reason in creating the desire for peace, the organization relied on artistic means of publicizing peace. The founders of the WILPF had long protested the use of the aesthetic in the service of war and sought to recoup art for the forces of peace. Addams explained in a 1907 talk that

> war, desiring to impress the human mind with the courage of the soldier, his readiness to die, his willingness to surrender all to patriotism, has called to its aid music, the march and the gold-bedecked uniform. All through the centuries [men] have clothed warfare in high sounding language and it has always had behind it noble emotions. ("New Ideals of Peace" 106)

These images and the associations they create between battle and grandeur efface the suffering and loss that accompany war. The WILPF actively promoted alternative forms of artwork and entertainment that might disrupt popular, mechanized, emotional responses to symbols of war.

To this end, the U.S. WILPF Executive Committee established the National Art Committee, headed by Elizabeth Johnson. In her initial report of the committee's work, Johnson echoed Addams's sentiments about the importance of aesthetic appeals in cultivating peace:

> Warfare could never exist without the glamour of uniforms, flags, insignia, music, and the beat of drums ... the hypnotic influence of rhythm, color, form. And so Art comes to the front in time of war to fire the imagination and stir the heart ... in a word, to create "Morale." We need its help if we are to build up a "Morale" for Peace!

With Johnson's leadership, the committee composed the following resolution for adoption at the 1924 annual WILPF meeting:

> Resolved: that during the coming year a part of our National program shall be an effort to make Peace popular by popular means, and that we shall lay great stress upon concrete demonstrations through the arts, including its light as well as its serious forms, in order that imagination may be touched and hearts fired with something of our zeal, and that we may secure first the one thing needful, The Will to Peace. (qtd. in Woods, "Minutes" 5)

According to the committee, artistic efforts to promote peace should include both the so-called fine arts and widely accessible, everyday forms such as "musical comedy, vaudeville, popular songs, movies, and the comic pages of the daily press" (E. Johnson 1). Through common forms of art, the committee believed, attitudes of broad populations are molded. While

> these [forms] may not constitute art in a high sense, . . . they are forms which affect the daily life of millions, coloring thought and establishing emotional trends. . . . [They are] a force to reckon with seriously if peace sentiment is to become widespread and deep. (E. Johnson 1)

The efforts of this committee were already well established, thanks to the earlier work of the Woman's Peace Party, the predecessor to the U.S. WILPF. In 1915, the WPP's Committee for the Encouragement of Artists, Musicians, and Writers of Productions Promoting Peace published a four-page list of artistic resources for peace activists. The list includes novels, poems, plays, music, pictures, statues, books, monthly periodicals, cartoons, and numerous other resources, all available through the organization for any group or individual interested in the pacific cause. In addition, the publication lists trained readers who would attend local meetings and perform recitations on peace themes. This list notably includes writer Zona Gale, a speaker and organizer for the Woman's Peace Party and later for the WILPF (Thomas).

In addition to the written word, the WILPF emphasized the persuasive power of visual rhetoric. Elizabeth Johnson urged her fellow WILPF members to focus on the power of the visual in creating sentiments for peace: "World cooperation founded upon world justice must become visual in terms of beauty if a better world order is to rest upon the solid basis of popular support. Let the graphic lessons of art transfer the dramatic appeal of war to Peace!" (3). Under Johnson's leadership, the committee involved producers of visual popular culture in peace efforts, largely through national contests such as the World Peace National Poster Competition in 1924. While this contest was open to all artists, specific appeal for entries was made to producers of everyday or common art forms: "It was to rank and file artists and to students that we made our direct appeal," Johnson explained. This appeal came through "ten thousand announcements" sent to "practically every art school, club guild, centre, alliance, museum, and department in the country" (2) in order to ensure the participation of those whose work most directly influenced the populace.

Marion Craig Wentworth's *War Brides*

Reflecting this strong belief in the persuasive power of the visual, theater became one of the most important mediums through which the WILPF promoted pacifist sentiments during the 1920s. One of the earliest publicity efforts by the U.S. WILPF involved the production of Euripides' *Trojan Women* at the Little Theater Company of Chicago (Thomas 47).[6] The best-known playwright working with the WILPF during its first decade was Marion Craig Wentworth, whose plays *War Brides* and *The Dreamers* became the most popular of WILPF-sponsored peace plays. Wentworth, speaking at the annual conference of the U.S. WILPF in 1923, explained the importance of aesthetic appeals to emotion in cultivating a receptive audience for peace: "War could not exist without the glamour of music, uniforms, flying banners, and the roll of drums. Can the Peace Movement become widespread without similar aid? Movement, color, music, form—good art rightly used is needed to touch the imagination and stir men's hearts" for peace (qtd. in U.S. Section, "Art Gives Her"). Proponents of peace, in other words, had to create artwork that associated words, music, and images with peace in order to counter artwork that had been used wrongly for war.

Wentworth attempted such a creation through her drama *War Brides*. The play tells the story of Hedwig, a new wife and expectant mother whose husband has been called to war. Set in a "peasant's cottage in a war-ridden country" in Europe, the play begins with women "aristocrats and peasants, side by side" working in the fields gathering grain, baskets of grapes, and loads of wood—a harmonious image of women as the sustainers of life, even in a time of war. This image, however, is soon disrupted by the patriarchal presence of military power. In the first few moments of the play, stage directions indicate that "a cheer is heard" offstage. The cheer, we learn through Amelia, a nineteen-year-old peasant girl, comes from a crowd gathered to witness a mass wedding ceremony, an effort on the part of the nation's leaders to create a next generation of soldiers. Through these mass weddings, young women became "war brides" so that soldiers might "lay the seeds" for future generations before heading to battle and to almost certain death.

Throughout the play, Wentworth associates militarism with foolishness and deception while emphasizing that women are at the mercy of militaristic leaders. Heads of church and state subordinate all else to battle. Even the wedding ceremony for war brides is merely a pause in the march to war. One recently wed young woman, Minna, provides a glimpse of the power and omnipresence of the war machine in her description of the war brides' ceremony: "There were ten of us. We all answered in chorus. . . . Then the priest made a speech and the burgomast and the Captain. The people cheered and then our husbands had to go to drill for an hour" (18). The women do not speak individually—that privilege is reserved for the men who lead the clergy, the local government, and the military. Not impressed by this kind of ceremony, Amelia resists the pressure to become a war bride herself when Lieutenant Hans Hoffman implores her to marry him before he leaves for the front.

Wentworth uses Hoffman's character to critique the perverted patriotism generated by militaristic nationalism and the self-aggrandizement characteristic of the military. Upon Hoffman's stage entrance, stage directions explain that he is "accustomed to having the women bow down to him." When Amelia protests the idea of marrying him because she does not know him, Hans responds with superficial arguments of patriotism and military expediency: "We can't stop to think of such things now, Amelia. It is wartime. This is an emergency measure" (18). The entire patriarchal government, Hans proceeds to argue, has issued orders for women to perform service to their country through marriage: "Pretty girls like you should marry. The priests and the generals have commanded it. It's for the fatherland." The argument, based on the authority of army men, church men, and the "father" land, demonstrates how disempowered women have become in wartime. To emphasize this far-reaching disempowerment, Amelia's mother hesitantly assents to the idea of her daughter being a war bride. With "a far-away look," she tells her daughter, "It is for the fatherland, Amelia. Aye, aye, the masters have said so. It is the will and judgement of those higher than us. . . . You will not say no when your country bids you! It is your emperor, your country, who asks, more than Hans Hoffman" (19). Women in wartime, the play suggests, have little choice.

The central character of the play, Amelia's sister-in-law Hedwig, is another female casualty of militarism. Hedwig, we learn through dialogue in the play, had been engaged and married before hostilities started and is expecting a child by her husband, Franz, who has been called to war. Her character, strong-willed and vehemently opposed to militarism, provides a mouthpiece for the pacifist-feminist arguments of the WILPF. Her first line in the play is a "contemptuous" "Ha!" pronounced in response to the distant cheering at another war brides' wedding ceremony. Her marriage and her pregnancy— both accomplished before wartime—provide a powerful contrast to the militaristic impulses behind these marriages of national expedience. She confronts Hans about his desires to marry Amelia, arguing that war brides are simply "breeding machine[s] . . . to breed a soldier for the empire; to restock the land [with] food for the next generation's cannon" (19). Women and their children, in Hedwig's eyes, are positioned by militaristic thinking as material to be rationally managed for the benefit of the war machine.

Hedwig also articulates arguments that the WILPF used to critique the exclusion of women from international political channels. Hedwig argues to Hans,

> Are we women never to get up out of the dust? You never asked us if we wanted this war, yet you ask us to gather in the crops, cut the wood, keep the world going, drudge and slave, and wait and agonise, lose our all and go on bearing men. . . . You use us and use us—dolls, beasts of burden, and you expect us to bear it forever dumbly; but I won't! (19)

She proceeds to argue against war from the perspective of women and mothers, elaborating on the anxiety of waiting for a husband's return and the extreme financial burden if he does not, leaving his wife to raise a child by herself. Hedwig personifies the conditions the WILPF protested in their formal resolutions and manifestos; through her character the WILPF can put a "human face" on their arguments for change in international relations.

Amelia, upon hearing Hedwig's arguments, refuses to marry Hans, who then reports Hedwig's "treasonous behavior" to Captain Hertz, the local "military head of town." Like Hans, Hertz represents the arrogance and foolishness of the military. His character bolsters the WILPF's argument that the war is an "old man's war," conducted by those of a stagnating generation. The stage directions indicate that Hertz "is well on in years, rheumatic, but tremendously self-important." In response to Hertz's command that she remain quiet in the future, Hedwig again argues that women have been silent too long in international affairs:

> You tear our husbands, our sons, from us—you never ask us to help you find a better way—and haven't we anything to say? . . . If we can bring forth the men for the nation, we can sit with you in your councils and shape the destiny of the nation, and say whether it is to war or peace we give the sons we bear. (23)

The captain responds to her argument with laughter.

The one-act play ends with news of Franz's death in battle. Hedwig, overcome with grief at the loss of her husband and not wanting to give birth to another soldier for the war machine, commits suicide. The play is heavy with pathos, yet it served as a popular channel to raise sentiments for peace and to pronounce women's arguments against war. After opening in New York in 1915, the play toured coast-to-coast and proved so popular that a movie version of it grossed over $300,000 before the U.S. entered the war (Tylee, Turner, and Cardinal 13). While the play ultimately did not prevent the war, it helped raise awareness of injustices toward women who had no voice in international politics and provided realistic, inglorious images of war's debasement of women and families.

Beyond their ability to stir emotions for peace, theatrical productions were advantageous to the WILPF because they could be supplemented with direct appeals for action. Trained curtain speakers would often take the stage after the final curtain of a pacifist play and appeal to audience members to act on their emotions. As WILPF member Harriet Thomas reported in 1915, "During the appearance at the Majestic Theatre in Chicago of Madame Nazimova in [Wentworth's] 'War Brides' permission was granted by the management for curtain speeches after each performance" (47). The professional acting abilities of Nazimova were complemented on this occasion by the oratorical skills of Grace Abbott, who would later head the U.S. Children's Bureau of the Department of Labor, and Sophonisba Breckenridge, University of Chicago professor and later dean of the Chicago School of Civics and Philanthropy. To provide further channels for audience members to act upon their responses to the play, four thousand copies of the WILPF's platform were distributed in the lobby of the theater. Artistic and informational tactics thus complemented one another as the WILPF used the play to stimulate emotional impulses and supplied copies of the platform to provide rational suggestions for peace work.[7]

Through their use of theater and the arts to promote peace, the WILPF sought to connect aesthetic experiences with political and social ends. Such work challenged the use of literature and drama by university English departments, which, as James Berlin has argued, were at the time attempting to distance the aesthetic from lived experience through "a new conception of the nature of poetics, a conception that defines the aesthetic experience in class terms while isolating it from other spheres of human activity, most explicitly the political and scientific" (*Rhetorics* 4). Rejecting what Pierre Bourdieu calls the "pure gaze" of aesthetic appreciation that judges art apart from

actual experience, the WILPF understood aesthetic texts as critical instruments in the formation of attitudes toward important political and economic
issues, particularly as those issues affect the international environment.

Promoting Peaceful Rhetoric in International Education

Art was not the only thing wrongly used in the service of war, according to
leaders of the WILPF. Antagonistic international relations were also maintained through formal practices of education around the globe. As part of
their attempts to create a kairotic moment for pacifist arguments, the WILPF
actively promoted methods of education that fostered sentiments for peace
in future citizens. In 1924, the WILPF resolved to counter militarism "by
shaping the instruction given our children in such fashion as to create in
them a determination to promote a peaceful and cooperative world civiliza-
tion rather than a barbarous world of conflicting national units" (*Report of
the Fourth Congress* 3). In a similar spirit, the official program of action for
1915 had recommended that members work with teachers to "write on the
walls of every school-room, 'Above all Nations is humanity'" (*Report of the
International Congress* 111). Teachers, the WILPF hoped, might inscribe the
message of peace in the classroom through their textbooks and curricula.

History, Language, and Peaceful Education

The WILPF's educational reform efforts frequently concentrated on refuting the militaristic rhetoric of nationalism that threatened democratic education. *Pax,* the newsletter of the U.S. WILPF, warned members in 1924 of
the threat to education posed by the sloganeering of numerous national
education organizations. More specifically, the newsletter warns of the "propaganda and fear and prejudice" informing plans for National Education
Week ("Plans for 1924–5"). The writers fault the proposed program—which
was initiated by the U.S. Bureau of Education, the National Education Association, and the American Legion—for including ethnocentric, militaristic statements such as "Revolutionists, Communists, and Extreme Pacifists
are a menace to [the Constitution's] guarantees"; "America First"; and "An
illiterate who obtains only second hand information is a tool of the radical."
To counteract the sentiments informing the proposed program, the WILPF
organized a concurrent "Armistice Week," designed to "bring to the teachers and the children a realization that there is more than one point of view
on patriotism and good citizenship" ("Plans for 1924–5").

WILPF members were particularly disturbed by the militaristic rhetoric
of history instruction. The presence of such rhetoric was not accidental. As

Sproule has recently demonstrated, the National Board for Historical Service (NBHS), with the blessing of the Wilson administration, had turned *History Teachers Magazine* into a channel for anti-German propaganda in the teaching of high school history classes. Among other things, the NBHS used the publication to urge teachers to "emphasize that Germany presently enslaved ten times more people than had labored in servitude in the old American South" (Sproule 12). At the same time, Wilson's Committee for Public Information spread "the impulse to teach history as a warrant for current political policy" (Sproule 12). In addition to these overt moves to influence teaching practices, history textbook writers of the period often limited their perspectives on world conflict. Reflecting the concerns of many WILPF members, Fannie Fern Andrews asserted that American history textbooks

> place far too much emphasis upon the political and military phases of history, and far too little upon the social institutions which have influenced the destiny of our nation. The development of our resources, and of our industries . . . should be taught as our constructive achievements, and our wars as merely their temporary interruptions. (qtd. in Woman's Peace Party, *Report* 14)

In response to the militaristic bent of organizations like Wilson's Committee for Public Information and the NBHS, the WILPF's proposals for educational reform focused on loosening state influence on curricula and on internationalizing the production and distribution of textbooks. Helene Schen-Riez, an Austrian delegate to the 1921 WILPF Congress in Vienna, suggested that the creation and circulation of textbooks only *within* geographically separated areas maintained divisive hostility in international relations:

> As long as every nation, every town, every village, compiles its own textbooks, they will always build up barriers between mind and mind. Why have separate textbooks at all? Here is a world full of nations that have produced wonderful thought, lovely books and the master minds of all ages. Why not pool them and distribute them all over the world? (*Report of the Fourth Congress* 39)

Collaborative writing, editing, and circulation of histories might minimize the bias of nationalism and regionalism.

The language of history instruction, the WILPF believed, was also an impediment to international peace. As recent theorists of critical literacy have argued, language is integral to the development of identity and worldview:

> It is through language that we come to consciousness and negotiate a sense of identity, since language does not merely reflect reality but plays an active role in constructing it. As language constructs meaning, it shapes our world, informs our

identities, and provides the cultural codes for perceiving and classifying the world. (Giroux, *Schooling* 46)

Working from a similar understanding of language and identity, the WILPF advocated respect for language difference in the composition of textbooks, particularly history textbooks. More specifically, they asserted that students should study their history in their own languages. Balch, for example, praised the work of her contemporary Adolf Ferriere of Switzerland for his empowering practice of composing histories in the native dialects of various populations. Balch explained that, as a result of Ferriere's composition of the histories of southeastern European countries in the dialects of their people, no longer will "the children of these lands have . . . to learn their own history in the languages of their oppressors." Instead, these children were able to read their histories in the language that constructed their lived experience (WILPF, *Report of the Third International Congress* 43). History, and the language used to compose histories, should not be imposed from without if international good will is to be cultivated.

Peaceful Curricula

Not only were textbooks problematic, so too were curricula into which those textbooks were incorporated. To change militaristic curricula, the WILPF wrote course materials for instructors to integrate into their classes. These materials ranged from general collections of famous thoughts on peace to fully elaborated courses. For example, the U.S. WILPF's Committee on Education composed a collection of "quotations showing the folly, the uselessness, the waste and the stupidity of war, from great statesmen and generals [and] quotations from the great religious teachers of the world teaching love and human brotherhood." These quotes were "arranged in the form of leaflets for distribution among teachers, appealing to them to teach according to their religion or as great statesmen urged them or as generals have in the end told them to do" (Blake).

The U.S. WILPF Committee on Education also designed a full course, entitled *Education for World Mindedness,* for students at Woodbury High School in New Jersey. The course included "a series of Programs given for the 900 students during the morning assembly periods on two or three days a week during the school year 1926–27" (3). Organized around the theme "The Contribution of Various Racial Elements to our Complex American Life," each "class" session focused on a particular country or ethnic group and integrated presentations from various disciplinary areas. For example, the program for October covered "Contributions of the Italians to Our

Complex American Life" and included presentations by the art department on Italian art; the English department on Italian literature; and the training department on Italian Folk Dancing (U.S. WILPF, *Education* 3). Lesson plans also reflect the WILPF's belief in the importance of art as an appeal for peace. Several plans call for instruction in diverse musical styles, such as the Glee Club's performance of black folk songs in February's program, "Contributions of the Negro to Our Complex American Life" (U.S. WILPF, *Education* 11).

Other attempts to influence curricula involved the WILPF in debates with school boards and other administrative bodies. A list, "Suggestions for Good Will Day, May 18, 1926," distributed from the U.S. headquarters reveals the WILPF's belief in the importance of cultivating attitudes toward peace within school administrations. The first two items on the list recommend that members "get leading people to accompany you to call on the Board of Education to ask that the schools celebrate Good Will Day with appropriate exercises" and "[i]nduce leading people in your community to offer their services to the Board of Education to speak to the children in the schools on Good Will Day on the importance of World Cooperation."

The organization also hoped to involve institutions of higher education in creating world sentiment for new internationalism. The WILPF called on universities to provide education in peaceful methods of international relations. An educational plan-of-work for the WILPF in 1927 suggests that universities develop "correspondence courses on international affairs and the peace movement." "Could not one of the great universities," the writers of the plan-of-work ponder, "be led to experiment along this line or to try University Extension work in this field?" *(Proposals)*. While the WILPF hoped universities would become more involved in the process of educating for peace by offering university extension or correspondence courses, in the absence of such offerings, the WILPF devised a "syllabus for study at home, available for farmers' wives, working people, and others who are discouraged by anything that appears to them as too 'high-brow'" *(Proposals)*. The language of adult education for peace had to break from traditional academic models in order to reach the broadest of audiences.

Substantial reform in the curriculum of higher education, the WILPF argued, should also include training the body so that students become mentally and physically receptive to peaceful methods of negotiation. Physical education, like all components of education, should foster thoughtful international citizenship. The physical discipline of military training, women of the WILPF suggested, inculcated inflexible mental habits, rendering students incapable of properly assessing arguments or determining just positions. In a 1923 article, for instance, WILPF member Anna Garlin Spencer suggests that "mentally, military training leads towards a swift obedience, which is often useful, but does not secure the democratic expression of free and rational choice." Furthermore, Spencer continues, military training rejects "the basic fundamentals of good citizenship, . . . human sympathy and a cooperative spirit" because it revolves around "the psychology of killing" (2). Rather than positioning the body as a tactical component in orchestrated destruction, physical education, Spencer stresses, should train students to view the body as a vehicle for enacting cooperative citizenship.

Not surprisingly, the U.S. WILPF protested the National Defense Act of 1920 that proposed to expand military training through "Citizens' Military Training Camps" and mandatory military training in colleges and universities. If "Citizens' Military Training Camps" were to dot the American landscape, the organization argued, the Department of Agriculture should be called upon to establish "non-military citizens' training camps" to "give instruction in constructive citizenship such as reforestation, life guard service, fire fighting, etc." (U.S. WILPF, "Report of the Literature Committee" 2). WILPF members also critiqued the plan to involve colleges and universities in military training. In a 1927 letter to leaders of various national women's and peace organizations, U.S. WILPF Executive Secretary Dorothy Detzer asserts that the Morrill Land Grant Act, on which supporters of the National Defense Act based their arguments supporting military training in universities, in fact stood in direct opposition to such training. To refute supporters' use of the Morrill Act, Detzer quotes the following passage from Representative Justin Smith Morrill's speech in support of the act in the 1862 Congress:

> Our military "crown jewels" are manufactured at West Point at government expense; . . . the exercise of holding the plow and swinging the scythe are every bit as noble, artistic, and graceful as postures of the gymnasium drill. . . . We have schools to teach the art of man-slaying and to make monsters of deep-throated engines of war, and shall we not have schools to teach men the way to feed, clothe, and enlighten the great brotherhood of man? (qtd. in Detzer, "Letter" 1–2)

Morrill, according to Detzer, envisioned his act as a means to counter the appeal of militaristic images by replacing them with glorious images of productive physical labor in the form of agriculture. It was erroneous, then, to use the Morrill Act in support of military education. WILPF protests were not without impact. After extensive pressure from the WILPF and other peace groups, the 1923 Wisconsin legislature made military training optional in its twenty-six land grant colleges (Hochstein).

Educational Institutions for Peace

Realizing the slow pace of change within institutions of education, the WILPF sought to educate international youth through college clubs, junior leagues, and WILPF-sponsored schools. By the early 1920s, WILPF-related peace clubs were common features at many women's colleges, including Smith, Radcliffe, and Simmons (U.S. WILPF, "Report of Executive Secretary" 1). For younger learners, the WILPF set up "Junior Leagues" that engaged students in study, discussion, and community projects. Topics for discussions listed in the WILPF's 1923 "Eight Outlines on International Problems to Be Used as a Basis of Study and Discussion for Young People's Groups" include "Social and Economic Laws," "Psychological and Spiritual Laws," "Unrest and Progress," "War and Progress," and "Youth and War" (Junior International Leagues Department). Suggested community projects attempted to involve youngsters in various writing and speaking practices that would promote peace. Proposed activities included peace-related essay contests; pageants and dances for peace; international pen-pal programs; Esperanto clubs; and sessions devoted to critiquing military posters and advertisements. Junior Leagues were also used to advance the link between peace and recreation through the development of peace games, peace toys, peaceful plays and films, and "patriotic celebrations" for peace, including peace-focused parades, "vespers," and observances for the July Fourth holiday (Junior International Leagues Department).

On other occasions, the WILPF developed their own institutions of peaceful education, including several international summer schools devoted to education in international strategies for peace. The first WILPF-sponsored summer school in 1921 focused on "Education for Internationalism." The school, which was attended by approximately three hundred students, consisted of activities designed to create like-mindedness and instruction aimed at facilitating international communication for peace (*Report of the Second International Congress* 188). Social outings designed to create a sense of identification among the students were central to the endeavor. According to WILPF records, the school provided the opportunity for "[a]ll sorts of excursions" such as "two concerts [featuring] the singing of the 30 girls from the 'Ancoats Girls' Choir.'" Furthermore, "the school was fortunate ... in being held during the Mozart Festival Week, when daily concerts and a magnificent Reinhardt performance of 'Everyman' were additional delights" (Swanick 187).

Yet WILPF-sponsored schools were not merely social occasions. WILPF schools also focused on training teachers in methods of international communication and understanding. Because many WILPF members had professional teaching experience, the organization recognized the limitations of teacher training and agreed with Vilma Glucklich, who explained the situation of teacher education to her colleagues at the WILPF meeting in 1924 this way:

> As an old teacher I see one of the greatest obstacles to a growing pacifistic public opinion in the fact that only a small minority of teachers are aware of their great responsibility in this question [of peace education]. Therefore I think that great effort will have to be made in order to give to those teachers who are willing to work on our lines the best possible information about the best methods for such work. (qtd. in *Report of the Fourth Congress* 112)

To further this effort, Glucklich proposed that the WILPF's international headquarters, during its "slow months" in summer, "could very well take in six to eight young teachers from abroad, whom a scholarship would enable to come there to study for six months." While there, Glucklich suggested, teachers might take courses through the Institut Jean Jaques Rousseau, which would give "the necessary scientific foundation for pacifistic education" (WILPF, *Report of the Fourth Congress* 112). At the same meeting that Glucklich presented her proposal, the Executive Committee of the U.S. WILPF named as one of their projects for the coming year "the establishment of . . . a series of summer schools in 1925 for teachers on the Atlantic and Pacific Coasts and the Great Lakes" (Woods, "Minutes").

WILPF-sponsored instruction for teachers typically focused on rhetorical methods for promoting the international exchange of ideas. The first week of the 1921 summer school provided instruction in peace pedagogy by elaborating on how to initiate the "development of peaceful and beneficent life" within the young child (Swanick 187). Lessons included an overview of "the dangers of suppression of personality, the uses of cooperation as against the struggle for existence, [and] the psychology of the herd" (Swanick 187). Part of this instruction also stressed the importance of a free press, with an afternoon dedicated to several presentations on "The Contemporary Press" (Swanick 187). The school also provided suggestions for content in peace-friendly courses. According to the report of the school, the second week addressed "*What* to teach: past and current history, self-government in schools, the League of Nations and other forms of political association, [and] the economic cooperation of nations" (Swanick 188). The 1924 summer school continued this focus on rhetorical machinery for peace, featuring sessions on the function of literature in cultivating pacifism ("Internationalism in Art," "Cosmopolitanism in French Literature," "Goethe, the Great Internationalist," "Changing Attitudes Toward War in English Literature"); the role of the press in the formation of public opinion ("Internationalism and Public Opinion," "The Press and Internationalism"); and educational methods of promoting peace ("Education for Peace," "Symposium: Education and Internationalism") (*Report of the Fourth Congress* 125–30).

Through several other educational forums, women of the WILPF helped each other learn how to use rhetorical tactics to promote peace. Annual meetings of the U.S. WILPF, for example, often provided training in publicity methods and public speaking. In 1927, the national office hosted a forum for branch leaders on "Spreading WIL Ideas," and, in 1929, the annual meeting included several sessions dealing with publicity and the training of volunteer workers (Pois 301). State branches also joined the effort. In 1923, the Pennsylvania branch reported plans "of starting a training course for speakers" (U.S. WILPF, "Pennsylvania"). That same year, the New York branch held a "Speakers' School." This school covered not only public-speaking tactics but presented WILPF members with substantial arguments they might employ on topics such as the outlawry of war, the dangers of preparation for war, and the need for international intellectual cooperation. The impressive list of instructors for courses in the New York school featured John Dewey, Will Irwin (a well-known muckraker journalist), and WILPF leaders Harriet Stanton Blatch and Frances Keller (C. Miller). By 1925, training effective speakers had become a national concern for the organization and the national executive board had established a course of instruction for WILPF speakers (Woods, "Minutes").

By the mid-1930s, the publicity and educational practices developed by national and international leaders of the WILPF were taught to new members on a fairly regular basis, thanks largely to the work of WILPF Executive Secretary Dorothy Detzer. Detzer published and circulated instructions for various communicative endeavors, such as organizing deputations and peace meetings, writing letters and resolutions, and interviewing congressmen. Her 1936 "Peace Pressure Primer" functioned as a rhetorical handbook of political persuasion for women activists in the WILPF, providing instruction and suggestions for designing both individual documents and larger publicity campaigns (Pois 380).

The Limits of Publicity and Education as Political Strategy

That the WILPF's efforts to influence public opinion had an impact is evident from the resistance they met from the press and the government, yet the impact of these efforts was hampered by many significant challenges. One of the biggest challenges arose from women's ambiguous position with regard to existing political structures of international relations. While the WILPF may indeed have had the support of innumerable women's organizations, and while the organization may have been able to widely publicize the reforms its members wished to see in international relations, it lacked real power in the mechanism of political change because so few sympathetic women were present in legislative and diplomatic bodies. Without representative voices in the central, official spheres of government, the organization's rhetorical power remained marginal. This lack of power is reflected in the argument Julia Grace Wales put forth to support her proposal for a conference of neutral nations. In that argument, she suggests that such a conference would lift "the programme of pacifism into the realm of serious political consideration. As a proposition made seriously from governments to governments, it would gain a hearing, it would have a psychological effect, such as no private propaganda could ever give it" (*Continuous* 6). Wales essentially acknowledges that discussion and endorsement of her plan within official governmental channels is far more likely to lead to results than is the kind of "private propaganda" employed by the WILPF. While the exclusion of pacifist views from official political bodies hampered all pacifist groups— of men and women—it was particularly troubling for the WILPF, whose members were doubly excluded from the "realm of serious political consideration" by their gender and their political stance (Wales, *Continuous* 6). The WILPF found itself in the position of what Nancy Fraser calls a "weak public"—a public "whose deliberative practice consists exclusively in opinion-formation and does not also encompass decision-making" ("Rethinking" 75). The impact of public opinion as influenced by these weak publics, Fraser explains, "is strengthened when a body representing it is empowered to translate such 'opinion' into authoritative decisions" (75). No such body existed to translate the WILPF's ideas. The organization could voice all manner of persuasive protests, but it had no way to ensure that these protests were heard and acted upon by policy makers.

Their position outside of official governmental channels meant that WILPF members had to rely on statesmen to take up their causes, something that did not happen very easily. In fact, statesmen tended to treat members of the WILPF politely while viewing the organization's protests as a minimal threat to the status quo. Indeed, politicians' attitudes toward the arguments of the WILPF were probably similar to Harvard philosopher William James's approving but ultimately belittling reaction to Jane Addams's book *Newer Ideals of Peace,* in which she formulated many of the ideals upon which the WILPF was founded. According to James, the book displays the work of "a deeply original mind, and all so quiet and harmless! Yet revolutionary in the extreme" (qtd. in Schott 6). Women in the WILPF could indeed espouse radical ideas to statesmen who could, like James, still view those women as "quiet and harmless."

The weakness that resulted from the WILPF's lack of official power is evident in the experiences of WILPF envoys who met with various international leaders following the Hague Congress. Based on their conversations with these statesmen, the envoys composed a "Manifesto" urging neutral nations to initiate a conference of mediation based on the Wales Plan. The manifesto expresses confidence in the likelihood of the Wales Plan coming to fruition. The envoys assert that "we are in a position to quote some of the expressions of men high in the councils of the great nations as to the feasibility of the plan" (Addams, Balch, and Hamilton 163). The manifesto continues with quotes from some of these men: "'You are right,' said one Minister. . . . 'Yours is the sanest proposal that has been brought to this office in the last six months' said the Prime Minister of one of the largest countries" (163). As a result of these words of support, the WILPF's leaders felt they had significantly influenced diplomatic thinking. These feelings were bolstered by the words of President Woodrow Wilson who, shortly after his visit with the envoys, delivered his famous Fourteen Points speech, an argument that included several of the proposals for peace espoused by the WILPF (Addams, *Peace and Bread* 59).

While the proposals of the WILPF may have had an impact on the words of traditional diplomats, the action taken by those diplomats proved less than encouraging. Based on the response of Wilson, for example, the organization "considered that the United States was committed not only to using its vast neutral power to extend democracy throughout the world, but also to the conviction that democratic ends could not be attained through the technique of war" (Addams, Balch, and Hamilton 59–60). Yet the president soon contradicted his fourteen points by advocating a larger army and preparedness for war. Disillusionment is obvious in Addams's remark that

> the persistent tendency of the President to divorce his theory from the actual conduct of state affairs threw [the WILPF] into a state of absolute bewilderment. During a speaking tour . . . he called attention to the need of a greater army, and . . .

> openly declared that the United States should have the biggest navy in the world.
> (Addams, Balch, and Hamilton 60)

While the WILPF initially received encouraging words from statesmen, those words were not binding since the women had no power to negotiate international policies. Indeed, as Addams herself acknowledged, "Perhaps the ministers talked freely to us because we were so absolutely unofficial" (Addams, Balch, and Hamilton 97).

To be sure, the WILPF recognized its lack of power. Yet the organization, in order to maintain its extensive membership, stopped short of officially advocating the immense alterations that some of its own members believed were necessary for permanent peace. The conflicting impulses to advocate radical change in official structures of international government and to amass widespread public support are evident in the WILPF's efforts to compose a plan for permanent peace after World War I. To this end, the Executive Committee of the WILPF established a special committee to propose "A New International Order." Following extensive study, this committee concluded that there was a need for a revolution in the organization of international relations. "The complexity and the interdependence of the mechanisms which regulate the life of human society are such that one cannot touch one part without disorganizing the whole," the committee report explains. "Therefore," the report continues, "a New International Order demands a complete reorganizing of the world, and Peace can come only as the result of such reorganization" (Cahier Committee 3). Speaking for the committee, chairwoman Gabrielle Duchene rejects a reformist approach:

> We believe that it is practically impossible to obtain lasting and useful reforms without a change of system. . . . How long will governments be under the domination of trusts, of capitalistic interests? Not only nations and individuals but also institutions are acting in such close interdependence that partial reforms cannot be efficient; the whole system has to be reformed. (Cahier Committee 96)

Reflecting this belief in the need for systemic change, the committee report includes an extensive, socialist plan for establishing new venues of international organization and detailed explanations of the "minimum conditions" required for a peaceful world order, including the end of "the exploitation of the middle classes, the industrial workers and the peasants by capitalism" (3).

An economic and political restructuring of the current world order, the committee believed, would enable the development of extensive communicative means for international education and deliberation. The current "venal press," which, the report boldly asserts, "in all countries disseminates its paid-for lies," would "collapse with the fall of the form of political and economic organization which supports it" (Cahier Committee 12–13). An official communicative network, based on methods similar to those used by the WILPF, might then develop: "There might then arise . . . a vast informative press which without being the slavish organ of the world government, would set forth and discuss events and problems from the point of view of the League of Peoples and of the general interests of humanity" (13).

Through these new economic, political, and communicative structures, the committee suggests, the concept of nations as bordered and bounded interests might disappear. Rather than competing for economic and political superiority, nations would work to phase out the divisive forces that structured their existence: "It is at once the duty and the interest of nations to help one another until the time when they shall unite in a single federation" (Cahier Committee 4). The restructuring of international power relationships by removing national divisions and the communicative structures that maintain those divisions, the committee report argues, would foster "human brotherhood which cannot be limited by frontiers" (4).

The committee's attitude toward divisive constructions of nationality and their hostility toward the international press surely resonated with the critiques proffered by WILPF leaders, yet these leaders ultimately rejected the committee's plan. Following a "brief" discussion, the 1924 WILPF congress voted not to endorse the report unanimously, electing instead to include on it the names of "such Sections of the WILPF as should decide to adhere to it," thus significantly reducing its force (*Report of the Fourth Congress* 163). The congress then unanimously endorsed a more reformist-oriented manifesto written by the British section and supported by Balch and Addams. This manifesto, rather than calling for a radically new international order, "affirmed the 'first principles' of the WILPF" (Pois 172). While, as WILPF historian Anne Marie Pois suggests, the manifesto "performed the function of strengthening the WILPF's identity as an international pacifist organization by advocating principles of non-violence, social and economic justice, and international organization," it also circumscribed the impact of the organization's work (174).

Although the decision of the WILPF leadership not to endorse the radical plan reflects the presence of traditional forces in the organization, it also reflects the leadership's realistic understanding of the need to maintain membership numbers. As Susan Schultz Huxman puts it, "as movements work their way from the task of enthusiastic mobilization to maintenance, they must become more practical and less visionary if they wish to escape oblivion" (94). Pushes for reconfigurations of capitalism did not sit well with the U.S. WILPF, which feared that the increasing tide of public opinion against anything possibly related to communism would result in the organization's blacklisting—a risk Addams and other leaders wished to avoid in order to keep at least a presence, if not an officially empowered one, in the discursive arenas of international politics.

Despite their struggles to create widespread support for change, the challenges posed by the WILPF to the rhetorical status quo of international diplomacy remained applicable throughout the following decades, and, one might argue, remain relevant today. Writing in an introductory essay to a 1945 edition of Addams's *Peace and Bread in Time of War,* John Dewey articulates the timeliness of the rhetorical challenges posed by Addams's thought as it had informed the WILPF almost twenty-five years earlier:

> the instruction and the warning [in Addams's thought] is against adoption and use
> of methods which are so traditional that we are only too likely to adopt them—
> methods which are called "terms of peace," but which in fact are but terms of a
> precarious interim between wars. The instruction concerns the need for adoption
> of methods which break with political tradition and which courageously adventure
> in lines that are new in diplomacy and in the political relations of governments.
> (Introduction xi–xii)

A need for new rhetorical methods of international relations still exists today, over eighty-five years after the formation of the WILPF. The WILPF's critiques of diplomacy and the rhetorical structures of international relations remain frighteningly apropos, suggesting the immense tasks still to be accomplished by those who share the WILPF's vision.

Seeking Full Measure
The League of Women Voters
and Partisan Political Communication

4

The League's records reveal what actually happened to those women
who, having sought so long the right to share in shaping the common
destiny, then faced a prolonged struggle to give full measure to their hard-
won political status. . . . With such circumstances furnishing the context,
the infant organization was forced to assess its objectives. One clearly was
to promote the political education of newly enfranchised women citizens.
Another was the establishment of some *modus vivendi* with the political
parties that would yield access to opportunities for women to take part in
the governing.

> —Louise M. Young, *In the Public Interest:*
> *The League of Women Voters, 1920–1970*

As the WILPF struggled during the late 1910s and the 1920s to change restrictive channels and procedures of international relations, other women
struggled to change restrictive channels and procedures of American electoral politics. When the Tennessee legislature ratified the Nineteenth
Amendment in August 1920, American women who had long labored for
suffrage quickly discovered that although they could now cast their votes,
the opportunity to do so existed in a constrained, male-dominated partisan
system. Partisan resistance to suffrage had hinted at the difficulties women
would face after gaining admittance to the voting booth. As National American Woman Suffrage Association president Carrie Chapman Catt observed
in 1917, "It has been the aim of both dominant parties to postpone woman
suffrage as long as possible. . . . The party machines have evaded, avoided,
tricked and buffeted this question from Congress to Legislatures, from Legislatures to political conventions" (*An Address to the Congress* 18). Women
had waited on party politicians for decades—observing, agitating, protesting, and petitioning while officially powerful literate practices (including the
act of signing the Nineteenth Amendment into law) rested solely in the hands
of male partisans. As a result, Catt explained, "Many of us have deep and
abiding distrust of all political parties" (*An Address to the Congress* 18–19).

Anticipating the difficulty of integrating former suffragists and their concerns into partisan American politics, Catt called for a successor organization to the NAWSA that would train new women voters in electoral procedures and further the interests of women within the platforms and administrative structures of political parties. This successor organization, proposed first by Catt in 1919 at the annual meeting of the NAWSA, became known as the League of Women Voters.

Women watching as Governor Edwin P. Morrow of Kentucky signs the Anthony Amendment. Courtesy of the Library of Congress, Prints and Photographs Division [LC-USZ62-110212].

Suffragists' distrust of partisan politics grew in the face of party actions in the years after suffrage. After suffrage, as before, male partisan leaders seemed to have a stranglehold on the topics and methods of political discussion. Suffragist and charter member of the LWV Catherine McCulloch even suggested to her newly enfranchised sisters that the suffrage struggle might not have been worth the effort:

> [Suffragists] might not have thought it all worth their while if they could have believed we were rescued from the Scylla of husbandly dictation only to rush wildly to the Charybdis of the Amalgamated-Union-of-Republican-Husband's Control or to the Ancient-Order-of-Democratic-Married-Men's dominance. Being bossed by one husband is not as unpleasant as the polyandric arrangement of being domi-

neered over by a combination of 10,000,000 husbands on one side or 12,000,000 on the other.

To many former suffragists, political parties appeared as impenetrable as well-established fraternal orders, populated by entrenched men who refused to view women as colleagues and coworkers.

The frustration of the newly enfranchised resulted in large part from the refusal of the Democratic and Republican parties to engage issues about which many former suffragists felt strongly. Political historian Kristi Andersen argues that in the period after suffrage, parties narrowed their definitions of the political in an effort to exclude women's concerns. Many party officials responded to suffrage by "tr[ying] to redefine politics so that women's activities and interests were clearly distinguished from men's; as a result, the space occupied by 'real' (male) politics constricted" (166). Community improvement, civic betterment, and the rights of married women were seen as women's work or private matters, and thus not granted prominence on party platforms.

Party elites also denied women positions as decision makers within party structures. To be sure, parties made gestures to embrace newly enfranchised women, but these were, for the most part, merely gestures. The Democrats named over one hundred women to their San Francisco convention in 1920, yet these women served "mainly as alternate delegates and very few [were] from pioneer suffrage states" (L. Young 48). Both parties actively worked to establish women's divisions that were staffed by women and dedicated to recruiting women voters, yet these divisions lacked teeth because they were not truly under women's control. As Anna Harvey explains, women's divisions were initially appointed by male party elites. "Even after women were admitted to party posts that were elected by both male and female voters," she elaborates, "male party committees retained the power to nominate candidates for these positions" (206). Moreover, "several documented instances exist of male party elites using their control of women's divisions to remove outspoken or otherwise troublesome women. In their stead were appointed women who were widely reputed to be much more receptive to the wishes of male party elites" (Harvey 206–7). As late as 1927, no woman had been appointed to the all-important resolutions committee at either political convention. As a League press release noted at the time, women consistently lacked a voice in "the one committee [the resolutions committee] . . . which more than any other is responsible for the party's declaration of national issues" (LWV, "Women in the Political Parties" 2). Lacking a voice in this committee was particularly dangerous because the committee not only determined which issues candidates would champion in upcoming elections, it also established the legislative initiatives the party would pursue in the immediate future.

By the end of the decade, many women who had worked hard within the parties were disillusioned. Emily Newell Blair, a former suffragist and devoted Democrat, had championed women's work within political parties after suffrage through a strategy she called "Boring from Within." This strategy involved reforming party practices and preferences by increasing women's visibility within political parties. Yet, less than a decade after suffrage, Blair retired her office in the Democratic Party, complaining that partisan attitudes toward women had actually declined since the passage of the Nineteenth Amendment (Freedman 523).

Establishing a Nonpartisan Ethos

Because party elites held tightly to their privileges, women needed to create a space from which they could critique the existing political order and voice their arguments about political issues. What Royster points out about nineteenth-century African American women writers holds true for women trying to enter political parties in the 1920s: "As people of low status or of no status or privilege, given the habitual hierarchies of power, . . . they are deemed unimportant and made invisible or non-entities" (63). In order to make women visible, audible, and legible in the discursive structures of electoral and legislative politics, the LWV needed to carve out rhetorical territory where they could establish authority as speakers and writers on political matters. The organization effected this rhetorical authority by constructing itself as a "nonpartisan" organization. From their position outside of political parties, LWV leaders hoped, women might champion legislation they found important but that political elites typically ignored.

The LWV also hoped to use their nonpartisan location to advocate reform of what they saw as ineffective methods of political communication. Similar to the WILPF, the LWV identified the revision of ineffective rhetorical models of political debate as one of its principal goals. Political discussion and change, League leaders argued, were limited by political parties' enslavement to the process of procuring votes. LWV founding members Catt and Jane Brooks argued in 1919 that because political parties "are necessarily forced to adapt their platforms to an appeal for votes," they are inherently "conservative and slow-moving." Thus, "an outside group, non-partisan, unpartisan, and all partisan," was necessary to "agitate and educate, without fear of favor, on behalf of the needed changes in our fundamental system" (Brooks and Catt 1045). Candidates and elected officials who identified themselves with a party and relied on party support for elections could not afford the rhetorical and political experimentation of expressing controversial or cutting edge opinions. Only an outside organization could pioneer legislative and communicative reforms in the tightly ordered world of traditional politics.

While parties constricted the definition of the "political," the League set itself up to expand that definition, prioritizing issues that political parties tended to overlook. According to Connecticut League leader Katherine Ludington, the new organization would allow women to move beyond the limited scope of political discussion within parties: "The desire . . . to unite women on such questions as lie outside the programs and scope of the political parties, was the mindspring of the National League of Women Voters" (qtd. in Connecticut Woman Suffrage Association 1). From this united point beyond party control, women might continue to work for legislation of interest to them. The initial organizational plan of the LWV addressed several of these issues by including committees on the legal status of women, child welfare, women in industry, and American citizenship (a committee that encompassed educational and electoral reform and food supply and demand).[1] Similarly, resolutions passed at the first meeting of the new organization in 1920 included calls for a federal department of education, an increase in teachers' salaries, the passage of the Sheppard-Towner bill for infant and maternal health, and an end to discrimination against women in civil service.

From their nonpartisan space, the LWV also sought to challenge the tenor of political debate by minimizing threatening and divisive discourse in political arguments—a change they believed would encourage greater public participation in politics. The LWV's critiques of partisan communication in many ways mirrored the arguments the WILPF deployed against conventions of diplomacy. Connecticut LWV officer Gertrude D. Smith, for instance, argued that organizations of men in politics rely on scare tactics to bring about political ends, using "the threat of tightening the purse-strings or creating fear of unemployment" to influence legislative work (3). Rather than rely on intimidation, Smith maintained, "women are trying to use only the method of public opinion expressed in an orderly and open way" to influence legislative work. Most male-run political organizations, including political parties, were too impatient to employ the practices of negotiation and education necessary for influencing public opinion, so they reverted to threats as political argument. "Public opinion is slow to form and hard to mobilize," Smith acknowledged, but she maintained that "it is the right way in a democratic country" (3). The LWV hoped to expand the role of citizens in determining the nation's course of action by removing scare tactics from the rhetorical practices of political discussion.

These changes would not be easy given the longstanding traditions of confrontation in partisan politics. Electoral traditions, Catt explained in a 1930 speech, were infused with a spirit of animosity similar to that revealed in a well-known Ben Franklin anecdote that recounts the story of two quarrelsome men who lived in the Eddystone Lighthouse. So antagonistic were their interactions that "neither wanted ever to see or to hear the other again, so one had gone to live in the tower while the other occupied the ground floor, and for six months they had not met" ("Mrs. Catt's Address" 2). Franklin's tale, according to Catt, illustrates the confrontational spirit that pervaded partisan bodies in the 1920s. Catt envisioned the LWV as an antidote to this antagonism and a force that might "drive from its midst any spirit of Eddystone that appears" and "wage war against such spirits in the home circle, all legislatures, and Congress." "With political fly brushes," she urged, women of the LWV must "swish every buzzing Eddystonean spirit" ("Mrs. Catt's Address" 2).

Despite their stinging critiques of parties and the empowerment they derived from working outside of partisan structures, League leaders stressed that women should ultimately aim for voice and power *within* political parties. While such a stance initially seems contradictory, it reflects the bind that newly enfranchised women found themselves in with respect to partisan politics. For better or worse, political power was situated squarely within the parties, a fact the LWV clearly understood, even if it did not fully approve. League officials readily admitted that "parties are the great nominating bodies that choose the candidates whose names appear on the ballot" (Connecticut LWV, "Why Do We Say 'Join a Party'?" 4). Recognizing that legislators and their agendas came from within powerful parties, the LWV encouraged women to "Join a Party."

Yet the LWV's advocacy of women's participation in parties resulted not from a desire merely to have women's involvement in politics mimic the behavior of men. Rather, the LWV hoped that women might spearhead extensive change within parties by making them more receptive to progressive legislative programs. As Catt explained of the new organization in 1919, "it is hoped and believed that all political parties will adopt the program of the League of Women Voters as their own" ("Why Not Leave"). The goal, then, was to use the LWV as a means to reform priorities and procedures within political parties. Catt, in fact, expressed a hope that the LWV might make itself obsolete within five years, having given women full voice and power within a reformed sphere of partisan politics.

Catt on "Political Parties and Women Voters"

Perhaps the most elaborate explanation and justification of the League's stance and purpose vis-à-vis political parties came in Catt's address to the first congress of the LWV in 1920. The speech, which was subsequently published and widely distributed in pamphlet form, demonstrates careful negotiation of the rhetorical context of partisan electoral politics. Political parties, perhaps rightly, saw the development of a national group of nonpartisan women as a threat to their dominance. Shortly after Catt announced her plan for transforming the NAWSA into the LWV, the fledgling organization encountered strong resistance from politicians and the popular press. In "hostile editorial comment" across the country, former suffragists were charged with "ingratitude, even treachery, in setting up an organization to compete with parties" (L. Young 34). Although the power of partisanship was lessening from its heyday in the nineteenth century, it remained a powerful force in shaping public opinion and thus not a force the LWV could ignore.[2] Responding to this sensitive rhetorical climate, Catt crafts her talk to deflect partisan criticism of the new group while also rallying members to embrace a nonpartisan stance.

Carrie Chapman Catt.
Courtesy of the League of
Women Voters of Illinois.

Catt carefully patterns her speech, blending strong critique of parties with suggestions that the LWV wished to cooperate with those parties. She begins by suggesting that partisan resistance to the LWV was the result of problems in communication experienced by both the LWV and the political parties. Catt explains that "we are so stupid on the one hand that we can't express an idea so that other people will get the same understanding we have, and on the other, we are so stupid that we can't take in other people's ideas as they understand them" (Address 2). After what seems like an acknowledgement of fault on both sides, Catt clearly places primary blame for the continuing acrimony on political parties: "The people who are interested in enrolling large numbers in political parties have expressed here and there rather cutting criticism of the League of Women Voters. They have represented it according to their own viewpoint, which is a different view from that which we hold" (2). While Catt acknowledges that the founders of the LWV may not have expressed their purposes clearly, she makes plain her opinion that partisan leaders are at fault for distorting the public's perception of the LWV.

Not wanting to offend parties too much, however, Catt quickly follows this accusation with a gesture of cooperation. After suggesting partisan responsibility for acrimony toward the LWV, Catt commends partisans for their work in securing the vote for women. Because "there was no possible way of ever getting that vote until the political parties were willing that [women] should have it," Catt explains, "ratification would not have been possible without their aid" (2). This acknowledgement of party participation in the suffrage movement, however, is not devoid of critique. Although the statement credits parties for their assistance in securing the passage of the Nineteenth Amendment, it simultaneously registers a complaint about the slow pace at which parties responded to women. The parties were willing that women should have the vote, Catt goes on to clarify, only after "suffragists had worked with political parties for almost sixty years" (2). Furthermore, Catt suggests that women's work with parties in the suffrage battle happened not out of mutual respect, but rather out of necessity—because "there was no possible way of ever getting that vote until the political parties were willing." Cooperating with parties, Catt implies, had never been a particularly pleasant feature of political action for women—it was, however, unavoidable.

Catt then offers assurances that the LWV was not intended to discourage women's participation in traditional partisan politics, but these assertions are undercut by a critique of traditional partisanship. In fact, Catt dedicates much of the rest of the speech to demonstrating that party structures at the time posed a serious threat to political communication, particularly for women citizens. The potential for practical disenfranchisement of women as a result of party dominance, Catt argues, had become evident through limited partisan response to women's enfranchisement in western states. Despite their enfranchisement in several states beginning in 1869, women of the American West remained relatively powerless within political parties. Explaining the results of an NAWSA study of women's involvement in political parties after suffrage in western states, Catt notes that "although the women had been voting for many years in some of the states, and they were enrolled in parties, their positions were pretty largely those of a mere ladies' auxiliary" (Address 3). These women suffered, Catt suggests, from the absence of an organized, nonpartisan group of women that could agitate for policies and legislation outside of entrenched partisan networks. Because "the old suffrage associations had gone to pieces [in the wake enfranchisement in these western states] there was no common body that could ... bring political influence to bear" on behalf of women within those states (3).

According to Catt, the struggles of women in western states should be a lesson for the wide range of American women assembled as the LWV. The disempowerment of women vis-à-vis political parties across the nation, Catt warns, "may happen in the future and especially if the women do not go into the political parties with the intention of being something more than a me-too inside those parties" (Address 4). Instead, women must make a concerted effort to attain rhetorical power within parties:

> women must persuade men to respect and to have confidence in the capacities of women. . . . Because women have the vote, it doesn't follow that every man who is an election district ward or a county chairman has suddenly become convinced that women can do things as well as men. (4)

Throughout the speech, Catt emphasizes that increasing women's power within political institutions would require an organization, such as the LWV, to apply pressure to parties after suffrage.

Catt also uses the speech to lay out a second, critical line of work for the LWV: encouraging American women to participate in the project of opening political discussion to women. According to Catt, the LWV "must stimulate other women to forward movement and encourage them to increase self respect" (4). The struggle after suffrage, in other words, would involve overcoming resistance from women as well as men:

> The mass of women will be hesitant and timid and doubtful of themselves. . . .
> [T]hey will be content to stand back and not use the power and the brains and the

consciences that they have. They will be content to think that everything they find ready made to their hands is all right, no matter how wrong it may be. (4)

Catt charges her listeners and readers to counter this situation by helping women recognize weaknesses within the American political process and by preparing women to participate in eradicating those weaknesses.

To illustrate the kinds of problems women might encounter as they attempt to work through party structures, Catt provides a vision of how parties might try to exclude women from the rhetorical activities of greatest political consequence—the writing and speaking practices involved in composing platforms and selecting candidates. She describes the hypothetical entry of a new woman voter into a political party thus:

> Probably when you enter the party of your choice you will find yourself in a sort of political penumbra where most of the men are. These men will be glad to see you and you will be flattered by their warm welcome, . . . but if you stay still longer and move around enough . . . you will discover a little denser group, which we might call the numbra of the political party. You won't be so welcome there. . . . Those are the people who are planning the platforms and picking out the candidates, and doing the work which you and the men voters are expected to sanction at the polls. And if you stay long enough and are active enough, you will see something else—the real thing in the center, with the door locked tight, and you will have a hard, long fight before you get behind that door, for there is the engine that moves the wheels of your party machinery. (5–6)

Because of restrictive party structures, Catt suggests, newly enfranchised women should expect to remain several levels removed from the conversations of greatest consequence, leaving them with the "privilege" of sanctioning the proposals of party men. The vote alone could not give women political power because it did not provide persuasive power within the engines of electoral politics.

Despite her haunting vision of silenced partisan women, Catt stresses that women should work within political parties. No matter how despicable party attitudes toward enfranchised women might be, those parties maintained a stranglehold on political action in the first two decades of the twentieth century. Catt's realization of this situation is reflected in the advice she offers in the speech shortly after detailing how tightly parties will guard against women's full participation. The parties, Catt counsels, "are going to carry your legislation into law and you must be part of those parties. You must move right up to the center of the thing and get your influence there" (Address 6).

Once again, though, Catt's recommendation that women work through party structures comes with a strong critique of partisan methods. The LWV's ultimate goal, she continues, is to challenge the kind of partisanship that had controlled American electoral politics prior to the Nineteenth Amendment. Catt identifies two types of partisanship. One "is the kind [of partisanship] that reasons out that a certain platform has more things in it that you endorse than any other and that this party has more possibilities of putting those things into practice than any other" (Address 6). The LWV would advance this first kind of partisanship. Doing so, however, would require that the organization overthrow the prevailing patriarchal form of partisanship, a form which, according to Catt, "makes you a republican or a democrat because you were brought up in those parties and your grandfather and your father were in them" (6). Unthinking tradition is the guiding principle in this kind of partisanship: "You don't know the antecedents of your party, but you know they were right. You don't know what is your platform or what your party stands for but you are for it" (6). The LWV, Catt emphasizes, should work to eradicate this second, predominant model of partisanship: "I hope that the League of Women Voters will so do its work that it will teach this nation that there is something higher than the kind of partisanship that 'stands pat' no matter what" (7). Through the intervention of a nonpartisan group such as the LWV, partisanship might come to mean not blind allegiance to a party, but support of the party that puts forth the most comprehensive and desirable platform.

While she carefully weaves calls for former suffragists to revolutionize partisan politics with statements that might appease party elites, Catt also articulates a rationale for the gender-specificity of the LWV. She argues that new women voters are well suited to dispel traditional partisan allegiance, to encourage thoughtful political communication, and to invigorate the process of public opinion formation on matters of political importance. To fulfill their promise as political leaders, however, women required a gender-specific space that would empower them to speak and write without the suspicion endemic to partisanship. Within the LWV, "Democrats from Alabama and Republicans from New Hampshire must be friends and work together for the same things and without doubt of each other's sincerity" (Address 7–8). From the nonpartisan space of gender solidarity provided by the LWV, women would be able to resist divisive partisanship while demonstrating how to work collaboratively for political goals.

To the very end of her speech, Catt carefully blends calls for women to challenge parties with assertions that they must work through parties. The closing paragraph perhaps best encapsulates the complex mediating position Catt hoped the LWV would come to hold between women voters and political parties. In these final remarks, Catt provides words of encouragement for members of the fledgling LWV. Members must prepare to withstand the disbelief and ridicule of men who will be unable to see political participation in anything other than restrictive partisan terms: "I must further warn you that only about one man in twenty-five will be big enough to understand that you, a republican, can work with you, a democrat, in a non-partisan organization and be loyal to your respective parties at the same time" (Address 7). Not only would women in the League face skepticism based on traditional partisanship, they would face it based on sexism. Party leaders, Catt predicts, would doubt women's ability to succeed in an endeavor in which men had repeatedly failed (7). Despite the doubts of partisans, women were obligated to press forward. In the face of critique from traditional politicians, women of the LWV should battle for a higher principle: "Important and compelling as is the power of the party, the power of principle is even greater" (7).

While these words seem to provide a moral charge to battle against political parties, Catt's next words soften her blow to partisanship. The LWV's work, she proposes, should effect the reconfiguration, rather than the elimination, of partisan structures. The reconstructive efforts of the LWV would create parties that facilitate rather than inhibit the expression of the will of well-informed voters. "Whether our Nation attains [a higher] welfare," Catt argues, "depends upon the conduct of the voters who compose the parties. Independent, intelligent, lofty principled voters make great parties and great parties make great nations" (Address 8). The LWV, in other words, would shape political discussion and influence the political process by preparing voters for informed use of party mechanisms.

A Punch and Judy Show

While Catt's speech received a fair amount of public attention, the LWV needed many avenues to spread their critiques of party dominance. The first step in increasing the desire of new women voters to challenge traditional partisanship was to convince them of the disservice done to them by political parties. The League often relied on humor and dramatic methods to present their arguments against blind partisanship. In the decade after suffrage, local, state, and national branches of the LWV composed and performed numerous skits as a way to further their critique of political parties.

In order to depict the absurdity of political machinery in the early 1920s,

Mary Gray Peck of the New York City LWV composed *How We Make Them Love Us, or Pitfalls in Politics: A Punch and Judy Show.* The play includes satirical portrayals of party politics, as indicated by the cast of characters at the beginning of the play. In addition to Punch and Judy, the play includes

MR. POLITICAL MACHINE, Proprietor of the Elephant Dry-Cleaning
   Outfit and the Donkey Spray Tank.
WADFIRST MAYFLOWER, Engineer of the Dry-Cleaning Machine.
MIKE TAMMANY, Teamster of the Spray Tank.
MAJOR VOTE-THE-STRAIGHT-TICKET, Chief of Police.
REPUBLICAN LANDSLIDE [and] DEMOCRATIC LANDSLIDE, Two escaped
   lunatics

By indicating that Mr. Political Machine is the "proprietor" of both Republican and Democratic establishments in the play, Peck suggests the monolithic nature of party politics. Both parties are run by the same proprietor, allowing little room for variety or difference in strategies or platforms. The only significant difference between the parties at the time, Peck's characterizations imply, was the class-base upon which each constructed their dominance. Mike Tammany is a "teamster," suggesting the power the Democratic party derived from organized labor, while Mayflower is an "Engineer," suggesting that the organization catered to the interests of professionals—a suggestion supported by the direction that he be clad in "capitalism costume" (11).

The two main characters of the play, Punch and Judy, represent the forces of tradition and reform in electoral politics. Punch is "the old fashioned voter" recently married to Judy who represents "the National League of Women Voters" (1). Punch, as the representative of old-fashioned politics, has many friends who are traditional partisans. Peck describes these old allies as "bachelors" who resent Judy's presence in Punch's house (3). Judy's character, on the other hand, embodies the nonpartisan methods of political influence the LWV wished to promote. When the newlyweds move into Punch's home in the first scene, Judy discovers that it "is in dreadful disorder" (2) and sees it as her responsibility to straighten things out. Similarly, when Punch announces that some of his partisan friends will be visiting, Judy informs him that she has been "well-trained in good manners" by LWV leaders and so will know how to communicate effectively with them. She assures Punch that she plans to follow LWV advice: "Carrie Chapman Catt says, we must appeal to [partisans'] minds and convince them of the justice of our demands" (2) Judy thus represents the new woman voter, trained in the rhetorical practices of partisan political influence while also highly skeptical of that influence.

Judy also promotes the LWV's goal of initiating collaborative political reform activity among U.S. women's groups. This goal was partly realized through the efforts of the first LWV president, Maud Wood Park. In 1920, Park created the Women's Joint Congressional Committee (WJCC), a powerful forum for women's voices in national politics. The WJCC served as a women's lobby in which vast numbers of women could organize in support of particular pieces of legislation. Over the course of the 1920s, the committee involved between ten and twenty-two national women's organizations (the number of member organizations fluctuated during the decade)—and represented an estimated ten million women. The WJCC's Lookout Committee monitored congressional sessions for measures that might be of interest to women. News of noteworthy legislation was then circulated nationwide via the WJCC's member organizations. As a WJCC press release touted in 1921, "This committee acts as a clearing house for information concerning bills pending in Congress. Through it women from one length of the country to the other are kept in touch with the progress of legislation in which they may be interested" (Women's Joint Congressional Committee, "Press Notice for 1921").

Park's early plans for a national network of women's organizations clearly inform Judy's lines and actions in the play. When Political Machine offers to help Judy with her housecleaning "at a moderate figure," Judy informs him that she has already enlisted the help of "Mrs. Working Woman" and "her friends," including "Mrs. Consumers' League, Miss YWCA, [and] Mrs. Federated Clubs" (4). Judy, as a representative of the LWV, plans to coordinate interested groups of women in a larger project to improve political procedures. As she explains to Political Machine, "Maud Wood Park [first president of the LWV] says we must join forces with them, and they will help us in every way" (3). The national network of women publicizing their perspectives on electoral matters would, Judy suggests, lead to change.

In addition to elucidating the goals and methods of the LWV, the skit cautions its audience about the steadfastness with which political parties would resist women's input and offers extensive critique of traditional partisanship. At one point in the play, Tammany and Mayflower vehemently assert in unison that Park and Catt "are criminals [and] ought to be jailed. Maud Wood Park is trying to put me out of business—Mrs. Catt ought to be hung! They all ought to be hung! Hanging is too good for 'em!" (5). Mr. Political Machine even levels the charge of bolshevism against Judy, reflecting the red-baiting attacks women's organizations suffered during the period. Perhaps the most biting critique of traditional partisanship, however, comes through the characters Democratic Landslide and Republican Landslide. The Landslides, who are described in the dramatis personae as "two escaped lunatics," dart about the stage dressed in ridiculous costumes. Republican Landslide enters "wearing an elephant's head, covered with streamers, carrying a horn, banner, etc." Democratic Landslide accompanies him "wearing a donkey's head, ringing bells and braying" (6). Together, the two "career about the stage," proclaiming their intentions to usurp complete power. "[T]ooting horn, ringing bell, [and] braying," they "knock Judy on the head" while exclaiming "WOW! I'm King of the United States! WOW! I'm King of Europe! WOW! I'm King of the World! WOW! I've wiped every damn thing off the map!" before exiting in a "pandemonium of noise" (6). Peck's portrayal of diehard partisans as egomaniacal warmongers speaks volumes about the LWV's frustration with the divisive and procrustean modus operandi of political parties.

The play concludes by emphasizing the reform work the LWV is poised to perform in the political arena. Unable to persuade Judy to accept the services of either Tammany or Mayflower, Mr. Political Machine calls for the assistance of Major Vote-the-Straight-Ticket, who is appropriately dressed as a police officer. Straight-Ticket informs Judy that the parties "are the only housecleaning agencies authorized to work in this town, and you will have to employ them" (8). Judy refuses adamantly: "I WON'T TAKE EITHER OF THEM. I AM GOING TO RUN MY OWN HOUSE!" (8). In response, Straight-Ticket exclaims, "Young woman, you are a menace!" and hits her on the head with his nightstick (8). Despite three violent attempts to change her mind, Judy remains insistent that she, like the LWV, will not work through corrupt party machinery. The Devil then comes to take Judy away because he has heard she is a bolshevist. Judy, however, convinces the Devil that the true bolshevists are Mr. Political Machine, Tammany, and Mayflower. The play closes with the Devil sending the partisans to eternal damnation.[3]

Throughout the humorous scenes of the skit, the larger message is clear— the League is determined to work outside of and perhaps in spite of the established parties. Yet it is interesting to note the contradictions in the play's message. The strong resistance Judy encounters suggests that the pressure-politics approach promoted by LWV leaders might not be particularly effective given the power of tradition. Audience members probably wondered how characters like those portrayed in the play could ever be "persuaded . . . to respect and to have confidence in the capacities of women"—the goal Catt established in her speech to the inaugural meeting of the LWV (*Political Parties and Women Voters* 4). Furthermore, given the critiques of people like Katherine McCulloch, who expressed dismay at the parties' treatment of women as subordinate wives rather than political colleagues, it seems counterproductive to represent the relationship between male voters and the LWV through the marriage of Punch and Judy. On the one hand, this choice merely reflects the popular generic conventions of a "Punch and Judy Show," yet the genre itself is informed by the same kind of sexism the LWV protested in the operation of political parties. As I examine in greater detail below, the early texts and rhetorical practices of the LWV often reflect the contradictions and limitations of the historical moment in which the organization began.

Getting the News to Women Voters

Political parties were not alone in raising the ire of the LWV. The fledgling organization held the popular press accountable for much of the dysfunction in American politics. The newspaper, the League argued, was the primary means by which the American public learned about political matters, but the majority of pressmen failed to meet this responsibility ethically. In a 1922 report entitled "Newspapers and the Getting of News," Massachusetts League leader Florence Kitchelt presents damning evidence of newspapers corrupting democracy. The report, based on a 1922 LWV-sponsored conference on international journalism, begins by stressing the importance of the newspaper to an informed, involved citizenry: "In the *Atlantic Monthly,* Walter Lippmann said that 'the newspaper is in all literalness the Bible of democracy, the book out of which a people determines its conduct. It is the only serious book most people read. It is the only book they read every day'" (1). But this bible, Kitchelt laments, perpetually misleads the public. For democracy to succeed, Kitchelt asserts, "we, the people, [must] have facts upon which to base that public opinion which our government is expected to translate into action" (1). The press, however, "is muddied by prejudice, partisanship, subversive propaganda, and suppression of facts" (2). The situation was made more deplorable by the time constraints many Americans faced. "The woman voter with three children and all the housework, where shall she obtain knowledge and where shall the wage-worker with scant leisure?" asks Kitchelt (1). Being properly informed, in other words, was a luxury given the state of popular news reporting in early twentieth-century America.

The news at the same time was corrupted by many factors, most notably by economic and political interests. Kitchelt argues that "news is a commodity, to be sold as silk and pig iron, not by the yard and ton, to be sure, but by the column, by the inch, by the word" (3). Within domestic politics, the buying and selling of news meant that the wealthiest group or party could control the editorial slant of the paper, leading to news that is "unreliable, misstated, partisan, controlled toward a certain policy, and suppressed in important particulars" (2–3). When a local editor decides "for a few hundred local readers" or, more significantly, when an Associated Press editor decides "for a whole continent" what information deserves attention, his choices, Kitchelt stresses, are often prompted by the preferences of the paper's owner, "whose financial assets the paper must both guard and augment" (5). Journalistic bias, Kitchelt is careful to mention, was also evident in papers with partisan leanings: "We get contrary stories of the same political event in Democratic and Republican papers" (4–5). Relatedly, Kitchelt continues, government staff and elected officials often have a hand in crafting news favorable to themselves: "Governments . . . desire to give certain impressions, to cultivate certain opinions, and therefore they arrange their statements for the public with that point in view" (5).

These deplorable conditions of journalism necessitated the intervention of an organized, principled group like the LWV. Kitchelt suggests that the organization might intervene in two particular ways. First, it might focus on reforming the relationship readers assume toward their daily newspapers. Americans tended to passivity in their reading. According to Kitchelt, "We shout and subside with our daily press, either to make unjust war on Mexico, or to live in careless ignorance of the causes of the industrial war being waged all about us" (10). A critical step in reforming the journalistic practices that publicly promote injustice and ignorance, Kitchelt urges, involves educating the American public in methods of critical media analysis: "The best way to reform the papers is to reform first ourselves, the reading public." More specifically, Kitchelt advocates that courses in "how to read the news" be conducted for both the young and the adult student. Such courses might help Americans to "read with discrimination—and distrust on occasion" so that papers might feel pressure to reform their processes of selecting and circulating news. Kitchelt recommends that "every local League of Women Voters . . . make a study of its neighborhood press, and educate the voting citizen in the use of the newspaper as a preliminary to the use of the ballot" (12).

In addition to teaching women how to use the press intelligently and democratically, the LWV endeavored to produce publications to circulate "unbiased" political information to the American public. LWV leaders realized that women lacked this all-important access to political information. Given what they saw as the deplorable state of public information provided by political parties and the popular press, the League developed its own publication and circulation networks in order to involve women in political discussion, debate, and persuasion. In these endeavors, Dewey's theories about communication and democracy particularly appealed to the League because, like many new women voters, he recognized that political discussion was ruled by excessively powerful political parties during the 1920s. Writing in *The Public and Its Problems* (1927), Dewey laments that

> instead of individuals who make choices which are carried into effect by personal volition, there are citizens who have the blessed opportunity to vote for a ticket of men mostly unknown to them, and which is made up for them by an under-cover machine in a caucus whose operations constitute a kind of political predestination. . . . The public is so confused and eclipsed that it cannot even use the organs through which it is supposed to mediate political action and polity. (120–21)

Reviving democracy, Dewey suggests, would require improving channels of political communication:

> If the Great Society is to become a Great Community . . . so that an organized, articulate Public comes into being, the highest and most responsive art of communication must take possession of the physical machinery of transmission and circulation and breathe life into it. . . . [F]or democracy . . . will have its consummation when free social inquiry is indissolubly wedded to the art of full and moving communication. (112)

Improvement of society and democracy can only be accomplished, Dewey argues, with "the improvement of the methods and conditions of debate, discussion, and persuasion" (114). The LWV made such improvements their ultimate goals.

League Publications

Although Kitchelt does not address the issue directly in her report, the LWV believed that popular media were particularly oppressive to women readers because of what they presented as "appropriate to women"—primarily beauty, entertainment, and society-page fare. In protest of what popular newspapers tended to publish as items "of interest to women," the LWV produced a spoof newspaper, the *Ballot Box Review*. This paper presents a gendered world turned on its head. One headline in the *Review* announces "Legislature Grants Jury Service for Men." The article that follows repeats arguments that were commonly made against women serving on juries but applies them to men in order to reveal the absurdity of those arguments. For example, the article reports that "Senator Sneed," speaking in support of the legislation, asserted that "in the states where men serve as jurors there is not the least intimation that manhood has lost any of its sensitiveness, that chivalry is decadent or that men have [been] contaminated and stained by jury service" (1). It seems absurd to argue that men would be contaminated by such service; so too, the LWV suggests through this satire, was it absurd to argue that women would be.

The *Review* also includes a mock "Ladies' Page . . . devoted to the alleged interests of women." In a satirical column entitled "Household Hints," the *Review* reports that "Mrs. Bozo Snyder writes of a new way to remove grease spots. She says: 'Take a pair of sharp scissors and cut around the spot in a wide circle. Care should be taken to keep the fingers out of the path of the scissors." Similarly, in a mock beauty advice column written by "Miss Minx," one letter asks, "I have tried in every way to get rid of freckles as I am otherwise an attractive girl of neat appearance. What do you suggest?" In response, Minx writes "Did you ever try skinning?"

League leaders did more than critique the press, however; they developed their own publications to help women become more knowledgeable citizens. League-sponsored newspapers and periodicals served numerous important functions in the development of the organization. These functions were similar to those served by the African American periodical press in the nineteenth century, which, Royster has explained, "helped the community articulate its own problems, deliberate its own needs, celebrate its own achievements, and identify strategies capable of effecting change in the larger sociopolitical context" (218).

One important step in encouraging new women voters to get involved in politics was fostering a sense among them that they were part of an extensive, interactive network. At the national, state, and local levels, League publications developed quickly with the purpose of establishing such a network. The national LWV, for instance, contributed monthly reports to the *Woman Citizen*, a national periodical devoted to the interests of women's organizations such as the YWCA, the NAWSA, and the GFWC. These regular contributions to the *Woman Citizen* strengthened the LWV by inspiring widely dispersed members with the success stories of various Leagues. In April 1921, the monthly report of LWV activity in the *Woman Citizen* included a survey of work accomplished by Leagues across the country. "We Are Coming Hundreds of Thousands Strong" features brief reports from state and city Leagues and pictures of state League chairwomen. The compilers of the report suggested that readers engage the briefs and the pictures as they would a "march" of the state Leagues, similar to what women might witness if they attended a convention. The photos and summaries serve a purpose similar to a parade at a national LWV convention—they are intended to rally women together around the work of the LWV. As the compilers further explain,

> The dominant note of all of these reports is that of women in massed formation and prepared for action. Each state League of Women Voters is in the pages to follow speaking up as at roll-call. . . . Every state has been urged to tell what it considers its best, or worthiest or most significant [activity]. . . . When the evidence is in, the sum of experiences, it is expected, will make a guide for future work, will stimulate, enlighten, encourage. (1159)

The authors assert that through this article the League "is making its *apologia pro vita sua*"—charting a course for its entire membership (1159).

By 1922, the League's monthly reports had developed into a four-page monthly newsletter, the *Woman Voter,* which appeared as a special section of the *Woman Citizen.* According to Elizabeth Hauser, then secretary of the national LWV, this newsletter was

> devoted to systematic information about plans, persons, and happenings such as would scarcely furnish material for magazine articles, but which will still contribute to the success of the things the League stands for, by bringing all state Leagues into closer touch with one another and with the national organization.

The publication was presented not as a newspaper to attract women readers through coverage of sensational stories or beauty treatments but as a means of connecting diverse women in the discussion of political activity. Hauser also emphasizes that "every woman voter is invited to join the news-gathering staff and to send to Washington headquarters any bit of news, any pertinent comment, and any suggestion for betterment, which will help to strengthen interest in the work of the League." Reflecting the interactivity the LWV hoped to achieve through its publications, Hauser encourages her readers to contribute to the discussion of politically relevant information rather than simply receiving it from the newsletter.

During its first decade, the LWV expended great effort and expense to enlarge the political horizons and rhetorical abilities of women voters. While the national office of the LWV published and circulated monthly and weekly bulletins that reached an estimated 250,000 subscribers in the early 1920s, local and state Leagues also published periodicals, including over twenty different titles by 1922 (Fletty 8; "Leagues in Journalism" 18). Women in many cities and towns received national, state, and local publications in an effort to edify their political knowledge and increase their ability to enter into conversation on current political topics. A League member in Cleveland, for example, regularly received national LWV publications (including the *Woman Voter*), the *Ohio Woman Voter,* and the *Cleveland Voter* ("Leagues in Journalism" 18).

Like their predecessors in suffrage and temperance organizations, leaders of the LWV realized the importance of controlling their own media outlets. Without such control, it would be immensely difficult to publish and circulate political information to women because mainstream media outlets typically regarded political news as men's news. League publications were designed specifically to deviate from what popular news organs portrayed as "women's interests." Accordingly, articles included in LWV periodicals were "a far cry from the typical 'woman's page' which editors have for so many years insisted on, out of their preconceived notions of what women like or at least ought to like" ("Leagues in Journalism" 18). Rather than the domestic or etiquette issues that popular newspapers tended to put on the "woman's page," League publications approached issues of political and economic interest to women. According to Minnie Brewer, editor of the Clarksdale, Mississippi, *Woman Voter,* national, state, and local LWV organizations strove to produce media outlets in which "every variety of economic, historical, and political question receives attention" ("Leagues in Journalism" 18).

In this spirit, many LWV publications kept members abreast of legislative campaigns at the state and national level. The national LWV's *Legislative News* provided an update of congressional action on all measures officially supported by the national organization, including the Child Labor Amendment and the Sheppard-Towner Bill for Maternity and Infant Health. Specific publications were also developed to respond to the urgency of different legislative situations. During the months when the Connecticut state legislature was in session, the Connecticut League published a weekly overview of legislative action, informing readers of bills supported by the League and reporting how different representatives voted on those measures. In the case of particularly controversial bills, national, state, and local Leagues distributed "Briefs for Action." These short pamphlets provided an overview of the status of the bill in the legislature (in committee, on the floor, etc.) so that members knew when to exert influence. Leagues at all levels often supplements "Briefs for Action" with shorter leaflets, called broadsides. Broadsides could be produced and distributed rapidly and thus were an efficient means of raising extensive support when a crucial vote was expected (Fletty 10).

The League also developed texts—most notably the questionnaire and the survey—to gauge and publicize the political opinions of officeholders and candidates on League-supported legislation. As might be expected, such literate practices disturbed many partisans. The League's public rationale for gathering this information, therefore, explained the work as "fact-finding" designed to provide voters with details about candidates and legislators so that they might make more informed choices at the polls. Other explanations, particularly those circulated among League members, constructed these literate practices as acts of political advocacy. The purpose of a candidate questionnaire, explains the author of a 1928 LWV member's handbook, is three-fold. First, the questionnaire serves voters "by providing accurate information about the candidates and their views on public questions, particularly those in which women are most interested." Second, it serves the candidate "by providing a fair and dignified means for the expression of their views in a way to reach large numbers of voters." Third, it serves the legislative interests of the LWV "by interpreting the League and its program to the candidates and the public" (LWV, *Get Out the Vote* 18). The questionnaire, in other words, could be used to publicize the LWV's program and to persuade candidates to support the LWV's agenda.

Through both content and form, the LWV designed its texts to engage women in the political arena. The ultimate goal of League publications, first LWV vice president Marie Edwards explained, was to "make government interesting, stimulating, and serviceable to the person who is indifferent" ("Excerpts" 2). More specifically, the organization sought to expand political discussion to include the new woman voter, who had little or no previous incentive for political participation. Accordingly, LWV leaders emphasized the need to translate difficult ideas into language that a wide audience of women could process and put into practice. Because specialized language might effect the removal of women from political communication, the League eschewed technical or complex language in their texts. During a lecture delivered to a League-sponsored "Civics Study" at the University of Wisconsin, League member Mrs. Henry Youmans explained the importance of language in education for civic participation. More specifically, Youmans called for a "more vital kind of teaching" to replace the traditional pedagogy of school civics courses which were "taught in about the same way as Latin is taught"—in other words, in unfamiliar language and completely removed from lived experience (qtd. in "Civic Study"). Rather than relying on this "dead language" approach to instruction in citizenship, the League published and circulated articles in what they considered to be an accessible style. This accessible style sought to engage women in political issues by using "terms of living rooms and offices rather than of libraries and academies" (Sherwin qtd. in Brumbaugh 31). The vocabulary of LWV publications, in other words, derived from the lived experiences of women. A study of League publications by the Carnegie Corporation in the late 1920s suggests that the League had succeeded in their attempts to engage a broader public. The study reports that League texts were "well adapted to the needs of the layman and non-student" (qtd. in LWV, "The League as Publisher").

In addition to using vocabulary familiar to many new women voters, LWV publications followed particular formats in response to their audiences. New women voters, LWV leaders recognized, might be discouraged from participating in politics if they needed to wade through complex and lengthy explanations of electoral processes or legislation. One of the most common genres the LWV employed was the informative pamphlet, a genre "designed to give authoritative treatment that is nevertheless simple and brief" (Brumbaugh 31). One reviewer of League publications asserted that LWV texts were "as directly usable as a cook-book" ("Your Vote and How to Use It" 34). If the reader followed the clear directions—the recipes—provided in League publications, she could produce the desired legislative result. The similarity between League publications and cookbooks also reflects the League's desire to link their texts to the lived experience of women, many of whom were responsible for food preparation in the home.

To ensure that their publications used widely accessible style and formats, the League established a reading committee to review all national publications before they were circulated. This committee made a regular practice of returning drafts to writers with suggestions for revision. Reading committee notes in the national LWV archive indicate that revision suggestions tended to focus on simplifying the language of a text so it could be readily understood and appreciated by a nonspecialist audience. One committee member comments to the writer of a pamphlet, "Domicile and Citizenship of Married Women," that the "explanation of the differences between settlement, residence, and domicile seems too long. . . . [I]t might be given in one brief paragraph. Most of our readers would require and want less detailed information." Another member remarks about the same pamphlet,

> I would suggest an opening paragraph to arouse interest in the subject. . . . For instance, the first question in my mind was, 'Why should I be interested in so technical a subject?' . . . Such an opening paragraph, it seems to me, should relate the subject immediately to our common experience. (Judd)

To get the attention of American women, many of whom lacked motivation to participate in political affairs as a result of previous disenfranchisement, writers of LWV texts had to appeal directly to the lives and immediate concerns of those women.

Nonpartisan Broadcasts

The League also used the new technology of radio as part of its rhetorical practices of political engagement. Radio technology expanded rapidly in the 1920s, providing a means of publicizing political concerns outside of long-established newspapers and their partisan biases. As Michael Sproule has recently noted, "Between 1920 and 1924, broadcasting accelerated from a handful of stations to 600 licenses granted; during the same interim, the number of radio sets in use rose from approximately 60,000 to 3 million" (33). Enthusiasm for the power of radio to carry political information to a previously inaccessible audience of women grew during the 1920s at the national offices of the LWV. At the April 1927 annual meeting of the League, M. H. Aylesworth, president of NBC, announced his support for a radio program to be hosted by the League on a weekly basis. In January 1928, the League began to broadcast its "Voters' Service," presenting weekly discussion panels about contemporary political issues via twenty-three radio stations across the country.

The LWV's zeal for radio as a nonpartisan means of increasing women's participation in political discussion is evident in the proud words of second LWV president Belle Sherwin. In a brief talk launching the Voters' Service, Sherwin articulated the LWV's belief in the democratic and educational promise of radio broadcasting:

> Tonight the League of Women Voters is at supper at this hour in many cities and states, united by the magic of radio in a citizenship school as novel in circumstance as it is familiar in purpose and policy—namely to throw more light on practical problems and pressing political situations, and to do so without partisan prejudice. Sight unseen the members of the League are all agog with interest tonight in the possibilities of citizens learning through this new medium how to become more intelligently a part of government by the people. With applause unheard we welcome the very great opportunity offered. ("Radio Address" 3)

As Sherwin's address suggests, the Voters' Service complemented the educational efforts of League publications. Through radio technology, the LWV hoped "to familiarize the public with the issues of the campaign, and to educate them for intelligent reception of partisan discussions" (Aylesworth). Using new technology, the League worked to prepare citizens with the knowledge to assess the information they received through partisan channels.

The content of the Voter's Service programs, and the terms in which the

LWV explained these programs, showcased the complexity of the LWV's nonpartisan rhetorical stance, promoting political dialogue while carefully tiptoeing around partisan censure. The service was not designed to replace information provided by parties, but rather, Sherwin explained, "to supplement and round out what the political parties give [by] presenting . . . men and women who are recognized specialists in important phases of domestic and foreign politics" ("Radio Address" 3). Addressing the audience of the first broadcast—an audience that undoubtedly included many skeptical party men—Sherwin constructed the Voters' Service not as the LWV's attempt to challenge established political parties, but as a forum of nonpartisan experts and specialists. To help maintain this nonpartisan ethos, Sherwin cautioned invited speakers that "the purpose of the Service is to inform and clarify but not to *promote* any platform or point of view." Instructions provided to speakers emphasized that, although speakers "are not required to be unpartisan," they should attempt to "present fairly all points of view which are important as factors in the development of the issues before the country in the campaign year" (Sherwin, "Information for the Convenience of Speakers"). Furthermore, cooperation, not partisan confrontation, should guide the programs: "all speakers will *discuss* subjects not debate them. They will aim to suggest ideas not to argue for them. They will raise questions and not always answer them." To avoid the kind of animosity prevalent in party disagreements and, no doubt, to protect themselves from the wrath of parties, the League presented its radio program as a time of collaborative inquiry rather than sustained debate or divisive partisan argument.[4]

Sherwin also envisioned the Voters' Service as a medium for increasing collaboration and dialogue among women voters. She urged members and listeners to get involved in the radio conversation by "talking back to us. . . . Tell us what subject you want to hear about, what speakers you would like to listen to" ("Radio Address" 3) In this way, Sherwin suggested, women listening to the program might become agents in their own continuing political education: "You can double the value of this new course in adult political education by making known what information you are conscious of needing." To enhance this educational potential, the LWV assisted members in organizing "listening-in classes" that would function "as a means of continued discussion" (qtd. in "Tune-in Tuesday").

Not only did the radio provide a technology through which the League could involve a much wider audience in political conversations, it also strengthened women's sense of participation in a national network of political communication. In a Voters' Service address commemorating the tenth anniversary of suffrage, Ludington convened a national meeting via the airwaves: "The League of Women Voters has never seen a day like this! From California to Maine, we are *together* as if we were in one room, thinking the same thoughts, honoring those who made this day possible, appraising the use which we have made of the tool they put in our hands" (Ludington, "A New Tool" 1). Voters' Service programs enabled League members to hear one another on a weekly basis and, through that shared listening time, participate in a weekly national meeting.

It was no easy task to prepare texts, both published and broadcast, upon which political knowledge could be built and political consciousness formed, yet it was one that the LWV strongly believed new women voters required. In the absence of meaningful sources of political information for new voters, the LWV created its own publications and distribution networks. These networks would, the LWV hoped, unite women voters in the discussion and support of legislation that political parties minimized or overlooked. A nonpartisan network would thus open up a space from which new women voters could challenge party domination of the topics and methods of political communication.

The LWV as Counterpublic

Fraser argues that, as a central strategy in their efforts to challenge dominant modes of public discourse, competing publics create "parallel discursive arenas [and] invent and circulate counterdiscourses, which, in turn permit them to formulate oppositional interpretations of their identities, interests, and needs" (*Unruly Practices* 123). She offers Mary Ryan's study of women's voluntary associations in the nineteenth century as an example of how this process works within diverse publics: "Ryan's study shows that, even in the absence of formal political incorporation through suffrage, there were a variety of ways of accessing public life and a multiplicity of public arenas" (116). Even after official political incorporation, a large number of women continued to work through competing publics to prepare themselves for full political participation and to advocate changes in the electoral system so that they might "give full measure to their hard-won political status" (L. Young 1). I conclude this chapter by examining the struggles and rewards that accompanied the LWV's attempts to create a "parallel discursive arena" from which to challenge partisan politics.

The Perils of Nonpartisanship

In the eyes of its founders, a nonpartisan LWV would function beyond traditional boundaries of the electoral sphere as a counterpublic to the dominant partisan system. According to an early LWV pamphlet, the LWV operates on the beliefs that women

> should study public questions, not as good citizens only, but as WOMEN citizens; that there are matters for which women are peculiarly responsible; and that an organization of women is necessary in order to give these matters the emphasis in government that their importance demands. (*Principles and Policies* 1)

Members of the LWV developed women's counterdiscourses—manifested in their publications and broadcasts—to critique the restrictive literate practices of partisan politics.

As one might expect, the LWV regularly clashed with the members of the partisan public. These clashes were particularly vitriolic when they touched upon the meaning of the term "nonpartisan." Especially troubling to parties, and to some LWV members who wished to maintain partisan ties, were the League's seemingly contradictory objectives to work for "the development of a higher order of citizenship among women" and for "the holding of voting women together for legislative ends" (Brooks and Catt 1018). The organization claimed to provide nonpartisan training in citizenship, while simultaneously advocating particular reform measures and legislative planks within political party structures. In the 1920, 1924, and 1928 presidential election years, the LWV composed a "Woman's Platform" of legislative demands and presented it to leading party conventions in order to pressure parties to include those planks in their official platforms (Harvey 109–10). While this "Woman's Platform" was not directed at any particular political party (and thus could be defended as "nonpartisan"), it was intended to influence partisan actions—an intention that partisan leadership did not respond to kindly.

The League's promotion of legislative reforms disturbed partisans in other ways as well. While the LWV claimed not to endorse candidates, League-circulated information about particular measures inevitably resulted in certain candidates appealing more than others to women voters. Furthermore, the organization often found it difficult not to support more progressive-minded candidates over more conservative ones. Shortly after the founding of the organization, during the 1920 elections, for example, the LWV officially opposed the nomination of anti-suffragists James W. Wadsworth, a Republican candidate for Senate from New York, and Frank Brandegee, a Senate candidate from Connecticut. This decision to take an official stance on candidates created great hostility from parties and offended several party-active women. While the League would refrain from officially endorsing candidates later in the decade, its stance on different political issues and the information it circulated about where different candidates stood on those issues surely swayed voters for or against particular candidates.

Furthermore, the League's presentation of "facts" was far from neutral with regard to legislation or candidates' positions on legislation. Despite League claims that their Voters' Service broadcasts aimed to present "all points of view," the speakers and topics included in the service generally reflected the LWV's progressive political agenda. Speakers who participated in the first year of the service included Franklin D. Roosevelt on the history of presidential campaigns; Senator Frederick H. Gillett on the World Court; Senator Robert LaFollette on "The Progressives and Labor in the Campaign"; C. C. Merrill, Secretary of the Federal Power Commission on "Power and the Public"; and numerous speakers who provided instructive overviews of congressional activity, including lessons on the "machinery of Legislation" as well as specific updates on particular progressive measures (LWV, "Speakers in the Voters' Service").

The nonpartisan descriptor attached to the LWV's discursive endeavors also led to conflict within their counterpublic. Many LWV leaders believed that nonpartisan education for citizenship should focus solely on teaching women the procedures of voting (how to register, how to mark a ballot, etc.) and could not justifiably co-exist with advocacy of particular legislation. At the League's 1922 national convention, several leaders suggested that the League focus on one aim or the other, not both. Lucy Miller, head of the Pennsylvania LWV, argued that the organization should focus on educating its membership about electoral and governmental procedures and on working to improve these procedures. To this end, she moved that a "Department of Efficiency in Government" be the League's chief department and that the departments concerned with specific social legislation, such as the committees on child welfare, social hygiene, and the legal status of women, be abolished (L. Young 65). In response, future League president Sherwin argued that participation in campaigns for specific legislation was essential in motivating women to pursue political education and thus could not be separated from it (L. Young 65). Such conflict over the League's nonpartisan stance would, as I explore further in the next chapter, continue throughout the decade.[5]

If the League's nonpartisan stance distressed some of the organization's supporters, it certainly ruffled the feathers of the partisan faithful. An early article about the new organization published in the *Woman Citizen* summarizes partisan resistance to the idea of a League of Women Voters:

> Ever since the project [of the LWV] was broached by Mrs. Catt [in 1919], interest in it has steadily grown. For the most part, that interest was based upon an intelligent appreciation of the intent and purposes of the proposed organization. . . . [S]uch opposition as was voiced was all projected from the same base—"women should not be lined up in a woman's party against men." (Brooks and Catt 1018)

To combat what they saw as an amassing of women into a women's party, partisans attacked the credibility of the LWV and its leaders. Like the WILPF, the LWV was included on the "Spider Web Chart" and labeled by many traditional politicians as a threat to American democracy, despite the fact that the organization pledged support to the American war effort.

It is important to consider how League leaders responded to this hostile political climate in their initial formulations of the organization and its purposes. All arguments—including arguments articulated through the counter-discourses of a competing public—are intimately connected to the contexts in which they are constructed. As V. N. Volosinov explains in *Marxism and the Philosophy of Language,* any utterance—written or spoken—is the product of both the speaker (or writer) and the audience(s) that speaker (or writer) addresses. Every utterance, according to Volosinov,

> *is a two-sided act.* It is determined equally by *whose* word it is and *for whom* it is meant. As a word, it is precisely *the product of the reciprocal relationship between speaker and listener, addresser and addressee.* . . . A word is a bridge thrown between myself and another. If one end of the bridge depends on me, then the other depends on my addressee. (86)

The arguments counterpublics construct to justify their practices inevitably respond to the interests and biases of other publics operative at the time. League leaders' configurations of the organization responded to their relationships with multiple competing publics. Not infrequently, the LWV leaders' descriptions of their purposes reflect the political backdrop of powerful parties and strong nationalism in the World War I era. League leaders attempted to justify their project in terms that political leaders and party men (often the same people) would find difficult to critique—those terms, unfortunately, were sometimes ethnocentric and elitist. Catt and other founders of the League justified their new organization in part by playing on contemporary popular fears of espionage and military weakness. In Catt's initial articulation of the LWV, warnings of an immigrant-based "literacy crisis" threatening American democracy appear side-by-side with calls for the newly enfranchised to embrace the LWV's goals of reforming partisan politics and promoting progressive legislation.

An Opportune "Literacy Crisis"

In "A Nation Calls," an address delivered to the 1919 Jubilee Victory Convention of the NAWSA and subsequently published in pamphlet form by the LWV, Catt urges suffragists to continue working together even after the culmination of the suffrage campaign. She uses the celebratory occasion to pose several important questions to the group assembled before her. Once suffrage is attained, Catt ponders in the speech, "Can we ... desert the woman industrial worker in this crucial moment when exploitation and sex conflict threaten her security? Is it not our duty to stand by her and her cause for the sake of all womanhood?" (5). Responding to her own questions, Catt urges the women of the NAWSA to reconfigure themselves as an advocacy organization that might further progressive labor legislation. She explains that the time is ripe for women to take on this active role in promoting women's concerns: "normal evolution and the quickening influences of war have made a new world for women and that world is calling to women voters to keep pace with the new demands" (4). The time had come for women to work together for the benefit of all women.

While a constitutional amendment legalizing woman suffrage would do a great deal to improve women's status as U.S. citizens, much work remained to be accomplished in other areas of the law. Although legal conditions for women had improved greatly since the origin of the NAWSA, women still had to confront the "curious relics [and] little forgotten oversights" in the legal codes of various states (4). Catt provides several examples of such relics: the age of consent, which at the time was eighteen in Wyoming but only ten in Florida; a woman's claim to guardianship over her children, which she had in Illinois but lacked in Louisiana; the status of abuse as grounds for divorce, which was sufficient cause in most states but not in South Carolina; and the legal length of the workday for women, which in Colorado was eight hours but in Alabama went as high as sixteen hours. A League of Women Voters, Catt stresses, could advocate for the unification of these laws, based on "the best and clearest" ones (4–5).

Catt's argument about the potential legal impact of the LWV, however, takes up only the first quarter of her speech. Most of the remaining three-quarters explains that a League of Women Voters is needed to combat a literacy crisis threatening American political life. Caught up in the nationalistic fervor of the recent world war, Catt proclaims illiteracy a force "more menacing to the future security of our country than any other" (8). According to Catt, illiterates provide "hothouse growth potential" for foreign espionage and seriously compromise the military power of America. To illustrate the threat of illiteracy, Catt quotes figures from a report of the Secretary of the Interior: "There are 700,000 men who cannot read or write who may be drafted within our Army within the next year or two." These illiterates constitute a serious threat to American security because "they cannot read their orders posted daily on bulletin boards in camp. They cannot read their manual of arms. . . . They cannot understand the signals or follow the Signal Corps in time of battle" (8).

"Foreign born" illiterates, Catt suggests, are particularly dangerous and pose an "almost insurmountable handicap to war preparation" (9). She relays the story of a "group of Italian and Slavic men" who could not properly participate in military drills due to difficulty understanding orders given to them in English, and she provides details about a commander of a machine gun regiment to whom "a group of illiterates and foreign-born were sent." The commander had sent most of these illiterates away after a few days "because they could not be trained to handle a machine gun until they had first been taught enough English to understand instructions" (9). On the civilian front, Catt argues, illiterates hamper women's patriotic participation in the war effort. The committee to enroll women for war service, according to Catt, "was hindered by . . . perplexing misunderstandings" that caused non-English-speaking women to be "easily convinced by troublemakers that the Government intended to conscript them into munitions factories far away from their homes and their children" (10). Through several other examples, Catt paints a frightening picture of an illiterate-immigrant menace to national security.

Catt also constructs those not able to read and write English as threats to the progress of political institutions and the reform of partisanship. Illiterates, she indicates, had long provided fodder for corrupt political party men: "Not only would woman suffrage have been established many years ago, but political corruption . . . would have been stamped out in all its worst manifestations long ago, had these millions not offered dangerous temptations to unscrupulous men" (13). Immigrants, as much as corrupt partisans, thus take the blame for the prolonged suffrage battle.

Catt's arguments and examples appealed to the strong anti-immigrant sentiments of the time. With the congressional override of the vetoed immigration bill in 1917, national policy came to stipulate that "all aliens over sixteen years of age, physically capable of reading, who can not read the English Language, or some other language or dialect, including Hebrew or Yiddish" would not be permitted to immigrate to the U.S. (Gere 20). In identifying literacy as a requirement for legal immigration, the bill reflected worry among political elites that a burgeoning immigrant population would inhibit the traditional functioning of American democracy by bringing the threat of communism to the country. Such xenophobic anxiety could be used to the advantage of the LWV. To fight the "menace of illiteracy," the NAWSA, Catt argued in 1919, should reconfigure itself as an organization to teach literacy in English and the ideals of American democracy. Catt thus initially offered the LWV as a "patriotic" attempt by newly enfranchised women to "use their new found freedom to make their nation safer for their children and their children's children" (*A Nation Calls* 22). Reflecting both the fear of foreigners and the war fervor of the times, Catt presents the LWV as a means for women to serve their country: Soldiers "have fought 'over there' for the spirit of democracy. Shall we not give over to them a country in which democracy is realized by a people speaking one language, reading its own ballots, and honoring one flag?" (22).[6]

While a substantial portion of the address relies on narrow patriotic sentiments to justify the formation of the LWV, Catt did not neglect to use the occasion to critique partisan politics. The indictment of illiterate immigrants, in fact, provides Catt with an opportunity to discredit traditional partisanship. It was deplorable that illiterates made war preparation difficult, but, Catt suggests, the war itself was caused by the even more deplorable corruption of political parties: "had political parties stood for American ideals in their practice as well as in the brave words of their platforms and made war on corruption instead of using it secretly each to beat the other, we would never have had a war" (14). Furthermore, Catt accuses, partisan leaders encourage uninformed "bloc" voting among illiterate immigrant populations:

> Political committees driven madly by the push and whirl of a campaign have little time for ethics. . . . [As a result] the ends justify the means . . . and the system as it exists is utilized to the full with as little actual knowledge of the facts allowed to leak out as possible. (15)

Big business is also to blame for the uninformed traditions of voting. Men of commercial America, Catt argues, "make contributions to parties or candidates' expenses, in a spirit of self preservation. In exchange for contributions they received assurance that no legislation shall disturb the even tenor of their way" (16). Often, this money is used to influence voting blocs—party machines, supported by big business dollars, provide material incentives (cash, gifts, etc.) to immigrant groups in exchange for their uninformed vote. Catt goes so far as to call big businesses and manufacturers "contributors to political confusion" (17), suggesting that illiteracy among immigrant groups is a threat to American democracy not because of foreign-led political radicalism, but because of partisan-led, big-business-financed political obfuscation. The real danger for American democracy, in other words, is not immigrant illiteracy per se, but political illiteracy—or the inability to use language to participate actively and critically in political life. Political parties, Catt suggests, perpetuate political illiteracy.

Like women's clubs before it, the LWV was deeply ambivalent about immigrants. Gere has discussed at length the ambivalence of "white middle-class clubwomen" toward immigrants in the late nineteenth and early twentieth centuries. A clear "tension . . . between embracing and spurning immigrants" permeates Catt's speech (Gere 59). Despite an extensive description of the danger posed by illiterate immigrants to the American way of life, Catt ultimately rejects the term "Americanization." The term should be eliminated, she asserts, because of its patronizing connotations: "Let us begin by eliminating the word 'Americanization'! That word . . . sounds too much like oppression, whereas the only way to succeed in making true Americans is to give them incentives to be Americans in all the senses that word implies" (*A Nation Calls* 19). Yet shortly after she rejects the term "Americanization" because it seems too oppressive, Catt proposes nine rather ethnocentric methods for addressing the "menace of immigrant illiteracy," including an "Oath of Allegiance" as a condition for enfranchisement; the establishment of English as a national language; the implementation of stricter processes of naturalization for the foreign born; and a civic education test as a precondition for voting (19–23).

The LWV's second national president, Belle Sherwin, would explain the notions of education, citizenship, and literacy quite differently than Catt had in 1919. According to Sherwin in 1928, the League "used to say 'education,' was essential to the success of democratic government and by education meant 'literacy.' Now we are more convinced that 'education' is essential and means a continuing of political education" (qtd. in Mabie). Beyond learning English and the rules for being a good American citizen, Sherwin clarifies, "political education consists in experiencing a relation to government and acquiring information and a capacity to act in that relation in the public interest" (qtd. in Mabie). For Sherwin and many other LWV leaders, the goal of the LWV was not a narrowly defined process of immigrant assimilation but a multifaceted effort to further effective, rather than nominal, political literacy among women—a goal the following chapter examines in detail.

The Limits of the League

As Catt's initial justification of the League hints, membership in the LWV was not egalitarian. The organization reflected the fact that history, experience, and context always inform one's understanding of what counts as a public matter of significance. As Iris Marion Young has suggested,

> People necessarily and properly consider public issues in terms influenced by their situated experience and perception of social relations. Different social groups have different needs, cultures, histories, experiences, and perceptions of social relations which influence their interpretation of the meaning and consequences of policy proposals and influence the form of their political reasoning. (408)

The League could not speak for or to all women voters. Membership and participation were determined in large part by class, race, ethnicity, and political preference.

The League's arguments about its ability to represent the interests of women citizens effaced significant political difference among those women. First of all, members and leaders of the League tended to be white and middle or upper class. While the LWV promoted labor legislation and engaged many issues related to the working class, its status as a voluntary association meant that its leaders had to have a substantial amount of leisure time to dedicate to the organization. Working women simply did not have the resources required to be active League members. Second, many women chose to work actively within political parties and, as a result, protested the formation of the LWV. Ruth Hanna McCormick, suffragist and leader of the GOP's Women's Division in 1920, maintained that the League was unnecessary because it duplicated efforts women were making through work within established party structures. Similarly, the Women's Republican Club of New York sent resolutions to major newspapers protesting the formation of the LWV. According to these Republican women, the LWV was "a nonpartisan party" that served only to foster "dissension between men and women voters whose interests are identical" and thus constituted "a menace to our national life" (qtd. in L. Young 34).

The gender-specific nature of the organization was also problematic because it muted the variety of issues that interested American women. While the LWV claimed to represent the interests of women voters at large, many women voters organized in competing associations with significantly different political agendas. When the LWV attempted to unite women behind a legislative program, they encountered substantial resistance from members of the National Woman's Party who argued that labor reform in the interest of women required an Equal Rights Amendment to the Constitution rather than piecemeal, protective measures applied only to women workers. In their attempts to unite women behind a legislative program that favored protective labor laws, LWV founders perhaps underestimated the variety of sometimes-conflicting interests among politically active women, a situation that weakened the impact of the organization's claims to speak for women voters.

Furthermore, the League's claims to support the interests of women in the political arena floundered when it came to the subject of women candidates. One of the organization's primary purposes was to procure more powerful voices in government for newly enfranchised women, yet its nonpartisan stance precluded it from supporting women candidates. While women candidates made modest gains in state legislative offices in the two years after suffrage, they had much less success in building their presence in national political bodies.[7] In the 1922 elections, for example, although sixteen women ran for Congress, only one woman succeeded, Winifred Mason Huck of Illinois, who was elected to complete the term of her father. Several defeated women candidates chided the LWV for holding to a nonpartisan stance and not supporting their candidacy. To many women, true power in politics would come only through increasing the number of women holding public office, yet the LWV could not openly support women candidates because such action would conflict with their professed nonpartisanship. In an attempt to resolve this conflict, the LWV added a paragraph to its program in 1924 urging the election of qualified women to public office:

> The League believes that qualified women in administrative office, upon boards and commissions, and in legislative bodies will contribute a necessary point of view to government in the United States and to its international relations. The League therefor urges the election and appointment of qualified women to positions in national, state, and local government. (qtd. in L. Young 74)

Beyond making this broad proclamation, however, the LWV did not officially endorse female candidates, a move that appeared counter to their goals of increasing the responsiveness of government to the concerns of women.

The ongoing debates over the LWV's nonpartisanship and gender-specificity manifested themselves in a proposal forwarded by Catt in 1922. Catt suggested that the organization consider dropping *Women* from its name and invite "progressive-minded men" to join the group in a larger endeavor to determine "an independent political policy for the nation" (qtd. in L. Young 49). As LWV historian Louise Young notes, this plan clearly contains "suggestive overtones of a third party" (49). Under this new configuration, the League would no longer be *non*partisan but *new* partisan. The proposal reflects Catt's disappointment at the gender-exclusive, nonpartisan organization's slow progress toward political power. Although Catt's plan for the development of a new party never came to fruition, it revealed the conflicting discourses the LWV espoused as it tried to establish itself as a powerful competing public and to provide newly enfranchised women with a voice in the conversations of American politics.

Rhetorical Education
for Political Influence
The LWV and Political Literacy

5

> We believe that as women we need the training ground given by the
> League of Women Voters: first, to teach us the facts about the contribu-
> tion we wish to make, and to enable us to form public opinion; second, to
> teach us how party and governmental machinery operates and how it can
> be improved so as to permit increasingly of the open expression of views
> at the right time for action.
>
> —Gertrude B. Smith, President of the
> Connecticut LWV, "Thinking Party Membership"

When political party leaders hesitated to appoint women to powerful administrative posts or to consider legislative concerns of importance to many
women, former suffragists responded by establishing the LWV. From its
location outside of traditional political parties, the LWV worked to involve
women in local, state, and national political discussions by training them in
techniques of political influence. While nonpartisan media might raise the
political intelligence of women voters, the LWV hoped to teach women citizens to do something with—to *act* on—that intelligence. Their goal, as
Ludington explained in 1920, was to "develop an intelligent and active electorate" (Connecticut Woman Suffrage Association 1). To this end, the organization developed educational methods to encourage women' participation
in electoral procedures and to train women as political rhetors.

Promoting Active Political Literacy

The LWV wished to prepare women for what they called "political literacy"
(Fletty 9). The League understood literacy to mean something similar to
Royster's definition of it as "the ability to gain access to information and to
use this information variously to articulate lives and experiences and also to
identify, think through, refine, and solve problems, sometimes complex problems, over time" (45). Political literacy, in this configuration, involves both
access to politically relevant information and, perhaps more importantly, the
active and strategic use of writing and persuasive skills in political arenas.

The League contributed to the development of women's political literacy in the decade after suffrage by increasing members' access to political information and by teaching them rhetorical strategies for political influence.

Because the LWV desired to cultivate active women citizens, their educational practices often involved women directly in the processes of political influence through experiential learning. Just as Dewey's understanding of the link between communication and democracy influenced LWV activity, so too did his emphasis on the link between active education and democracy.[1] According to Dewey, progressive education in a democracy should prepare citizens to conduct research, engage in debates, and enact solutions to problems alongside (or sometimes in opposition to) the officials they elect. Democratic education, Dewey argues, should not be based on "scholasticism"—by which he means a concern for theoretical arguments rather than the current experience of learners. Too frequently, he suggests, traditional educational practices remove learners from their immediate experience by teaching them ideas that have been developed by remote individuals:

> one has only to call to mind what is sometimes treated in schools as acquisition of knowledge to realize how lacking it is in any fruitful connection with the on-going experience of the students—how largely it seems to be believed that the mere appropriation of subject matter which happens to be stored in books constitutes knowledge. (*Democracy and Education* 342)

Rather than book learning, Stephen Fishman and Lucille McCarthy explain in their study of Dewey and composition instruction, Dewey advocates the teaching of concepts "not as isolated ends in themselves, but as interdependent tools for addressing pressing social problems" (66).

According to League historian Valborg Fletty, to instill in women the desire to do something with the political education they acquired through the LWV, "John Dewey's philosophy of learning to do by doing was adopted. Study was related to use and action.... The end sought was not mere interest in government, but doing something about government" (12). The LWV's *Handbook for League Workers* encouraged LWV officers to help members "experienc[e] a relationship with government" through experiential education methods such as field trips and participation in focused campaigns (15). League experiential education was geared to help women witness firsthand the rhetorical tactics of public influence. Field trips, for instance, involved small groups "visit[ing] for purposes of observation or of securing information" a variety of important sites, including courts; boards of education; and city, county or state legislative bodies. After observing these arenas of influence, LWV members were encouraged to follow up on the arguments they had observed by writing to or interviewing a legislator or other appropriate official (15).

A Deweyan pedagogy distinguished LWV education for citizenship from the instruction typically provided in academic settings. According to first national LWV secretary Elizabeth Hauser, the LWV "has for its purpose the education of women in political science, not the political science of textbooks and of schools, but the political science which relates government to everyday life" (qtd. in "The Mission of the League" 19). In fact, the LWV came to view academic approaches to education as a foil to their endeavors. According to early Connecticut LWV president Mary Bulkley, the LWV "understands the fascination and danger of academic opinions unqualified by practical experience" (11). When it came to education for improved democracy, Bulkley asserted, one could not simply study all of the time but instead must become directly involved in politics "because the political boss is not only studying, but working day and night to get what he wants" (11). The LWV hoped its educational campaigns would result not in good women students of politics but in actively engaged women voters who might collaboratively reform American politics.

Newly enfranchised women, the League maintained, were particularly well positioned to lead a Deweyan project of expanding democracy through political education. An early LWV press release claims that "since women are newly enfranchised and bound by no entanglements of political precedent or mental habit, they can approach the subject freely and fairly" (LWV, "League's Efficiency in Government Department"). Furthermore, according to League publications at the time, women "have so far no political habits and are therefore capable of acquiring good ones" (LWV, "Purpose of the League of Women Voters"). Women's lack of experience, these publications claim, thus actually bolstered women's credibility as political reformers. Political education also came under women's purview because, founding League official Marguerite Wells asserted,

> women are natural teachers. The kind of lives they have lived made them that. They are not impatient of arriving at results by the long method of education, line upon line, precept upon precept. It may even be a biological difference. The mothers must have faith in slow processes. (9)

Similar to the WILPF's justification of women's special role in promoting peace, the LWV's explanation of women's ethos as political educators derived from popular assumptions about women's roles as mothers.

Despite their claims about women's fitness as teachers of political literacy, LWV leaders could not overlook the fact that many newly enfranchised women appeared not to be overwhelmingly interested in political participation. Of the estimated twenty million new women voters, less than half of those registered went to the polls in November 1920. While voter apathy was strong among both men and women in the election, League leaders were particularly distressed by the low numbers of women at the polls and the paucity of women elected to office. Michael McGerr's study of the voting habits of men in the late nineteenth and early twentieth centuries suggests that the decline of party rituals, such as rallies and torchlight parades, led to the loss of a sense of belonging and brotherhood in the political process and, consequently, to a lower voter turnout among men. Women voters, LWV leaders believed, also lacked a sense of belonging to the political process but for different reasons. Women's relationship with political parties was not declining; rather, it had never really existed in the first place. Women needed to feel motivated to participate in a system that had long excluded them. As Louise Young notes, the LWV realized that "the ballot was merely the entry ticket to full citizenship, and the impulse to participate would have to be galvanized" (2).

Charles Stewart, Craig Smith, and Robert Denton explain in *Persuasion and Social Movements* that social movements, as part of their leaders' attempts to involve others in a cause, will "resort to rhetorical events and 'happenings' such as ceremonies, annual conventions, and anniversary or birthday celebrations" (64). The League's programs for political education initially included extensive plans for rhetorical events designed to foster "political socialization" in new women voters (L. Young 3). Through a process of political socialization, the LWV hoped to convince women that they were part of a significant group that was involved in a significant task. To raise enthusiasm for political involvement, LWV branches held birthday parties for new voters and presented them with a "Voter's First Birthday Souvenir Edition" of the League publication *Parties, Politics, and People* (LWV, *Practical Suggestions for a Voter's First Birthday Party* 9). New voter birthday parties publicly acknowledged young women as voting citizens and initiated them into the electoral process. Even the birthday cake reinforced the importance of what the newly legal voter could do. The cake, according to LWV instructions for conducting "voter's first" birthday parties, was to be "presented by the League president as a symbol of good citizenship, the knife as the tool or ballot" (*Get Out the Vote* 17). Birthday parties and other ritual celebrations helped the LWV cultivate a sense of responsibility for voting among women.

Sophia Horne and Elizabeth Honicutt with LWV fliers, Atlanta, Georgia, c. 1926. Photo courtesy of the League of Women Voters of the United States.

To further this sense of responsibility, the national LWV also circulated copies of a "voter's prayer" to state and local Leagues. The prayer encourages reverence for voting, particularly in local elections: "above all, teach us to pray for guidance before local elections as we are wont to pray in times of great national stress and panic" (LWV, "Press Release"). The prayer also reminds women voters of the struggles endured by their suffrage foremothers and, in the process, creates an obligation to vote: "help us, we pray Thee, to hold fast the measure of freedom bequeathed us; help us to carry on for others the fight they fought for us." The prayer closes by comparing the act of going to the polls to the journey of the Magi to see Christ:

> Give us wisdom to select leaders for the sake of our country's future; give us courage to support them and strength to elect them; and for the sake of Thy dear Son, bring to pass days set apart for election when we go reverently as went the Wise Men of old, guided by thy star to lay our gift of wisdom, courage, and strength before the cradle of humanity.

The voter's prayer implies that voting is a sacred duty, one owed to God and to the leaders of the suffrage movement.

Citizenship Schools and Institutes of Government and Politics

To further women's political socialization, the LWV designed and sponsored a variety of educational forums to acquaint women with the duties attending their enfranchisement. After the 1919 NAWSA convention, Catt and various faculty from the University of Chicago organized "a school of citizenship"—a series of lectures and discussions addressing topics such as political primaries, parties and party machinery, fraud in politics, campaign funding and finance laws, the judiciary system, and the distribution of power in the federal government. Leaders of the LWV attended this multiple-day school, listening to experts discuss important aspects of American politics. The school's lectures were subsequently published, along with supplementary lessons and study questions, in the *Woman Citizen*. These published courses expanded the LWV's efforts to prepare and motivate inexperienced and perhaps intimidated women for political participation. As the preface to one published lecture explains,

> The lesson . . . is going to be elementary in form. It is going to tell the politically educated suffragist a great deal that she already knows. But [these lessons] are not meant for the politically educated woman. They are meant for her next door neighbor who has "always believed in suffrage but never been active." ("Carrie Chapman Catt Course" 1086)

Like all LWV educational efforts, the article continues, "this is a course of action."

Based on this first school in 1919, citizenship schools—also called voters' schools—became a common endeavor for state and local Leagues during the 1920s. Citizenship schools were "short, simple, informing[,] chiefly designed to make clear the relationship between the individual voter and government" (LWV, "Educational Methods"). In many cases, this relationship could best be explained in local contexts, through the study of municipal government or school district systems. The Connecticut LWV partnered with Trinity College in 1922 to host a school of citizenship on "Efficiency in Government." Under this broad theme, the school provided sessions on "Progress in Science and Politics"; "The Distinctive Contribution of Women to Political Life"; and "The Social Aspect of the Courts." The school also incorporated a variety of sessions of local interest, including "The District System of School Management" and "The Proposed Civil Administration Code for Connecticut" ("Trinity College Offers" 1).

With a focus on teaching direct involvement, citizenship schools regularly incorporated experiential learning. The Boston LWV, for example, arranged a "Citizenship Day" as part of its annual citizenship school efforts. On Citizenship Day, LWV members and other interested voters gathered at City Hall to hear representatives from various departments of city government talk about what they do ("In Boston"). Other schools engaged women in applied learning activities, such as mock senates, elections, and judiciaries. The Massachusetts LWV set up "mock city government[s]" through which members "debated, decided and ruled in parliamentary fashion the entire season" ("State Leagues"). Similarly, the Indianapolis League hosted a school with a "mock Senate" in which each member of the class was assigned a U.S. senator to "impersonate" while debating a current bill ("State Leagues").

In addition to citizenship schools, the League sponsored institutes of government and politics. Institutes, the LWV hoped, might provide women with the opportunity for extended discussion of political issues between elections—periods when political parties traditionally lessened their activities. In contrast to parties, which organized for work around campaigns every two or four years, the League believed that "voting is an interest which cannot be developed purely for campaigning purposes, whipped up from time to time and allowed to stagnate in periods of comparative political calm" (Sherwin, qtd. in Mabie). Instead, the League asserted, "democracy requires a continuous process of individual political education."' Institutes responded to this need by "deal[ing] analytically with governmental machinery and issues" (LWV, "Educational Methods"). Typically developed in conjunction with colleges and universities, institutes cultivated sophisticated "background thinking" about important political topics such as international relations, industrial development, social hygiene, and municipal affairs.

Subjects covered in institutes and citizenship schools often dealt with communicative processes in politics. An institute developed in conjunction with Columbia University in 1923 addressed "Efficient Law Making," with sessions devoted to exploring "the composition and procedure of modern legislative bodies with attention to such proposed reforms as . . . expert bill drafting" (LWV, "Advanced Announcement"). Similarly, a citizenship school on "Foreign Affairs" hosted by Radcliffe College in 1924 considered structural constraints on international negotiation through topics such as "The Geographical Basis of International Politics," "Foreign Relations of the United States," and "International Organization" (LWV, "School of Politics: Foreign Affairs"). Within these larger themes, roundtables at the Radcliffe institute explored possibilities for reform through organizations such as the World Court and the League of Nations.

Other LWV schools aimed to prepare women to exert political influence by analyzing techniques of publicity and public opinion formation. An early LWV school of politics hosted by Radcliffe in 1922 focused on "Popular Control of Government" (LWV, "School of Politics: Growth of Popular Control"). Under this broad theme, speakers led discussions on topics such as the "Growth of Public Opinion in Democracies," "Popular Education in a Democracy," and "New Political Powers of the People." The LWV's specific concern for women voters and their relationship to partisan politics clearly informed this study of public opinion and democracy through sessions such as "Women's New Relation to Public Questions" and "Are Political Parties a Necessary Evil?"

While the LWV believed it was important to analyze existing methods of public influence, they also felt women needed to be trained to use those methods to advance their political goals. To teach women about publicity methods, the 1924 Radcliffe school included roundtable discussions on "Public Information: Sources, Circulation" and "Methods of Organizing Information to Stimulate Public Opinion" (LWV, "School of Politics: Foreign Affairs"). Other LWV-sponsored schools addressed the composition of persuasive arguments. As part of their state convention in 1927, for instance, officers of the Connecticut LWV attended "a training school for learning methods of formulating and expressing [an] opinion" on political issues (Bulkley 1). Such training programs taught women how to present a political argument in the manner the LWV desired.

Training also came through the accomplished women speakers who were frequently showcased at League schools. While many male faculty taught at LWV schools, prominent women were also extremely active in them. A school at Trinity College in Connecticut, for example, included sessions on women and jury service and women in industry led by Judge Jean Norris, city magistrate of New York, and Miss Julia O'Connor, president of the International Brotherhood of Electrical Workers ("Trinity College Offers" 1). Another school included talks by "Mrs. Bessie C. Fischer, a justice of the peace" and "Miss Opal Slater of the Yale Law School" discussing "Judges, Juries, Courts, and the People" ("Judges, Juries"). Exposing new women voters to such accomplished women educated those new voters and provided them with role models. As part of her talk on "Justice in the Courts," Fischer encouraged the 330 members of her audience to work toward securing more women justices. Women should not be intimidated from pursuing this office, Fischer argued, because of their limited employment background. The office, she stressed, does not require that its holder "be deeply learned in the law"; rather "it is vastly necessary to have a thorough course in the school of life so that one can weigh crime and the reason for its commitment in a big, well-balanced scale" (qtd. in "Judges, Juries"). Women, these female speakers suggested, can and should be active participants in political conversations.

Higher Education for Citizenship

The LWV envisioned an important role for higher education in their plans to increase women's political influence. Ultimately, the organization hoped to position itself as a channel through which higher education might enrich civic discourse. Numerous universities and other venues of higher education cooperated with LWV branches in this endeavor. The list of colleges and universities assisting in educating the new electorate through schools and institutes in the 1920s is quite impressive, including Yale, Virginia, William and Mary, Brown, Ohio Wesleyan, Trinity, South Carolina, Oklahoma, Minnesota, Bates, Iowa, Alabama, Washington University, the University of Chicago, and many others ("Where Citizenship Has Been Taught" 18–19).

University extension and adult/continuing education divisions were particularly receptive to LWV-sponsored citizenship courses. In the early 1920s, the St. Louis board of education included LWV citizenship courses, taught by LWV instructors, in their night school offerings. That same year, both Washington University and the University of Missouri worked with state Leagues to provide extension courses ("Survey of Citizenship School Work" 1339). In Massachusetts, university extension courses in "Women and Civics" used as their textbook the Massachusetts LWV publication the *Massachusetts Primer of Citizenship and Government* ("We Are Coming" 1159). The strong connection between the LWV and university adult education in the 1920s prompted *St. Louis Post-Dispatch* journalist David Lawrence to remark that the League "might as well be a university extension as a mere voters' organization."

Colleges and universities also assisted the LWV in their efforts to train new teachers of political persuasion. Sometimes these efforts took the form of individual sessions within institutes of government and politics. The League's institute at Columbia, for example, included a session on "Popularizing the Teaching of Government," which provided an in-depth roundtable discussion of "the most efficient methods of teaching others to teach" ("Institute" 1). In other cases, the LWV collaborated with colleges and universities to offer courses to train teachers in the methods of public influence. These schools, appropriately called League "normal schools," were "usually held at some large college or university, and ... attended by local [LWV] officers and their assistants" ("In the South"). League members attending these "normal school" sessions were expected to design citizenship courses in their localities based on what had been discussed. One such normal school was offered through the General Extension Division of the University of Florida. As leaders of the Florida LWV reported, "The fundamental idea of the school was to train women to assist in a wider spread course of civics next winter" ("In the South"). Similarly, five State Teachers' Colleges in Missouri held "an intensive short course in Citizenship" in cooperation with the state LWV("In Missouri"). These schools provided citizen-training credential certificates signed by both the State Normal Principals and the Missouri League of Women Voters.

The LWV attempted to situate education for citizenship in locales familiar to women. Thus, women's colleges were particularly important venues. Radcliffe College hosted yearly schools of politics throughout the decade, addressing many of the most pressing questions the League wished to bring to the attention of new women voters. Not only did activity at women's colleges attract local women to the citizenship school or institute, it also encouraged female students at the college to become involved in the LWV. By 1928, college Leagues were operational at eighty-nine institutions of higher education in twenty-eight different states—seventy at colleges and universities and nineteen at normal schools. To coordinate discussion among these collegiate groups, the national LWV office produced *New Voter,* a newsletter devoted solely to the activities of college Leagues. The national LWV believed college LWV branches could form an integral part of college education for women by linking the curriculum to real-life political experience and by providing women with a sense of agency in political life. According to first League vice president Ruth Edwards, "an active college league might be the connecting force between study of the theory of government and those examples of the breakdown of government which clog our courts and crowd charitable institutions" ("Excerpts").

With a firm dedication to integrating education for political participation into higher education, League members actively influenced curricula at institutions of higher education, especially those that catered to women students, such as normal schools and junior colleges. According to a 1922 report, the LWV wrote directly to such institutions and "urged" that they incorporate "live, modern courses in civil government and politics" (Edwards, "Excerpts"). Furthermore, in the spirit of experiential education, the LWV "urged that nearby communities be used as laboratories and that the pupils work in these political laboratories as they do in the scientific" (Edwards, "Excerpts"). The curriculum of normal schools was particularly important because women teachers might serve as conduits through which the League could further its goals of developing an educated citizenry. Referring to LWV work with normal schools, Edwards explained:

> All this has been done in the effort to create interest among the group of young women from whom we are to recruit our teachers in the next few years. There is no use in demanding the kind of course in the grammar schools which we wish to see put in until there are teachers trained to teach citizenship as a live and growing community interest. ("Excerpts")

Instruction in interviewing public officials, public speaking, testifying before legislative bodies, as well as in organizational tasks including writing petitions, resolutions, and other documents of parliamentary procedure, formed the core of the rhetorical curriculum League members promoted at normal schools and junior colleges. Boston League leader Grace Johnson, for example, taught courses in the rhetorical procedures of political influence at the Wheelock School, a normal school, and the Garland School for Homemaking, a two-year junior college that, according to its course catalogue, offered otherwise fairly traditional coursework for women in domestic issues such as cooking, child care, and interior decorating (Garland).

Johnson trained students at both schools in parliamentary protocol in order to familiarize them with official legislative procedures and the methods used in conducting meetings among women's organizations such as the League of Women Voters. According to course catalogues, these courses covered "writing [committee] reports" (*Wheelock* 31–32); "the management of a meeting; the making, amending, and disposition of motions; writing formal resolutions, . . . and constructing a constitution" (*Garland* 13–14). Such courses trained women to participate in political institutions and in women's organizations that worked to challenge those institutions.

Instruction at the Garland School also included Johnson's "English 7: Spoken English." In her lecture notes about the purposes of the course, Johnson claims that skill in writing and speaking will enable students "to be of influence in family, community, school, society, [and] in the world (internationally)" ("English 7"). More specifically, Johnson expresses her hope that this required course would accomplish several goals for politically active women:

1. That women—whether in private or public life—may have ideas, opinions, convictions, and may be able to express them clearly, convincingly, and graciously.

2. That we may raise the standard of thought and speech (in our houses) and in the community, in the street cars—on the street, in the hotel lobby, at the theatre, etc.

Other goals Johnson elaborates include developing effective research methods, increasing vocabulary to achieve subtleties of meaning, improving delivery and vocal style, and broadening interest in public affairs ("Lecture Notes"). In articulating these goals for "English 7," Johnson clearly responded to the historical context in which the League operated. On the one hand, she sought to strengthen women's writing and speaking skills in order to increase their political influence. On the other hand, she stressed the importance of women communicating "graciously," with a certain level of feminine, middle-class propriety.

Responding to the needs of her students, Johnson designed the course to assist and encourage those new to the world of political influence. Several of Johnson's lectures stressed the importance of entering public discussion, particularly for women. In her notes for her introductory lecture, Johnson identifies the course as an attempt to counter the efforts of the "unscrupulous person" who "makes poor cause[s] seem noble and fine." Because of such treacherous speakers, Johnson warns, "we need all skill and all knowledge that we may not be outdone nor undone" ("Lecture Notes"). Recognizing the animosity young women might face when speaking publicly, Johnson endeavors to prepare her students to respond to hostile audiences. She stresses that her students should know how to address audiences that are not quite ready to accept women's participation in political affairs. Johnson warns that, while former suffragists might be "sympathetic," other listeners would be "hostile, stolid, [and] rough." She provides examples of possible hostile audiences ranging from the "Young Men's Democratic Club" to "dog fight crowds and drunks" ("Lecture Notes").

Once she has warned her students about audiences they may encounter, Johnson provides lessons in speaking before unsympathetic listeners. Johnson's pedagogical archive reflects her awareness of the importance of cultivating a receptive audience in any rhetorical activity that is intended to challenge or change political habits. As Susan Wells has argued, "All speakers and writers who aspire to intervene in society face the task of constructing a responsive public" (329). Johnson recognized the enormity of this rhetorical task for her newly enfranchised students and endeavored to prepare them for it. She begins her lecture by identifying five possible persuasive goals of a talk: "to explain something, to make something clear"; "to entertain, to interest others as a matter of diversion"; "to convince others, . . . to convince them to believe"; "to stir the imagination . . . and to broaden the spiritual vision of [the] hearers"; and "to secure action of a definite character" ("Lecture Notes"). Any of these goals, she continues, is difficult to attain when addressing a hostile audience. There are, Johnson explains, specific rhetorical tactics called for by the unresponsive listener.

Johnson first recommends that, when faced with an unreceptive audience, "a speaker should maintain good humor at all times" in order to sustain an appearance of self-control. As an example of why good humor is needed when addressing a hostile audience on political matters, Johnson relays the story of abolitionist Henry Ward Beecher: "Under the most trying circumstances Henry Ward Beecher withstood the derision, hisses, and insults of [an] audience, without any show of ill temper and eventually he got a hearing and won their respectful attention" ("Lecture Notes"). Johnson also emphasizes that an unfriendly audience can only be persuaded by a speaker who knows her subject thoroughly and can present her knowledge clearly. Accordingly, Johnson's lecture covers methods of note-taking, filing, and organizing information. Course notes indicate that Johnson supplemented her lecture on approaches to hostile audiences with exercises in planning and drafting speeches, including the writing of "argumentative briefs"—preliminary documents in which students composed a concise statement of the subject and purpose of the talk, a one-sentence summary of the central idea, and a detailed outline of the talk itself ("Lecture Notes"). To inspire her female students as they embarked on these difficult composing tasks, Johnson references the speeches of League leaders Carrie Chapman Catt and Maud Wood Park in her lecture as examples of how newly enfranchised women successfully managed potentially hostile audiences with patience, good humor, and careful composition.

Reflecting the League's dissatisfaction with the partisan leanings of the popular press, Johnson used other class meetings to encourage her students to challenge the "propaganda" of the popular media. In lecture notes on "Propagandists' Arts," Johnson records her displeasure at the financial interests that determine what gets into print. A special interest, according to Johnson, "usually has money to pay trained men" to create propaganda. As a result, the citizen is "in the hands of such newspaper propaganda on *all* subjects" ("Lecture Notes"). Johnson then addresses "women and public affairs" and suggests to students that they might change the propagandistic bent of popular media by "read[ing] both sides"; "weigh[ing] arguments"; and "present[ing] [their] decisions in sincere and artistic" language ("Lecture Notes"). By learning strategies for critical analysis and argument, women could lead a charge against the corrupt communicative practices of popular journalists.

While her courses covered techniques of writing and speaking that could be applied to a variety of rhetorical occasions, Johnson was particularly interested in training her students to perform the kind of work they might do as politically active citizens. Her lecture notes on research reflect this desire. Worthwhile research, according to Johnson, involves discovering a topic with current political implications. In a lecture on choosing and investigating a topic, Johnson recommends that students consult government sources, such as state house records, congressional reports, publications of government departments, and the U.S. census. Timely and important topics, she suggests, cannot be accurately identified from reading popular media; rather, they can only be found in the primary documents of the political process. Reflecting the progressive educational spirit of the LWV, Johnson's courses also incorporated experiential learning, bringing students into the arenas in which they might deploy the arguments they developed in the classroom. The Garland School course catalogue indicates that students engaged in "Field Work" in conjunction with their studies of English. This field work took them to the state house, the public library, and the court house, allowing them to experience firsthand the arenas of communication they hopefully would engage in after graduation, perhaps even as members of the LWV.

Alternative Classrooms

The LWV's educational efforts moved beyond traditional classroom walls in order to reach even greater numbers of women. The Providence, Rhode Island, LWV attracted women by holding a citizenship school at the Outlet Department Store in Providence. This "Store School" ran for two weeks, three hours per day, and featured speakers on topics such as citizenship and the city; child welfare and citizenship; and "scientific temperance instruction" ("Store School"). According to the estimates of the Providence League, "from three to four hundred women were in attendance at the school for at least part of the time each day" ("Store School"). The technique of using stores as classrooms derived from the work suffragists had done to appropriate women's participation in consumer culture for political causes. Margaret Finnegan adroitly analyzes this appropriation in *Selling Suffrage: Consumer Culture and Votes for Women*. Suffrage activists correlated the motif of the smart woman shopper with the smart woman voter. As Finnegan explains,

> suffragists argued that penny-pinching women citizens would make government earn its keep, that comparison-shopping female voters would wisely choose among

political products. . . . With private shopping skills transformed into public assets, the new voters would make government sensitive to American concerns. (17)

The LWV continued these attempts to connect consumer culture and women's political participation by locating citizenship education within large department stores.

This consumerist choice of location, like suffragists' earlier arguments that women's experience as careful shoppers granted them ethos as voters, ignored the situation of working-class women, many of whom simply did not have the luxury to shop critically or to attend a citizenship school in a fancy department store. Partly in response to these limitations, the Rhode Island LWV also engaged local churches in their educational endeavors. In 1921, the Rhode Island League initiated "an all-sectarian movement to establish Citizenship Courses in the Churches." These courses covered subjects ranging from naturalization to "political terminology" ("Speeding Up the Schools" 1151). Because the church had been a critical venue for women's work in the past, the League saw it as a natural place to implement its educational program. The churches might also make citizenship education widely available to women of diverse class and ethnic backgrounds.

Later in the decade, the LWV delivered education for citizenship to the homes of individual women with the assistance of radio technology. The League believed expanding radio technology could be used to foster classrooms without walls, "a citizenship school on air" (Sherwin, "Radio Address"). As early as 1922, the Virginia League broadcast weekly programs discussing League-endorsed legislation. The enthusiasm expressed by Ludington, first chair of the national LWV radio committee, reflects the organization's high aspirations for this new educational medium:

> Think of these possibilities! There is a rich and promising field for investigation . . . in regard to the possible effect of broadcasting on the *content* as well as the method of adult education. Who knows what the effect may be of the new types of listeners—one may fairly call some of them students—which radio is bringing within reach of adult education? ("Report" 6)

Beaming faith in radio technology, Ludington announced the "start of a new project . . . a Citizenship School by Radio. . . . A school in which there are no teachers but only fellow-students in the great university of democracy; good citizens telling us stories of their own adventures in citizenship" (qtd. in "A Citizenship School by Radio").

Like previous LWV citizenship schools, teaching via the radio deviated from the pedagogical methods of the academy. According to the LWV's initial plans for the radio school, speakers would not pose as authorities but instead "might be described as everyday citizens telling stories from their own lives—humanly interesting stories—to other everyday citizens" (Ludington, "Something New"). Rather than lectures spoken by a teacher imbued with institutional authority, radio school sessions, Ludington stressed, would be narratives, "stories . . . of adventures in Citizenship" (Ludington, "Citizenship School"). Focusing on the tales of "everyday citizens," Ludington hoped, would promote the participation of all citizens in civic life. She introduced the first program in the eight-week radio school with the assertion that *"we need to change our focus:* we need to bring into range the great body of American Voters who are not only the foundation and the source of power of our Government, but who should be, each of us, a sharer in its processes" ("A Citizenship School by Radio" 4). The citizenship school by radio, like all League educational endeavors, was directed toward the end of encouraging action and involvement in democratic politics.

Political Literacy "Textbooks"

To supplement their instructional methods, the LWV developed an impressive array of educational publications. From bulletins and newsletters informing members about legislative matters to handbooks, manuals, and pamphlets full of instructions for expanding political participation, widely circulated educational texts constituted a large part of the League's efforts to foster political literacy.

Instruction for Voters

State LWV branches contributed to this publishing effort by issuing voters' handbooks—brief yet comprehensive guides to electoral procedures and governmental structures. The handbooks, as the author of the *Massachusetts Primer of Citizenship and Government* explains, aspired to be "elementary . . . bringing together in as terse a manner as possible the plan of our governing systems" (M. White i). A typical example of these handbooks is the Iowa LWV handbook for Iowa citizens entitled *You Are Democracy* (c. 1920). Much of the book is dedicated to instruction in how to vote, explaining qualifications for voting, legislative districts, registration and election laws, and ballot marking. Other chapters familiarize readers with political party organization through diagrams of party structure at the local, state, and national levels. Similarly, the New York State LWV's *Handbook for New York Voters* (1926) contains information on registration, election districts, and ballot marking. Other common handbook elements include glossaries of common political terms, annotated bibliographies on governmental topics, and charts illustrating common legislative tasks, such as the process of how a law is made.

Yet LWV handbooks do not simply provide for readers' passive understanding of existing political processes. *You Are Democracy,* as its title suggests, urges readers to be actively involved in the structures about which they read. To this end, the book includes sample forms on which readers are invited to record the voting behavior of their congressmen. Similarly, the *Wisconsin Citizen's Handbook* urges readers to pursue further studies, providing a chapter of suggested topics for study groups. These recommended programs of study are designed to involve citizens in state and local issues of political importance including "Wisconsin Laws Bearing on Women and Children"; "The Disposal of a City's Waste"; and "International Law and Arbitration" (Wood-Simons 77). The New York LWV handbook also recommends that its readers participate in bettering the system they are learning about. To this end, the text includes chapters on questionable campaign finance practices and corrupt party machinery.

Local Leagues supplemented state resources with guides to local government and elections. The LWV believed that women's participation in local politics was particularly important in challenging partisan domination of electoral and legislative matters. For the new woman voter standing outside the elite circle of partisan politics, "the most available points of access to the political process were in the community and precinct" (L. Young 51). Recognizing the importance of local politics in generating women's political activity, LWV vice president Marie Edwards asserted that "we have often asked ourselves and are asked, what are the essentials of citizenship? What is it that a woman should know before she votes? I should say knowledge of government as it touches her immediate surroundings. . . . In other words, her town and township government" ("Excerpts" 2).

Reflecting this belief, local LWV guides include a variety of political information, ranging from the political history of the area to a compilation of facts about upcoming elections. During the 1920s, the Cincinnati League published three editions of *Know Cincinnati,* a booklet covering governmental administrative structures, education and libraries systems, and city club organizations. In St. Louis, the LWV printed various editions of *The Voter's Guide,* each customized to the issues of different county and city elections. *The Voter's Guide* for 1928, for instance, compiled responses to LWV questionnaires sent to "all men and women who have filed as candidates for United States Congress, State Senate, and House of Representatives to be voted on in St. Louis County, and for County offices" (i).

To supplement book-length publications, the LWV composed and circulated a variety of instructional texts for new women voters. To cultivate "political literacy" among a wider swath of new voters, the LWV integrated their publications into correspondence courses. Marie Ames, director of the citizenship department of the national LWV, prepared such a course around her 1921 booklet *Lessons for the Study of Citizenship*. The course encompassed twelve lessons on subjects ranging from nominating and electing the president to the history of political parties. State Leagues also contributed to correspondence education. The Virginia League wrote and circulated *Ten Practical Lessons for Virginia Citizens,* a correspondence course featuring lessons on "What I Should Know in Order to Vote," "How Laws are Passed in the General Assembly," "How the Government of the United State Operates," "How the United States Government Conducts Foreign Affairs," and "Women and Government." To promote active understanding of and involvement in Virginia politics, course materials included timely political documents for study, such as the Constitution of Virginia; the rules of the state House of Representatives and Senate; and the most recent reports of the Secretary of the Commonwealth and the Superintendent of Public Instruction. These lessons encouraged women to enter contemporary political conversations by familiarizing them with the discursive conventions of state politics.[2]

Although LWV educational texts took diverse forms, they employed common formats designed to lessen the reader's anxiety about participating in politics. Complex language and terminology, therefore, have no place in the LWV's educational texts. A good example of the straightforward language typical of LWV publications is the Kentucky LWV bulletin *Kentucky Election Laws in Brief.* According to the preface of the bulletin,

> The language of the law has always been the bane of the layman. That is the only excuse this digest or syllabus of the Kentucky election laws has for being. It is an attempt to translate the language of the law into the language of the everyday life of the average citizen. (i)

The Kentucky LWV hoped that the exposition of laws would encourage new women voters to go to the polls and prepare them to be better voters than the majority of men, many of whom had exercised the franchise in ignorance. According to the bulletin, the LWV

> has set about to use every possible means of education for the recently enfranchised woman citizen so that she may exercise her newly acquired privilege with intelligence, rather than go to the polls like dumb driven cattle, as has always been the case

with a great many of our citizens who have borne the burden of suffrage far too lightly. (ii)

Women voters, educated through such LWV publications, might feel empowered to vote knowing that they were are prepared than the "dumb driven cattle" who had long monopolized the vote.

To lessen the intimidation of learning about complex political procedures, League writers often used a question-and-answer or debate format, thereby presenting issues not as one-way lectures but as interactive dialogues. The Cleveland League designed and distributed "dodgers," or small strips of paper, with information about voter registration in a question-and-answer format. The dodger lists then answers common questions about who was eligible to register, where registration took place, and where more information about registering could be obtained. The dodger makes the procedure sound as simple as possible in order to reassure readers that they could indeed participate.

In addition to making complex information more accessible to women, the League's interactive formats helped prepare women for political rhetoric. Women might be more likely to engage in political discussion, the League believed, if they were prepared with arguments they could employ in support of important legislative measures. With this in mind, the Connecticut LWV published "Objections Overruled!"—a document that refutes common arguments levied against an LWV-sponsored bill to establish jury service for women in Connecticut. After presenting an objection, usually in a single sentence, the pamphlet emphasizes the rebuttal in bold type and strong detail:

> THEY SAY: Women will be forced to listen to indecent evidence:
>
> WE SAY—They may read that same evidence in detail on the front page of daily papers. Most of such indecent evidence appears in divorce cases which are not tried before a jury in Connecticut. Such evidence may also occur in cases affecting young girls. Should women be afraid to listen in such a case? Furthermore the percentage of cases of a disagreeable nature is extremely small. (1)

Because the rebuttal is presented in detail, the reader would be prepared to argue in support of the legislation in her own conversations. She would be able to anticipate objections and reply to them quickly and fully.

Lessons in Publicity and Advocacy

Raising voting rates among newly enfranchised women required extensive publicity efforts on the part of the LWV. In support of these efforts, LWV members received substantial training in publicity techniques through national, state, and local offices. For instance, the national LWV published *Get Out the Vote: Why, When, How,* a text that provided LWV members with a clearly articulated rationale for the "Get Out the Vote" campaign, a list of important dates in the coming elections, and specific instructions for encouraging voter registration and turnout. The booklet served as a resource manual of publicity techniques by providing details of effective publicity tactics developed by various LWV branches around the country. The text explains, for example, that the San Francisco LWV sponsored a ceremony "to show the importance of coming of [voting] age." This ceremony involved "young Chinese, Japanese, and Europeans, all in native costume, participat[ing] in a patriotic program with the mayor and other officials while school children sang in chorus and motion pictures were made of the exercises" (10). Kentucky had enlisted the help of churches and arranged for the "reference by all ministers the Sunday before registration day to the duty of citizenship" (11). Some Maryland LWV members used even more creative means to rally voters by "paint[ing] each county's [voting percentage] goal on the barn roofs of the county" (11).

Another section of the booklet provides instruction in composing "Get Out the Vote" campaign materials. "Get Out the Vote" publications, the booklet suggests, need be concise and simple, aspiring to be "brief campaign fliers giving the facts, figures, and arguments of the campaign" with only "a few examples . . . for suggestive purposes" (23). To help members write these fliers, the authors analyze several samples that illustrate effective techniques of wording and formatting. Effective literature, the booklet stresses, need not be limited to traditional formats, such as the flier or brochure. League workers are encouraged to use innovative genres in order to reach an audience of women voters. For instance, the booklet suggests the nursery rhyme as a particularly effective means to grab the interest of women voters who, presumably through work raising children, would be familiar and comfortable with this genre. The booklet recommends that Leagues "Let Mother Goose Help" and adapt some well-known nursery rhymes to the purpose of motivating women voters:

> Tom, Tom the piper's son,
> Cast his vote and away he run,
> And called to all the folks he met,
> "I've voted. Have you voted yet?"
>
> Sturdy Boy Scout, come blow your horn,
> To wake all the voters on voting day morn.

Patriotism is what it denotes,

For service to country means getting out votes.

(27)

Rhymes could also be used to critique corrupt political party practices:

Taffy was a slacker, Taffy didn't vote,

Corrupt party bosses on Taffy they dote.

They know how he helps when he keeps the vote small;

Each vote counts for evil that's not cast at all.

(27)

Simple, memorable, and seemingly innocent nursery rhymes could thus be used to help the League critique parties and to encourage women's participation in political life.

Events, such as public forums and meetings, might also be used as publicity—a way to advocate for League-supported reforms and to interest new voters in the political process. Mrs. Robert Oliver of the Manhattan LWV wrote and circulated instructions for conducting an appealing public forum. According to Oliver, the success of an LWV-sponsored public forum, or any other LWV educational method for that matter, depends on a range of careful rhetorical choices and publicizing activities. A forum topic must respond to the moment, and it must encourage significant discussion: "Choose subjects of popular interest and those which are at the time engaging the public," Oliver advises. Furthermore, she counsels, "Be sure to get a subject that is controversial. People like a fight." Oliver then lists possible topics, all of which fit within the LWV's legislative agenda. In keeping with the LWV's belief that traditional partisan conversations were too antagonistic, Oliver also provides careful instructions for conducting discussion during the forum. She recommends that forum leaders ensure that no one person monopolizes conversation or intimidates others who might have questions to ask: "Do not let any one person ask more than one question until all have had a chance. Do not let any one from the floor make a speech from the floor under the pretence of asking a question." Such instruction in discussion leadership was essential to the League's effort to enact new models of political communication. Oliver's directions serve as a textbook for a new kind of political literacy.

In addition to teaching its members how to use publicity to motivate and engage voters, the LWV provided instruction in publicity as a political pressure tactic. Two common types of texts used by the LWV to advance its legislative goals were the candidate questionnaire and the survey. While some

League leaders were familiar with these tactics from previous suffrage and reform work, many League members required training to compose and use these genres effectively. In 1923, the national LWV convention included a session on how to write and use a candidate questionnaire. At about the same time, techniques for composing successful questionnaires became the topic of various League publications. In her article "The Question of the Questionnaire," League officer Marie Edwards explains the purposes of questionnaires in the national LWV newsletter, the *Woman Voter*. In addition to stressing that the questionnaire should be brief—"somewhere between the magic three and the classic nine" questions—Edwards clarifies the dual purpose of the questionnaire. A successful questionnaire is designed

> first, to emphasize for the candidate that certain issues loom large and important on the horizon of a good-sized group of women, which serves to impress the issues themselves more clearly on his mind; [and] second, to secure a real expression of opinion from the candidate so that the voting public may know how that candidate regards these issues.

Accordingly, the questionnaire should blend language that advocates particular measures with neutral-sounding language of inquiry. The questionnaire should get the facts, but it should also impress the opinions of the LWV upon the politician.[3] Because of this dual purpose, the genre of the questionnaire tended to confuse legislators. Edwards notes that "candidates are not quite sure why women want to know the things asked nor just what use they expect to make of the information." She does not, however, suggest that the genre be changed or its purposes altered. The conflicting presence of language that lobbies for particular measures and language that suggests a detached or objective search for facts may, in fact, have enabled women to be advocates without incurring the wrath of partisans.

While the candidate questionnaire pressured candidates to embrace LWV interests, the survey pressured office-holding legislators to act on those interests. According to instructional materials circulated by the national office of the LWV, a successful survey promotes legislative action and evaluates legislative performance while posing as a research instrument. A 1923 LWV pamphlet suggests that a survey "aims to measure work already done, and to recommend changes upon the basis of which improvement can be attained" (Moley 1). Furthermore, the pamphlet continues, the process of carrying out a survey provides two distinct benefits for the surveyor: it "give[s] the public the facts upon which it can judge its government and . . . place[s] before public officials facts and suggestions upon the basis of which they can improve their administration of public business" (Moley 1). The survey, then, was an interrogation tool through which the LWV monitored the work of elected officials.

During its first decade, the LWV composed a wide variety of political literacy "textbooks." These textbooks differed significantly from the textbooks typically used in teaching rhetoric and writing today; yet they were perhaps more attuned to the needs of their audiences and more clearly imbued with social purpose than the lengthy handbooks and readers that fill the pages of publishers' catalogues in the early twenty-first century. League publications taught specific skills of political literacy via brief, accessible texts that could quickly prepare new women voters to communicate effectively in a political realm that had long assumed their absence. These "textbooks," however, did more than teach women the standards of a new political discourse community—they helped women to challenge the distribution of power within that discourse community. As I explore below, the LWV developed other instructional texts to assist in the immense task of educating women for a new kind of political literacy—a kind that was not dominated by the writing and speaking practices of partisan elites.

Dramatizing Political Persuasion

While courses and publications were central to the LWV's efforts to increase the political literacy of American women, dramatic productions often took center stage as the organization taught women about political persuasion. The skit or play, the League believed, was one of the most effective ways to educate because this genre allowed for both learning and entertainment. The skit, according to the *Handbook for League Workers,* is appropriate for "1) Occasions requiring light entertainment; 2) Getting ideas across to an audience that would not listen to a speech on the subject; [and] 3) Varying the form of the League program and having a little fun in the League itself" (14). Yet entertainment, the *Handbook* stresses, should be a method of education, not an end in itself. The audience members of a League skit or play should be trained to see themselves not merely as viewers of entertainment but as students receiving an education through an engaging medium. In the preface to her 1921 LWV play *How Maggie MacTaggart Gained Her Citizenship,* Grace Bagley explains how the audience should interpret this unique use of the dramatic genre: "if you expect a play in the usual sense, you may be disappointed, but if you look for such information as is usually given in a book or in a lecture, you will not be bored and you will learn what every intelligent citizen should know" (3). The opening speech of the play similarly asks audience members "to regard [them]selves for the next three-quarters of an hour not merely as playgoers, but also as students" (3). The point of dramatic endeavors such as pageants, plays, and skits was not to cultivate artistic appreciation; rather, dramatic productions served to prepare women for public life through responsible and active participation in political conversations. LWV dramatic endeavors took many forms; however, chief among them were election plays, procedural plays, and issue-based plays.

Election Plays

Some of the LWV's earliest uses of educational theater aimed to teach women about voting procedures and to encourage the newly enfranchised to go to the voting booth. Writers of these "election plays" (also known as "Get-Out-the-Vote plays") often opted for a practical approach, covering the rules of voter registration, the mechanical operation of a voting machine, or the proper process of marking a ballot. *The Voting Machine,* a play composed by the Grand Rapids LWV, provides a demonstration of how to operate a voting machine and explains "the necessity of registration, . . . the duties of the various election officials, . . . and the illegality of advertising candidates within the polls" (LWV, "Skits and Plays" 1). The Massachusetts LWV's plays *Registration Day* and *Election Day* take similar practical approaches by incorporating extensive props and scenery in order to familiarize women with the physical landscape they might encounter in the voting process. Stage directions in *Registration Day* indicate that props should include "registration blank books, about 24" by 30", ruled in vertical columns, headings of which show the questions to be asked of each applicant" (2). Similarly, the directions for *Election Day* instruct that ballot props should be "printed on white paper and folded to be from 4 to 5 inches wide and from 6 to 13 inches long" and should be "enclosed in a sealed and labeled package" (2). The LWV hoped that carefully designed, realistic props would make the act of voting more familiar, and hence less intimidating, for the novice voter.

Humor was also used to ease the fears of novice voters. The Hartford, Connecticut, LWV's play *A Smock Election,* for instance, begins with a humorous bridge game that is interrupted by an LWV precinct worker who persuades the players to go register to vote. Act 2 provides an overview of the registration process, while act 3 involves audience members in a mock political convention. This convention, led by the bridge-player-voters from the first act, collaboratively composes a mock platform and nominates a mock slate of candidates. Nominated candidates include "such notables as . . . C.O.D. Bills for Collector, Samuel Spender for Treasurer . . . and Otto Grow for the board of Selectmen" (4). The platform drawn up by the characters is similarly whimsical, including planks for "a new municipal golf course with balls to be furnished by the city, traffic signals to be of fashionable colors, . . . [and] smocks for all city employees, regardless of sex, as an essential for a clean and beautiful administration" (4). While the play may not have stimulated deep political debate, it probably worked to dispel the shyness of new women voters by allowing them to witness registration and political convention procedures in a nonthreatening environment.

Procedural Plays

Dramatic methods could also be used to teach members about common League procedures and publicity techniques. One such play, entitled *How Not to Do It: A Non–Money Raising Interview*, centers on the character "Miss Meech," who, according to the dramatis personae is "a worker from the L. of W. V. (with an inferiority complex)" (*How* 1). The audience for Meech's fund-raising efforts, the script indicates, is a "Big Businessman," who responds to Meech's introduction with the dismissive line "Never believed in women voting—utter nonsense—silliest thing this country ever did" (2). While alerting women to the potentially hostile audiences they might face, the play also pokes fun at those audiences in an attempt to boost the confidence of the League member who may have seen herself reflected in Meech. From the outset, the skit is infused with sarcasm about the "Big Businessman." According to the prologue, "The Big Businessman is discovered, seated at a mahogany desk entirely bare of papers. He frowns in the manner of Jove" (1). His smugness and self-absorption contrast humorously with the apparent lack of work he has to do. Throughout the skit, the Businessman's words comically reveal the incongruity between the amount of material wealth and power he has accumulated and the amount of effort and intelligence he has expended. Denying Meech's request for money, the Businessman launches into a tirade against rising taxes: "They'll put us all in the poor house if they go on with this taxation business, and I'm under such heavy expenses all the time—my yacht, now . . ." Realizing the irony of his tirade in mid-sentence, the Businessman "checks himself, coughs, changes the subject" (3).

While the play eased women's dread of fund raising for political purposes, it also taught them to avoid common rhetorical errors in the fund-raising process. Mistakes that Meech makes in her solicitation include failing to provide specific budget figures, failing to connect League work to the local situation of the business being solicited, and failing to provide well-organized

League publications (such as explanatory leaflets and pledge cards) to the source being solicited. Most importantly, the play suggests, an interviewer cannot ramble. Because Meech is uncertain about the facts of the League, she cannot decide which facts to present and in what order to present them. As a result, she cannot respond to the Big Businessman's critiques. While the play is not a "lesson" in the tradition of classroom-based pedagogy, Meech's hapless bumbling and the Big Businessman's exaggerated pomposity create an entertaining educational event that surely promoted the LWV's vision of political literacy.

Other procedural plays taught political literacy by familiarizing women with the processes of legislative testimony. *How Maggie MacTaggart Gained Her Citizenship* (1921) conveys lessons on how to deliver arguments in favor of changing legislation. Specifically, this play presents arguments against a law that bound women's citizenship status to that of her husband. The narrator explains at the outset of the play that from the skit the audience should garner "such information as is usually given in a book or in a lecture" and should "learn what every intelligent citizen should know at the period of our national life when immigration and naturalization is the subject of heated discussion in Congress" (Bagley 3). Furthermore, the narrator acknowledges that the production is intended to persuade the audience to take up the cause "of changing a federal law which is unjust alike to the foreign-born woman, to the American woman married to a foreigner and to the United States of America" (4). The introductory material concludes by asking the audience to direct their attention to the processes of influencing legislation:

> The method of changing laws, how simple and invariable it is! Kindle the fire of demand in the home district of the legislator and when the flames mount high enough and the fire is hot enough, he will move, never fear. Remember, however, that success lies in the location in which the fire is kindled and by whom. (4)

Through the action of the play and the arguments of its central characters, League members, as both actors and audience, might come to understand how and where to create such fires.

The play proceeds to instruct women in the conventions of political discourse by presenting a hypothetical Senate Immigration Committee hearing on the Curtis Bill, a bill proposing to make a woman's naturalization status independent of her husband's. The opening scene depicts a legislative committee that, in keeping with the League's critiques of traditional political institutions, appears unresponsive and much in need of reform. "Members of the Immigration Committee are seen sitting in a semicircle with the

Chairman in the center at a small table. . . . The members of the Committee read newspapers, converse with each other, yawn, and in other ways exhibit their indifference" (7). From this point on, the scene involves League members in the discursive conventions of a legislative hearing. The stage directions indicate that "each proponent in turn as her name is called comes forward and gives name and address to the Chairman of the Committee. This is recorded by the clerk. This shows the proper procedure at a legislative hearing" (7). The play furthered the LWV's goal of increasing women's political literacy by translating into dramatic form what would otherwise have been an intimidating, dense text in the *Congressional Record*.

Issue-Based Plays

Issue-based plays instructed members in argumentation strategies they might employ in support of LWV initiatives. Topics of these issue-based plays archived in the LWV's papers include jury service for women *(Ladies of the Jury);* protective labor legislation *(Hour Legislation for Women, What Price Mothers and Babies?* and *A Woman's Jury on a Woman's Case);* efficiency in government *(Minnesota's Simplified Government);* and marriage laws *(Shall We Improve Our Marriage Law?).* Of all these topics, plays demonstrating arguments in support of the Child Labor Amendment were particularly popular. The Washington state LWV, for example, wrote a morality play to publicize arguments in support of the amendment. The play, called simply *Child Labor Morality Play,* portrays a "short allegorical sketch [and] an argument in favor of the Child Labor Amendment" (LWV, "Skits and Plays" 4).

Issue-based plays not only taught women arguments for particular policies, they also provided rebuttals to common objections. *A Family Takes Notice,* a skit about the Child Labor Amendment, depicts a debate among "A Farmer Father, a League Mother, a City Daughter running for the legislature, and a lawyer son, with the two women supporting the amendment and the two men against it" (LWV, "Skits and Plays" 4). The two female characters are politically involved and are, unlike their male foils, interested in social welfare legislation, an unsurprising gendered divide given the League's arguments about women's potentially reformative role in American politics. The purpose of the play is to convince the audience to support the Child Labor Amendment and, perhaps more importantly, to provide rebuttals to arguments commonly used against the amendment. As a summary of the skit explains, "Part I consists of disposing of the farmer's arguments that such an amendment would prevent children from working on the farm and Part II answers the son's doubts in regard to interference with states' rights" (4).

Skits and plays were also used within League meetings to educate members about the League's positions on issues soon to be debated in state and local legislative bodies. The Connecticut League, for example, involved members in a skit simply entitled *Legislative Sketch*. This skit reviews the contents of a League-sponsored bill that allowed for women to serve on Connecticut juries. Part procedural play, the skit demonstrates how the committee hearing for the bill would proceed, beginning with the clerk reading the entire text of the bill. The writers also include instruction on the proper manner of address in legislative assemblies and stress the importance of speaking loudly and clearly. At one point in the play, Mrs. Indiana Thomas rises to speak in favor of the bill and "omits to say chairman." In response, the chairman reminds her that she needs to begin her testimony, according to parliamentary procedure, by addressing the chairman. At another point, the character Sally Fanny Gleaton rises to address the chair and is asked by the clerk to speak louder and repeat her name (2).

The play covers more than procedures, however. It demonstrates substantial arguments for and against the bill, thus training League members to testify in support of the proposed legislation. Different characters speak for or against the bill as members of the committee guide the process of the hearing. The play also incorporates testimony from the opposition so that League members are prepared to rebut opposing viewpoints. One female opponent of jury service for women argues, "The least suggestion of being on a jury makes me tremble with apprehension. Why I might have to be locked up all night with a man. . . . Then I cannot refrain from mentioning that I might have to discuss delicate subjects with the other sex. I would be mortified to death" (3). In response, the chairman of the committee laughs and "recommend[s] that the lady who has just spoken so pathetically be given a dose of Madame Winslow's Soothing Syrup" (3). After another opponent testifies that she will not support the bill because her husband has told her not to, a committee member exclaims in disbelief, "Good Gracious, these shrinking violets!" (4). Portraying a favorable legislative audience and demonstrating the weakness of opposing arguments, the play encourages League members to speak publicly in support of the bill.

Nonpartisan Rhetorical Education as Political Strategy

Having just witnessed the success of their extensive educational campaigns in support of suffrage, the founders of the LWV maintained faith in their tried-and-true methods of influencing legislation. The organization put forth extensive effort during its first decade to expand these methods in the post-suffrage era. Between 1920 and 1930, a total of 1,194 voters' schools, citizenship schools, and institutes of government and politics were reportedly held nationwide (LWV, "Educational Methods"). League educational publications supplemented these schools on the national, state, and local levels, providing women with information for political influence.

This early educational work of the League had an impact, and the LWV saw several of its legislative goals reached before 1925. Largely in response to pressure from state Leagues, several states raised the age of consent, passed equal guardianship laws, and enlarged women's property rights in marriage. By 1925, some 426 LWV-supported laws had passed, and sixty-four LWV-opposed laws had failed to pass (L. Young 75). Nationally, the LWV was instrumental in bringing about several reforms, including the passage of the Sheppard-Towner Act for Maternal and Infant Health and the Voigt Act, which prohibited the interstate shipment of skimmed milk laced with coconut oil and sold as whole milk.

Due in part to League efforts, women also increased their presence in public office. Women in several states gained the right to sit in the state legislature, to serve on state university governing boards, and to hold public office. At the national level, the LWV helped pass the Civil Service Reclassification Act, which, while not eradicating all discrimination against women, helped open the civil service system to women's participation (L. Young 72–74). Furthermore, the LWV spearheaded a successful campaign for the establishment of a Women's Bureau in the Department of Labor.

The LWV's dedication to using education and public opinion as a means to gain political influence proved problematic, however, on several levels. First, despite their support for a Deweyan public with full publicity and open communication, the LWV's educational endeavors often worked to maintain a restricted version of political communication. For example, the LWV's use and teaching of parliamentary procedure in many ways reinforced the discursive conventions of traditional partisan politics. Jane Mansbridge has suggested that "the language people use as they reason together usually favours one way of seeing things and discourages others. Subordinate groups sometimes cannot find the right voice or words to express their thoughts" (119). Such silencing accompanied the LWV's choice to follow parliamentary procedure. While this procedure was a familiar element in the tradition of middle-class women's organizations, women who were not privileged enough to participate in these organizations, or to attend courses like Grace Johnson's "English 7," did not possess the specialized vocabulary necessary for full participation in this form of deliberative procedure.

Secondly, the League's educational work contained racist and xenophobic sentiments similar to those displayed by Catt in her warnings about "The Menace of Illiteracy" *(A Nation Calls)*. Although African American women did join the LWV, League educational endeavors rarely addressed their specific educational needs. Furthermore, LWV pedagogy clearly manifested anti-Irish sentiments. The cast of characters listed in A. J. McGuire's 1926 election play, *The Voter's Dream,* for example, includes "Mrs. Robinson, a club woman" and "Nora, the maid." Although Nora presents some arguments that help persuade Mrs. Robinson to vote, she is portrayed as a stereotypical, ignorant Irish immigrant. Her character embodies the corrupt power of the political boss and the patronage machine, and she explains her electoral decisions in terms of spoils promised to the men in her family rather than as the conscientious acts of an informed citizen. The audience's identification with the wealthy clubwoman, Mrs. Robinson, is furthered by the play's mocking portrayal of Nora's ignorance. When Mrs. Robinson asks Nora what she thinks of the Child Labor Amendment, Nora replies "Yes, I've heard tell of it all right, but I'm afraid be [sic] the time it's passed all the children will be grown up; so it's no use to pass it" (3). According to stage directions, Nora then exits the stage while the other characters laugh at her.[4]

Thirdly, the League's methods of education often seemed not to offer a serious challenge to the male dominance of American politics. Like the WILPF, the LWV was a "weak public" that had power to advocate but not to make official decisions. Because the organization lacked official power and had no clear plan for attaining official power, it was seen as too moderate by more radical women's organizations such as the National Woman's Party (NWP). While the LWV argued that its members could bring a distinct voice for women's concerns into male-controlled political arenas, other women reformers disagreed. Many former suffragists felt that the LWV's ambiguous "nonpartisan" stance and the educational work done under its auspices reinforced rather than challenged an oppressive political system. Former suffragist Anne Martin critiqued the LWV for what she saw as its complicity with partisan politics. In a 1925 article in the *Nation,* Martin argues: "There is no doubt that Mrs. Carrie Chapman Catt sounded the doom of feminism for many years to come when she urged the newly enfranchised American woman humbly to 'train for citizenship,' 'to join the men's parties,' 'to work with the party of your choice.'" Such instruction, Martin complains, put women "exactly where men political leaders wanted them, bound, gagged, divided, and delivered to the Republican and Democratic parties" (185). The political parties, Martin continues, represent the "most formidable . . . male dragons" in the path of women's advancement in political life (185). To feminists like Martin, it increasingly appeared that enabling women's participation in American politics required more than simply training them to work with and through the existing political channels. Real change required developing new structures more receptive to women's participation.

Catt herself struggled to come to terms with the subordinate position women found themselves in as they tried to gain powerful voices within civic discourse after 1920. While Catt championed a nonpartisan, advocacy-based organization of women, she also called for a powerful role for that organization in the official administration of government. As she explained in 1920, "The League of Women Voters aspires to be part of the big majorities which administer our government, and it also wishes to be one of the minorities which agitate and educate and shape ideas today which the majority will adopt tomorrow" (qtd. in Black, 250). As Catt and other founders of the LWV would discover, it is extremely difficult to speak as both a majority and a minority. The advocacy and educational work of women's organizations could easily be discredited by the greater political ethos, superior economic force, and official decision-making power of the established political organizations they confronted. And the LWV, it seems, had no clear plan for changing that situation.

The League's lack of official power was exacerbated by the fact that, since its inception, its leaders had struggled to match the organizing capabilities of political parties. As Anna L. Harvey has documented, leaders of both the Democratic and Republican parties in the late 1910s began to sense the inevitability of female enfranchisement and started organizing women within party structures. By the time Catt called for the transformation of the NAWSA into the LWV, the parties already had a substantial head start in the race to organize women for political action. The parties thus gained substantial control over women's votes, and partisan candidates had much less to fear from the LWV. In the late 1910s, Harvey explains, "male party elites created new positions within party organizations to tempt leaders of women's organizations to work for the parties. . . . These mobilization efforts by the parties would substitute *partisan* female leaders as the authoritative source of cues for group-based electoral behavior, rather than *independent* female leaders" such as those who ran the LWV (88). Early partisan efforts to mobilize women—undertaken while the LWV was still struggling as the NAWSA to secure enfranchisement for American women—significantly drained political ethos and membership resources from the LWV.[5]

The LWV's decision to embrace nonpartisan education as a strategy during the 1920s also made women's positions vis-à-vis political action more difficult in several ways. In the spirit of its professed nonpartisanship, the LWV effectively ceased endorsing candidates by the mid 1920s, focusing instead on educating women voters about voting, governmental procedures, and various pieces of legislation. While the decision not to endorse candidates was in keeping with the organization's expressed goal to work outside of the restrictive channels of partisan politics, it had the practical effect of lessening the pressure the LWV could put on elected officials to make legislative changes. The decision not to endorse individual candidates also had an impact on the power that women had within the parties because partisan women could no longer threaten an LWV-led mobilization of women's votes if parties did not respond to their demands. Legislative history in the 1920s seems to support the argument that the LWV's decision not to endorse candidates after 1925 was detrimental to the organization's political efficacy. The LWV, Harvey explains, "was successful between 1920 and 1925 in lobbying policy concessions for women as a group, but rather dramatically ceased winning concessions after 1925, and even saw earlier victories rolled back by the end of the 1920s" (156).

As the LWV continued to struggle against existing power structures, they also encountered challenges from other politically active women who found fault in their reformist approach to social issues. Disputes about how to improve women's working conditions, for instance, created seemingly insurmountable divisions among women's groups in the 1920s. The LWV advocated protective labor legislation that would ensure better pay, reasonable hours, and healthy working conditions for women. Other groups of women, most notably the NWP, argued that an Equal Rights Amendment was necessary to equalize working conditions and pay for men and women. As long as women were singled out as a special group among workers, the NWP argued, they would never be treated fairly in the labor market. The LWV, however, viewed the ERA as a threat to progressive legislative gains for women. Creating "equal rights," they feared, would lead to the repeal of protective legislation that benefited working women. Employers would not be willing to offer similar labor rights to men and, under the guise of "equal rights," would take them away from women.

Such disagreements over fundamental policy questions cast doubt on the LWV's claims that women could lead a united effort to correct faulty practices of political discussion. A 1926 national conference on women in industry revealed that women were more than capable of participating in hostile, divisive, and unproductive political conversations. Reporting on the conference in the *Woman Citizen* of 1926, LWV supporter Ethel Smith summarizes the animosity that filled much of the conference and that separated two large camps of women during the 1920s:

> It is a profoundly interesting fact, if not by this time a surprising one, that neither women's problems as such, nor industrial problems as such, can often be approached for public discussion in anything but a controversial spirit. . . . [T]here was an organized attack upon the conference and the Women's Bureau by a group of militant feminists, who staged an uproar which interrupted the proceedings and outraged the entire audience. (1)

The "uproar" Smith refers to involved protests by members of the NWP who pointed out that the program, sponsored by the LWV-friendly Women's Bureau, provided no speaker representing the perspective of the NWP. How could this conference, the NWP leaders objected, be about "women in industry" when it only included the perspectives of some women? The Women's Bureau and organizations sympathetic to protective labor legislation silenced their opposition. The rift between those women who supported protective labor legislation and those who supported an Equal Rights Amendment remained significant throughout the 1920s. Commenting on the schism in 1926, LWV president Sherwin explained, "The League and the Woman's Party are so diametrically opposed on fundamental questions of policy that there will never be any real alliance between them" ("Miss Sherwin Back from Paris Victory").

Opponents of the LWV's reformist approach also found the organization too slow and too bureaucratic. While first LWV president Park proclaimed with pride that "the League of Women Voters . . . has been willing to go ahead slowly in order to go ahead steadily" ("The Voter, the Press"), the length of time needed to achieve change through League procedure was simply frustrating to many women. In contrast to the textually extensive programs, planks, newsletters, memos, broadsides, circular letters, schools, plays, and institutes involved in the "middle-of-the-road" approach, the NWP believed in publicity through much more embodied, immediate demonstrations such as parades, flag burning, and hunger strikes. Waiting for the average citizen to be persuaded would mean waiting too long. Take bold steps to change the rules now, the NWP suggested, and the average citizen would learn to adjust.

In light of the powerful critiques issued by groups such as the NWP and the legislative losses the LWV encountered after 1925, I do not wish to present the organization as a rhetorical exemplar, free of faults or oppressions. Yet I also do not wish to dismiss their pedagogies of political literacy. Instruction in political procedures and communication were not enough to grant all American women immediate voice in domestic politics, but that instruction, as carried out by the League since 1920, has enabled many American women to get involved, both officially and unofficially, in American politics. For many women who would become active in formal political institutions (through legislative offices as well as appointed policy-making positions) later in the century, the League served an essential educative function. In 1972, "the League reported that eighty-nine of its members were serving in thirty-two state legislatures, which is an astonishing twenty-three percent of all women legislators" (Black 290). A 1983 study of women in state legislatures conducted by the Center for the American Woman and Politics indicates a similarly impressive impact: "57.5 percent of state senators and 49.7 percent of state representatives had belonged to the League at some time, as had 34.7 percent of women county commissioners, 17 percent of women mayors, and 17.9 percent of women in local councils" (Black 291). Naomi Black explains that, for these LWV members turned public officeholders,

> Nonpartisanship as practiced in the League provided training in distinguishing among political issues, in deriving and supporting preferences among policy alternatives, in publicizing and lobbying for these preferences. Meanwhile, both deliberately, as part of an educational process, and unintentionally, as part of finding out about issues and promoting them, the LWV provided a great deal of information about the functioning of the political process. (292)

In *Activist Rhetorics and American Higher Education, 1885–1937,* Susan Kates argues that historical study of instruction in composition and rhetoric is critical because such study can result in new perspectives on the present. "We are only now beginning to recover many of the pedagogical artifacts of educators and their students who confronted language and learning issues that are not dissimilar to those that students, educators, and educational policy makers face today," she explains (98). The language and learning issues faced by the LWV and the WILPF, I believe, are not dissimilar to those faced by students, teachers, and scholars of rhetoric and composition today. Many of us who teach rhetoric and composition in the twenty-first century want our students to become not only successful academic writers, but also active, literate citizens. As Bruce Herzberg points out, many instructors of composition and rhetoric now embrace a dual goal in their pedagogies: they want students to become better communicators and "better citizens, citizens in the strongest sense of those who take responsibility for communal welfare" (68). In designing curricula to meet this goal, composition and rhetoric specialists must address many important and challenging questions. Perhaps the most significant questions include, "What literate practices does someone need to know to be a responsible citizen? What literate skills can we teach students that will help them to be active citizens? What attitudes toward language should we foster in our students to help them see reading, writing, and speaking as tools to improve the worlds around them?" These questions about students are remarkably similar to those the LWV and the WILPF asked about newly enfranchised women in the late 1910s and 1920s. Thus, as I elaborate in the conclusion, I believe that the rhetorical and educational practices of both organizations not only enrich historical accounts of rhetoric and composition but also contribute usefully to contemporary pedagogical discussions in rhetoric and composition.

Conclusion
Learning from the Strategies and Struggles of the LWV and WILPF

> The historian is never simply writing an account of the past. She is also
> writing an account of the present and, of equal importance, a hope and
> vision for the future. In telling us what happened the historian is telling
> us what ought to happen now and tomorrow.
> —James Berlin, "Revisionary Histories of Rhetoric"

Literate practices employed and taught within organizations such as the
WILPF and the LWV provide fertile opportunities for study because those
practices reveal how groups of people collaborate in order to challenge the
configurations of power perpetuated through existing traditions of reading,
writing, and speaking. As Thomas Miller and Melody Bowdon have argued,
the dominant tradition of civic rhetorical practice "needs to be critically
reexamined to assess the limitations it imposed on public access and the
rhetorical strategies that were used to overcome them" (594). Such critical
reexamination bears on present rhetorical and pedagogical practice, particularly as a growing number of teachers and scholars work to reinvigorate connections between the university and its surrounding communities. In this
chapter, I consider how the literate practices the LWV and the WILPF used
to challenge the rhetorical limitations of diplomacy and domestic politics
might both enrich historical accounts of rhetoric and composition and suggest possibilities for contemporary pedagogy in rhetoric and composition.

Historical Significance
Understanding Counterpublics

The rhetorical efforts of the LWV and the WILPF are important for histories of rhetoric and composition in part because they shed light on how
politically disadvantaged groups can organize to protest their disadvantage
and to empower themselves as participants in the discussion of political
matters. Through these two organizations, a large number of women established forums in which their concerns and arguments held authority. Members of the LWV and WILPF developed what Lorraine Code calls a "rhe-

torical space"—a site from which participants can formulate and publicize agendas in ways they could not within dominant spheres of political communication. Code explains that rhetorical spaces are "fictive but not fanciful or fixed locations whose territorial imperatives structure and limit the kinds of utterances that can be voiced" (ix). While rhetorical spaces impose limits on utterances, they also provide an atmosphere in which those utterances meet with "an expectation of being heard, understood, taken seriously. [Rhetorical spaces] are the sites where the very possibility of . . . a discussion yielding insight is made manifest" (ix–x). The "territorial imperatives" women established through the WILPF and the LWV allowed for the voicing and serious discussion of political concerns that were often denied within the rhetorical spaces of traditional politics.

Within their rhetorical spaces, subordinate groups can develop and practice discourses of critique. Such critique, Jane Mansbridge suggests, often must originate outside of dominant publics: "because traditional public deliberative arenas are the most likely to draw on symbols that support a dominant order, democracies cannot rely on these arenas to produce the ongoing critique of power that they need" (131). Subordinate groups that aspire to become counterpublics and to challenge oppressive power structures must thus take on the responsibility of developing unique vocabularies, tactics, and arguments. Counterpublics also serve as "protected enclaves" in which participants "explore their ideas in an environment of mutual encouragement. They can then oscillate between these enclaves and more hostile but also broader surroundings in which they can test their ideas against the reigning reality" (Mansbridge 131). The rhetorical spaces developed by the LWV and the WILPF provided protected enclaves in which women could learn and practice rhetorical tactics to reform dominant institutions of political deliberation.

Although they provide some level of protection for their members, counterpublics inevitably maintain a complex relationship with their historical and cultural contexts. The practices the LWV and WILPF used to involve women in political discussion demonstrate that, even as a counterpublic constructs itself against dominant publics, it often remains heavily informed by those dominant publics. Although both organizations posited open discussion as the basis of participatory citizenship, they often relied on communicative procedures derived from traditional discursive arenas of politics, a practice that sometimes silenced certain groups of women. Enabling the kind of open participation that the WILPF and LWV supported requires special consideration for oppressed participants. As Iris Marion

Young explains, "A democratic public, however that is constituted, should provide mechanisms for the effective representation and recognition of the distinct voices and perspectives of those of its constituent groups that are oppressed or disadvantaged within it" (413). Yet the LWV and the WILPF limited participation in their organizations by adopting discursive procedures—most notably parliamentary procedure—that were familiar primarily to elite, white women. Many women thus remained disadvantaged within these counterpublics because they lacked alternative mechanisms for the expression of political views.

While the influence of dominant publics in some ways restricted the rhetorical scope of the LWV and the WILPF, in other ways it helped the organizations involve a wider swath of women in political discussion. Both groups appropriated then-current publicity tactics and communications technology to serve their progressive aims. The rise of communications technology, such as the electric press, the telegraph, the typewriter, the moving picture, and the radio, led to the development of several new professions in the early twentieth century, including mass journalism, public relations, and advertising. American universities responded to these new employment opportunities by developing coursework to train specialists in these areas. Katherine Adams explains that, by 1910, "universities [were] providing . . . specialized courses and majors: in journalism, public relations, advertising, public speaking, creative writing, film, and business and technical writing" (38). By the late 1910s, many of these university-educated specialists were employed in the publicity efforts of private corporations, political parties, and individual government officials. Eschewing these self-interested uses of communications technologies, the LWV and the WILPF worked to involve broad coalitions of women in what they saw as the intelligent and ethical use of mass publicity to increase women's influence in civic life.

The arguments the LWV and WILPF developed to bolster women's authority as political rhetors also demonstrate the complex gendered interactions that often occur between dominant publics and counterpublics. Working from popular notions of women as moral and maternal, the WILPF and the LWV identified themselves as "women's" organizations in order to establish an ethos from which to articulate ideas and beliefs that lacked expression in the existing idiom of male-controlled politics. This strategic deployment of cultural commonplaces, Rosemary Pringle and Sophie Watson suggest, is characteristic of emerging counterpublics: "Any connections among groups have to be constructed, articulated and maintained; they are not pre-given. Groups make these connections using the discursive frameworks available to their time and culture" (216). The choice to represent themselves as "women's" organizations, however, was not entirely enabling for members of the WILPF and LWV because this representation partly relied on dominant and restrictive constructions of gender—constructions derived from racist and sexist viewpoints.

When confronted by women who did not share their views, leaders of both the LWV and the WILPF surely realized that the term "women" can only serve as a partial signifier, never referring to all those gendered female but instead to a specific race and class of gendered subjects. Yet both groups chose to identify themselves as "women's organizations" because such an identification enabled a collective, if delimited, agency. For both organizations, the term "women" functioned as what Ernesto Laclau and Chantal Mouffe call an "articulatory practice"—a rhetorical strategy that enables identification among diverse group members by "partially fix[ing] meaning" and "temporarily arrest[ing] the flow of difference" (qtd. in Pringle and Watson 216). While such articulatory practices might prove politically strategic for some, they are often contested by those whose difference is effaced in the process of "arresting the flow."

Historical moments involving articulatory practices provide important sites for scholarly study aimed at developing a more complete understanding of how language intervenes between division and unity in political struggles. The "possibility of politics," Bill Readings asserts, lies in the careful examination of language and "*heard silences,* traces of radical dissensus within modes and structures of political representation, social communication, and economic accounting" (xxv). By focusing on "traces of radical dissensus" within the struggles of groups such as the LWV and the WILPF, scholarship might more fully address the differences that constantly challenge representation and counter tendencies toward homogenization and oppression.

The early work of the LWV and the WILPF also reveals how rhetorically disadvantaged groups, in spite of hostile climates and frequent disappointments, persistently employ writing, reading, and speaking to challenge dominant publics. From their counterpublic rhetorical spaces outside of traditional partisan and diplomatic politics, both groups engaged in practices of resistance that, although slow and sometimes unsuccessful, influenced popular opinion about progressive legislation and traditional methods of political communication. While few momentous speeches or world-altering treatises are associated with the early work of either the WILPF or the LWV, their work merits a place in the history of rhetoric because it illustrates the processes by which subordinate groups struggle to cultivate kairotic moments for arguments about political and social change.

The multiple, collaborative, and persistent rhetorical strategies used to create receptive environments for political and social change deserve greater attention within historical studies of rhetoric and composition. Without extensive preliminary rhetorical work, the famous texts that mark significant moments of change would not have received the attention of the broader public involved in the change. As Bruce Horner has argued, a rhetor's credibility, and thus a text's impact, depends upon numerous conditions: "Realization of one's economic, cultural, and social capital is contingent on institutional pre-conditions which delimit and authorize what one is 'entitled' to do, and whether one has 'recognized authority'" (174). Continued, widespread literate practices of public opinion formation, such as those engaged in by the LWV and the WILPF, can gradually change the institutional preconditions that limit who can speak and what can be said in a particular rhetorical situation, thus enabling authority for innovative political arguments.

Understanding the Present

The early work of the WILPF and the LWV earns additional historical significance by speaking to the challenges women currently face in their efforts to be active, critical citizens. The WILPF and LWV's critiques of partisan politics and diplomacy and the reforms that they promoted remain frighteningly appropriate today. The history of these groups highlights the strength of political traditions and their resistance to rhetorical innovation. Immense work remains to be done by those who wish to see an international arena in which nonmale, nonmilitaristic voices have a powerful presence and a domestic political scene in which partisanship and money are not all-powerful. Scholar of feminist citizenship Rian Voet has noted recently that women in the twenty-first century still face exclusion from political participation and decision making. Before women can be active citizens, Voet argues, they must have the ability to act as full citizens: "a full citizen in its most complete sense is someone who participates in legislation or decision-making in public affairs" (140). But women lag behind men in holding powerful positions in political life, both nationally and internationally. Ingeborg Breines reports in a 1999 UNESCO study of women and international peace movements that

> there are only 1 per cent of women elected heads of state and government, 7 per cent
> of women ministers (with very few women heading powerful departments such as
> ministries of foreign affairs, defence, the interior or finance) and some 11 per cent

of women parliamentarians. This century has seen fewer than thirty women prime ministers or presidents, and 99 per cent of the top political power is in the hands of men, as well as some estimated 99 per cent of the world's resources. (41)

Similarly, J. Ann Tickner concludes her recent study of women in global politics by asserting that "men predominate in elite positions of power in the realm of international politics, both at the intergovernmental and state levels; not only do they make the important decisions, they also set the policy agendas" (129).

To change this situation, women must continue to challenge the male monopoly of political power as the WILPF and the LWV have done; however, they must also consider how political discourse and positions of political power might be made more appealing to more women. In Voet's words,

> We can neither do without establishing decision-making positions for women, nor without changing the content of citizenship itself. . . . Woman-friendly citizenship implies a citizenship with which women can empathize, and one to which they can and want to be committed. . . . It implies a citizenship for which they can make time and in which they want to be active. (140)

In other words, women not only need to hone their rhetorical skills, they also need the opportunity and desire to be powerful political participants. Theorists of citizenship and political discourse such as Iris Marion Young, Ruth Lister, Kathleen Jones, and Ann Phillips have argued that enabling women as citizens today requires a critical reconstruction of the meaning of citizenship. Summarizing these theorists, Voet asserts that a "male bias" in popular understandings of citizenship must

> be corrected by rethinking the idea of citizenship from the perspective of the female and the feminist citizen. Among other things, this implies challenging the masculine founding myths of states, the idea of fraternity, the assumed necessary detachment of political actors from their bodies, backgrounds, group interests and group identities. . . . The images and the metaphors of citizenship need to change so that women feel included. (140)

An integral step toward this reconstruction of citizenship involves studies, such as this one, that explore previous challenges to the "civic tradition" as that tradition is conventionally constructed through a male-dominated perspective.

While certainly not without shortcomings, the WILPF and LWV's construction of women as caring, upright, moral forces in citizenship challenged traditional images and metaphors of civic participation. Anticipating recent feminist reinterpretations of citizenship, the WILPF and the LWV "illumi-nat[ed] the way in which the civic-republican conception of the citizen *was* 'aggressively male,' so that the exclusion of the female, far from being an aberration, was integral to the theory and practice of citizenship" (Lister 68). The practices these two organizations employed to challenge popular defi-nitions of civic participation as a competitive, confrontational activity might provide useful insights in the continuing struggle of women to gain power within a sphere that is, in many ways, still premised on their exclusion.

Pedagogical Implications

The early work of the LWV and WILPF also suggests avenues through which rhetorical education can contribute to civic discourse today. Indeed, these groups' rhetorical and instructional practices seem particularly relevant to contemporary education in composition and rhetoric given the strong push in higher education to link university instruction to civic life and com-munity participation. As I discuss in my introduction, the elevation of the great text and the individual author has left a mark on historical studies of rhetoric. Perhaps more important, however, is the impact this valuation has had in the classroom. One effect has been to distance composition classrooms from the "real world" writing occasions students are likely to encounter as active citizens. This distance will continue to grow, Ellen Cushman argues, as long as teachers of rhetoric and composition ignore everyday texts in order to maintain a privileged position for their research and for the classrooms in which they teach. According to Cushman, "so long as a select few gain en-trance to universities, so long as we differentiate between experts and nov-ices, and so long as we value certain types of knowledge" the composition classroom will remain distanced from the communities surrounding it (374).

The essays typically assigned in composition courses and included in composition anthologies maintain an academic area of expertise by creat-ing what Sharon Crowley has called "the myth of the academic essay." This myth, she explains,

> assumes that rhetorical situations are similar or the same across a range of certain
> possible settings, that instructors can forecast the parameters of such settings, and
> that students can adequately meet the terms of any given discursive situation by
> applying a handy set of discursive formulae. (233)

In many ways, the "myth of the academic essay" upholds elite professional values—a practice several scholars of composition and rhetoric have recently questioned. In the words of Kathleen Welch, "much of the teaching of writing has unselfconsciously formed itself after the static model of literary studies, with a canon to be revered and a language world divorced from all ordinary language use" (135). This kind of teaching establishes a literacy niche—a place where special forms of writing are expected and enforced. As a result, composition courses often do not adequately prepare students to meet the complex situations they will face as citizens, nor do they encourage students to use literacy as a means to actively promote change.

Instead of such courses, Nedra Reynolds suggests, "we need to offer students more and greater means of resistance to the thesis-driven essay, rigidly structured paragraphing, and the reductive emphasis on coherence and clarity" (71). For composition to engage literate practices of civic participation, she continues, "we need to rethink radically the forms of writing we find acceptable. The result might be the breakdown of some of the rigid boundaries that separate life and politics inside and outside the academy" (71). More and more teachers and scholars of rhetoric and composition are searching for ways to challenge these boundaries. Increasingly, Christian Weisser explains, teachers and scholars "are interested in moving beyond academic discourse, in both the classroom and scholarship, and toward the uses of discourse that might have more significance in shaping the worlds that we live in" (132). The collaborative literate practices I examine here represent such attempts to shape the world and thus provide alternatives to the genres that have long inhabited rhetoric and composition classrooms. The collective rhetorical practices of active citizenship ought to take a more pronounced role in rhetoric and composition courses so that those courses serve a purpose other than the production of individual, competitive, academic writers.

At the same time, scholars and teachers of rhetoric and composition might reimagine our relationship to the communities that surround our institutions. Faculty regularly participated in the educational efforts of the WILPF and the LWV, contributing their resources to projects aimed at improving local, state, national, and international discourse. Such projects, often absent from contemporary academic institutions that focus on research or on the teaching of undergraduate students, are critical for a pedagogy of civic engagement. As Henry Giroux has argued, lessening the chasm between academic institutions and the struggles of oppressed communities requires that higher education be re-envisioned "as a public resource . . . open to working people and communities that are often viewed as marginal to such institutions" ("Beyond" 250). Institutions of higher education, in other words, might be reconfigured so that they are not exclusive sites of professional credentialing but accessible centers for learning and community action.[1]

Calls for a re-envisioned, reinvigorated university are not unique to the writings of recent scholars. Jane Addams argued early in the twentieth century that university faculty had lost the rhetorical ability to engage their surrounding communities. According to Addams, professional academic regard for technical and research-oriented expertise had undermined the relationship between the university and the larger public: "So much is judged by the learning and technicality of the professor. . . . To such an extent has this progressed that today there are few university men who can address common people, owing to their estrangement from them." The focus on research specialization, Addams suggests, "has ruined their sympathies, and destroyed their power of association" ("Democracy and Education"). Faculty members were concerned with amassing ideas and transmitting them to students, but they were not paying enough attention to teaching students how to apply those ideas to vital processes of change in their communities.

Addams traces this predicament of the American university from the university's origins as a theological institution geared toward educating religious leaders. The shift from this initial religious mission to a more secular project marked the insulation of academia:

> As the college changed from teaching theology to teaching secular knowledge, the test of its success should have shifted from the power to save men's souls to the power to adjust them in healthful relations to nature and their fellow men. But the college failed to do this, and made the test of its success the mere collecting and disseminating of knowledge, elevating the means into an end and falling in love with its own achievement. ("Democracy and Education")

Addams recommends that, in order to regain a connection to the worlds around it, the university should work through organizations, such as settlements and voluntary associations, that focus on applying knowledge to practical problems. The settlement and similar voluntary movements "stand for application as opposed to research; for emotion as opposed to abstraction; for universal interest as opposed to specialization" ("A Function" 340). Women's organizations that derived from the settlement tradition, such as the WILPF and the LWV, would fill in where the university had failed, translating the abstract so that "common" people might apply knowledge to the pressing issues in their lived experience.

Service-Learning Pedagogy

If academics of the current century wish to contribute to the development of a more engaged, critical public discourse, we might also make attempts to become involved in that discourse by teaching in the midst of it. As Peter Mortensen has argued, if educators in composition and rhetoric are serious about exploring and expanding their place beyond the academy, attending to local concerns is crucial because "it is there that political and social issues of great consequence can be deliberated and acted upon" (195). One way to accomplish this goal is through service-learning pedagogy.

Service-learning courses employ assignments that enable students to discover the literate practices of civic engagement and to participate in community-related projects. Service learning, as articulated by many recent scholars, draws on traditions of experiential education similar to those embraced by the LWV and WILPF. In his study of service-learning initiatives in composition, Thomas Deans suggests that the progressive education movement in the late nineteenth and early twentieth centuries—the same movement within which the LWV and the WILPF located their educational practices—serves as a foundation for current service-learning pedagogy:

> Behind these contemporary voices in composition theory, one can hear the echoes of earlier educational movements, with none more important for service learning than progressive education. The chief philosopher of progressivism, John Dewey, is fast becoming *the* touchstone for service-learning practitioners. (29)

Drawing from Deweyan notions of progressive education and from more recent articulations of "critical literacy" as explored by Paulo Freire and his contemporaries, service learning has taken a wide variety of forms in American composition pedagogy. These forms reflect the productive integration of progressive education—which, as the experiences of the WILPF and LWV demonstrate, often lacked sufficient attention to class, race, and ethnic difference—and Freirian critical literacy pedagogy, a perspective on education that is dedicated to acknowledging and acting within the contexts of difference.

Deans identifies three major categories of service learning in the writing classroom—writing *about* the community, writing *for* the community, and writing *with* the community. These types of service learning are distinguished by the kinds of writing students are expected to produce in the course. Courses that employ the writing-*about*-the-community model typically ask students to participate in community service of some kind and then to write critically about those experiences, often using traditional academic essay forms.[2] The other two varieties of service-learning pedagogy ask students to produce at least one major assignment in a "nonacademic" genre, often in cooperation with a community group or agency. These courses operate under the assumption that "treating student writers first and foremost as citizens means finding real audiences and real occasions [and] re-thinking the purposes of the writing we assign and the kinds of resources, including textbooks, that we use" (Ervin 395).[3]

In both writing-*for*-the-community and writing-*with*-the-community approaches, traditional academic assignments, produced primarily for an instructor, are supplemented with, or replaced entirely by, scenarios in which the "text is not an end in itself but a performance measured by its personal and public consequence" (Peck, Flower, and Higgins 208). The end product is not an "original scholarly essay," but something that serves a definite purpose within communities beyond the academy. Writing-*for*-the-community courses, for instance, frequently ask students to produce a text in conjunction with a community agency as part of that agency's service to the community. Such projects familiarize students with nonacademic, and typically non-essayistic, genres of civic engagement. Similarly, classes that employ a writing-*with*-the-community approach involve students, teachers, and community members in a collaborative attempt to produce texts that will effect social change. The needs identified by the community members, rather than a scenario provided by a course instructor or textbook writer, determine the texts the students produce. Cooperative textual production, Wayne Peck, Linda Flower, and Lorraine Higgins suggest in their discussion of the community literacy center project at Carnegie Mellon University, encourages social change through "intercultural conversation" among community members, students, and university faculty. Intercultural conversation, in turn, promotes "a suspicion of colonizing rhetorics that work to impose a dominant discourse" and a generative "willingness to create hybrid texts" that challenge dominant models and forms of writing as traditionally taught in composition courses (211).

As Deans notes, the three categories of service learning value "distinctly different literacies, engage distinctly different learning processes, require distinctly different rhetorical practices, and result in distinctly different kinds of texts" (19). The service-learning approach most appropriate for a course will vary depending upon the goals of the course and the specific institutional and community contexts in which it is implemented: "Any one of the paradigms might work best within a particular local community or college context. Understanding the fitness, the *kairos,* of a particular approach to its particular context is the most pressing imperative" (19). Despite the variety of service-learning approaches, each represents a move toward a pedagogy of rhetoric that values the literate practices of civic engagement. In a service-learning model of pedagogy, the greatest pedagogical asset of teachers is not their ability to serve as founts of knowledge and judges of correct academic genres but their ability to facilitate interaction among students, organizations, and residents in the production of public discourses.

Of course, like any other pedagogical approach, service learning should not be embraced uncritically. The very name of the approach suggests the potential for elitist or paternalistic endeavors to be carried out under its banner. The term "service," Deans explains, "evokes not only the specter of unequal server-served relations . . . but also a gendered history in which women, both within and outside the academy, have been enculturated to submerge their selves in service to others" (23). A related danger attending service-learning initiatives in composition courses is the risk that the required writing course will be perceived as a service to local government and community agencies in much the same way as it has sometimes been labeled a "service course" for other academic disciplines. The composition classroom should not become a volunteer center—practitioners of service-learning approaches must carefully select and structure projects that provide opportunities to teach critical literacy skills. Courses must integrate service and learning.

In fact, traditional academic essay forms may be usefully incorporated into service-learning projects to ensure that service is coupled with learning. The critical analysis skills students can hone through techniques of academic literacy can serve them well in assessing and actively contributing to the goals and tactics of the communities they engage with as part of service-learning courses. Most teachers would agree that the goal of service-learning courses is not for students to embrace uncritically the rhetorical methods currently employed by the community groups with which service-learning assignments might bring them into contact. These rhetorical methods, like those used by the LWV and the WILPF, will hold their own oppressions and shortcomings. The practices of civic involvement must always be critically examined to see whom they exclude, and more traditional forms of academic writing can provide sites where this critique can occur.

Academic essays might also become points at which students consider their positions vis-à-vis the "clients" they "serve" in service-learning assignments. As Horner explains, "service learning projects can make visible the specific relationship of the realm of the academy, and work, and worker deemed 'academic,' to these other realms of the social" (179). The academic essay, Horner asserts, can serve a central purpose in the process of making these relationships visible. He explains that "it is . . . not academic discursive forms in themselves which have properties of impersonality and removal from social concerns. . . . Rather, it is the . . . reification of academic, and other, discursive forms that is to be combated" (182). In other words, academic essays are not inherently elitist; rather, the *myth* of the academic essay is. The academic essay can serve social ends if it is assigned with such ends in view.

The rhetorical and educational efforts of the LWV and WILPF thus suggest that we change the kinds of assignments we give to our students. As I explain below, these efforts also suggest that we reconsider the institutional location of rhetorical instruction for civic participation.

Interdisciplinarity

What the WILPF and LWV were trying to do for women in domestic and international politics is similar to what many instructors of composition and rhetoric would like to do for their students—motivate and empower them to participate as active citizens. The LWV and WILPF attempted to provide training that would enable their members to partake in various institutions of American and international politics (elections, public administration, community groups, political journalism, etc.). If we wish to train students for active participation in a democratic society, we also need to provide some instruction in the myriad rhetorical practices of domestic and global politics.

The numerous literate practices and the various means of delivery involved in the educational campaigns of the LWV and WILPF indicate, however, that any effort to provide education in the rhetorical practices of American and international politics must be interdisciplinary. Rhetorical studies, Steven Mailloux points out, already take place across academic departments:

> In contrast to departmentalized disciplines such as history, sociology, and biology, rhetorical studies is today an *inter*discipline located in fragmented pieces as subfields in various departments, primarily English and Communication, which have their own independent, professional disciplinary identities. (129–30)

These "fragmented pieces" of rhetorical study might be brought together in efforts to provide instruction in the rhetorical practices of active citizenship.

For example, the work of rhetorical specialists in English and communication might be coordinated in a curriculum that prepares students for political involvement. Lengthy campaigns aimed at changing legislation inevitably require rhetorical skill in both speaking and writing, with both modes of communication working to reinforce the other. The efforts of educators in composition and speech communication, thus, might be coordinated in a curriculum that links instruction in public speaking and community writing. Teachers in communications and English might also collaborate in offering rhetorical instruction in practices of dialogue. If we want students to be able to participate in a democracy, we must prepare them to speak and write in ways that invite varied response and continued conversations, yet our courses often ask for final products that we grade and return to the students, limiting the responses students' texts receive to grades and margin comments. The LWV tried to expand the conversations of electoral politics, and the WILPF attempted to break restrictive traditions of international negotiation—current instruction in rhetoric and composition might embrace a similar spirit of dialogue.

So how might we accomplish the teaching of rhetorical skills that further conversation? First, we might consistently provide students with real audiences to address beyond the teacher. As Susan Wells has argued, we must discover or construct public spaces in which our students' work will be read or heard by others; otherwise "[p]ublic writing . . . means writing for no audience at all" (328). The service-learning approaches to composition discussed above provide several ways in which we might accomplish this goal. We might also look for publication outlets for our students' work, be these outlets electronic or print. Only by creating scenarios in which students' literate practices will be received by a broader audience can we hope to teach them to anticipate responses that are more substantial and perhaps more meaningful than our individual comments.

Second, students would benefit from more sustained training in methods of leading discussions, either face-to-face or via writing. One distinct goal of both writing and speaking courses might be to increase students' facility with textual negotiations and textual interactions, focusing on texts (written or spoken) not as final products but as contributions to ongoing conversations. Julia Grace Wales and the WILPF attempted to teach diplomats new methods of negotiation so that, even in the face of war, international conversations might continue. The LWV provided instruction in discussion leadership so that League-sponsored forums would successfully engage a variety of perspectives and voices. We might also teach our students rhetorical methods to keep the conversation going.

Third, specialists in English and communication might pool their rhetorical savvy in the teaching of critical media analysis. Both the WILPF and the LWV spent much effort critiquing the biases of the popular press and developing publications that might counter the influence of the press in domestic and international politics. The ability to critique popular news sources and to present and circulate alternative sources has, as numerous scholars have illustrated, played a critical role in social movements throughout history. If we wish to enable our students to participate in such movements, these rhetorical skills should have a place in our pedagogies.

To this end, course readings and assignments might explore the relationships between financial interests and what get discussed as "civic issues." For both the WILPF and the LWV, challenging the biases of the mainstream press was intimately connected to funding issues. In the WILPF's "Report of the Secretary-Treasurer" for the 1920–21 year, for instance, Balch attributes the failure of the group's endeavor to publish and circulate its own newspaper to the financial strain such an endeavor entails:

> A great deal of time went also in getting out every second month a news-sheet or paper *(Pax et Libertas)*. . . . The time and money spent in this editorial work appeared to all of us who were at the Executive Committee Meeting of June 1920 to be out of proportion to our resources and *Pax et Libertas* was regretfully abandoned in favour of occasional pamphlets and bulletins. (qtd. in WILPF, *Report of the Third International Congress* 191)

Financial difficulties also plagued the LWV's efforts to provide alternative sources of politically relevant information. First LWV president Maud Wood Park reflected thus on the financial troubles faced by League leaders in the early years of the organization: "Our other great agony was over money. . . . [W]e were very desperate all that first year, and I remember perfectly, once . . . we had less than three dollars in our combined bank accounts" ("After Seven Years" 2).

That establishing alternative channels of communication was, and continues to be, so difficult suggests that successful channels deserve extensive scrutiny. In a time of advanced capitalism, wealthy interests tend to control channels of mass persuasion. But, as Adams concludes in her study of progressive politics and popular persuasion in the early twentieth century, "a powerful countering influence . . . could come from citizens trained not just in how to write correctly but in how mass persuasion works." Future citizens should receive both instruction in writing correctly and "an education on how those slants, twists, and distortions work" (150).

Teachers and scholars of rhetoric within English and communication departments might also work together to advocate for larger undergraduate programs in which rhetorical education for citizenship plays a central role in courses across the curriculum.[4] Responsibility for teaching the literate practices of political engagement should not rest entirely on the shoulders of specialists in communication or English departments; rather, it should be the concern of all departments. Beyond the obvious fact that one or two required courses in writing or public speaking cannot possibly expose students to the immense variety of persuasive skills needed for political engagement, political literacy should be an interdisciplinary concern because it involves participation in an array of symbolic systems other than writing and speaking. According to David Barton and Mary Hamilton, when participating in literacy events, whether those events are in the political realm or elsewhere, "people use written language in an integrated way as part of a range of semiotic systems: these semiotic systems include mathematical systems, musical notation, maps, and other non-text-based images" (8–9). Given the variety of semiotic systems involved in political literacy, we might work to develop linked courses in which students combine what they learn in a math or economics course, for example, with the persuasive skills for public participation that they learn in their composition or communication courses. Instruction in dramatic methods, music, and artwork from colleagues in other departments might also supplement the rhetorical education provided by communication and English departments, thus expanding the means of delivery through which students might contribute to political conversations. Through such interdisciplinary efforts, we can encourage students to think of instruction in writing and speaking not in terms of producing isolated speeches or papers but as part of larger semiotic campaigns to achieve political and social goals.[5]

The efforts of the LWV and the WILPF to involve great numbers of women in domestic and international politics also hints at several options for advanced, interdisciplinary courses that might serve the community as well as the academy. For instance, upper-division courses might use the expertise of rhetorical scholars in English, communication, and public relations to teach the skills of publicity campaigns for nonprofit groups or nongovernmental organizations. Other courses might incorporate rhetorical studies and political science to provide students with knowledge of legislative procedure so that students gain a better understanding of how laws are written, how they are interpreted, and how their language impacts lives. Such courses would assist future activists by familiarizing them with the discursive conventions of lawmaking. In addition, such courses might help future lawmakers and government officials to develop critical perspectives on their discourse communities and to work for change so that those communities become more amenable to broader public participation.

Internationalism

The rhetorical practices of the LWV and the WILPF also point to a need to internationalize current perspectives on the teaching of rhetoric and to consider several important questions about the global implications of what we do. For instance, in light of the restrictive constructions of literacy and patriotism that developed in the wake of World War I, we might consider how nationalism—indeed the very concept of nations—influences how we understand and teach literacy. Are there vestiges of Americanization or nationalistic aims in our literacy curricula? Who, both in a national and global framework, has the power to write and read documents of public importance—documents that determine public policy, laws, and political processes? Who has training to assess, discuss, and respond to these documents? Who benefits or suffers as a result? If, as Volosinov suggests, words serve as "bridges" between ourselves and others, what bridges, between which cultures, groups, and nations, do we enable and disable as a result of how we teach literacy?

Contemporary teachers of rhetoric and composition, Bruce Horner and John Trimbur argue, must "develop an international perspective capable of understanding the study and teaching of written English in relation to other languages and to the dynamics of globalization" (624). Teaching composition and rhetoric within the confines of the United States can easily mask the importance of international perspectives, isolating students from the language diversity of the world and from the power inequities that result from the privileging of one language over others. Horner and Trimbur suggest several means by which we might advance an internationalist perspective on rhetoric and composition. We might design composition courses that encourage students to think about language privileges; we might rethink the institutional, pedagogical, and research relationships among composition, ESL, and other languages in the academy; and we might develop stronger relationships between writing programs and writing instruction in other languages (621–22).

Margaret Himley has also recently addressed the need for internationalized instruction in composition and rhetoric. According to Himley, the current context of globalization in communication—a situation made more apparent and accessible to us and to our students through the web—suggests that our curricula ought to include courses that prepare students to read, critique, and contribute to information in a global context. Globalization, Himley points out, "depends on the circulation of texts, technology, and e-space." To prepare students for critical participation in this global context, she argues, students "need to acquire an understanding . . . of the ways texts move through production, distribution, and circulation" (60). If the need for critical readers and viewers of international information was critical when Jane Addams wrote of "Peace and the Press" in 1915 and when LWV member Florence Kitchelt wrote her critique of "Newspapers and the Getting of the News," in 1922, it is no less critical today when, as Himley explains,

> Students can access information instantaneously from around the globe, and need the geopolitical knowledge to assess that information, to frame it, and to challenge and critique it. . . . [A]s we would no longer plan a course without considering questions of gender and race, we need to consider questions of globalization. (61)

A Final Thought

The documents and stories I discovered in the archives of the WILPF and LWV are fascinating in their own right, but my ultimate hope is that this project does more than edify historical understandings of women's political and rhetorical activity in the early twentieth century. I hope my research contributes to the development of a curriculum that integrates literate practices of civic involvement. As Freire has argued, "the goal of critical education is to create a public sphere of citizens who are able to exercise power over their own lives, and especially over the conditions of knowledge production and acquisition" (Introduction viii). The LWV and WILPF provide case studies of the development of power over "the conditions of knowledge production and acquisition." When political parties, diplomatic circles, and the popular press did not admit their concerns into public discussion, these organizations developed their own channels of communication to create public discussion. I hope, then, that this project contributes to critical education by elucidating the relationships among education, mass communication, literacy, and power, and by encouraging the integration of rhetorical education and political engagement.

Notes

Works Cited

Index

Notes

INTRODUCTION

1.   Several feminist historians have begun to appreciate the continuity of women's participation in organization-based political activity after suffrage, and I am indebted to their work. These historians have argued that, although the Nineteenth Amendment "is the most obvious benchmark in the history of women in politics in the United States, . . . it is a problematic one" because focusing on the electoral arena means viewing women's political activity and their participation in civic discourse "through the conventional lens where male behavior sets the norm" (Cott, "Across" 153). Traditionally, historian Nancy Cott explains, narratives of feminism and women's activism in America claim that "after the achievement of the vote, the large coalition movement among women disintegrated; now insiders rather than outsiders, women (ironically) lost influence within the political process" ("Across" 154). Cott's work undermines these narratives of decline by positing a greater continuity in women's political activism and efficacy, particularly through women's continued involvement in diverse voluntary associations. Membership in these associations, which were designed largely, although not exclusively, for civic betterment, burgeoned in the period following the passage of the Nineteenth Amendment and remained strong into mid-century. Historian Susan Ware has also done much to chart women's activism in the 1930s.

2.   The names of these two organizations have changed during their lifetimes. As I elaborate in chapter 2, I use the name "Women's International League for Peace and Freedom" to refer to the organization that was initially called the International Committee of Women for Permanent Peace. I use the name "League of Women Voters" to refer to the organization that was known as the League of Women Voters of the United States from 1920 until 1944, when its name was changed to the National League of Women Voters.

3.   A selection of anthologies includes Karlyn Kohrs Campbell's two-volume *Man Cannot Speak for Her;* Jane Donawerth's *Rhetorical Theory by Women Before 1900;* Catherine Hobbs's *Nineteenth-Century Women Learn to Write;* Andrea Lunsford's *Reclaiming Rhetorica: Women in the Rhetorical Tradition;* Carol Mattingly's *Water Drops from Women Writers: A Temperance Reader;* Joy Ritchie and Kate Ronald's *Available Means: An Anthology of Women's Rhetoric;* and Molly Wertheimer's *Listening to Their Voices: The Rhetorical Activities of Historical Women.* Book-length studies include Anne Ruggles Gere's *Intimate Practices: Literacy and Cultural Work in U.S. Women's Clubs, 1880–1920;* Cheryl Glenn's *Rhetoric Retold: Regendering the Tradition from Antiquity Through the Renaissance;* Shirley Wilson Logan's *"We Are Coming": The Persuasive Discourse of Nineteenth-Century Black Women;* Carol Mattingly's *Well-Tempered Women: Nineteenth-Century Temperance Rhetoric;* Krista Ratcliffe's *Anglo-American Feminist Challenges to the Rhetorical Tradition(s): Virginia Woolf, Mary Daly, Adrienne Rich,* and Jacqueline Jones Royster's *Traces of a Stream: Literacy and Social Change among African American Women.*

1. BEFORE SUFFRAGE: RHETORICAL PRACTICES OF CIVIC ENGAGEMENT

1.   See, for example, Blair; Deutsch; Foster; Gere; Haarsager; Hewitt; Higginbotham; Logan; T. Martin; Mattingly; Rogow; Royster; and A. Scott.

2.   The organizations I discuss here do not represent an exclusive list, by any means, of the networks in which women across the nation participated during the nineteenth and early twentieth centuries. Two large networks that space prevents me from discussing at length, for instance, are faith-based organizations women founded within different Protestant denominations beginning in the early nineteenth century and the National Congress of Mothers (later the National Congress of Parents and Teachers [PTA]), founded in 1897. For more information on these and other organizations, see Sklar; and Skocpol.

3.   For more information on the history of women's clubs and organizations before the nineteenth century, see Baker; Blair; T. Martin; and A. Scott.

4.   During the mid-nineteenth century, Hobbs explains, "female academies, seminaries, and normal and training schools appeared, along with the prestigious women's colleges" (13).

5.   For a discussion of the restrictions on women's rhetorical education in colleges and universities in the nineteenth century, see Ricks; and Simmons.

6.   Controlling media was particularly important for African American women who were active in abolition work. Mary Ann Shad Cary, an African American abolitionist who helped African American immigrants settle in Canada prior to the Civil War, established the *Provincial Freeman,* through which she could publish and circulate her antislavery ideas (Royster 203). Jacqueline Jones Royster explains that, among African American activists, such publication practices "have constituted a counterforce to the more dominant 'official' voices that define the public agenda in a manner that usually excluded African American interests" (219).

7.   Channels for self-representation were much needed given the regularity with which popular publications included unflattering portrayals of club work. As Anne Ruggles Gere and Sarah Robbins point out, "Nearly all the newspaper and magazine representations of women's clubs portrayed them as groups of silly white middle-class women, simultaneously rendering African-American clubwomen invisible and trivializing the activities of all clubwomen" (646). These negative portrayals often took the form of satirical cartoons, suggesting that women were meddling, unsuccessfully, in men's business. *Harper's Weekly,* for example, published "cartoons featuring men holding babies and/or knitting while stern and umbrella-pointing women conducted meetings" (646). Similarly, the popular cartoon team of James Reed Parker and Helen Hokinson presented clubwomen as overweight incompetents who had trouble maintaining club budgets and who focused meetings on trivial issues such as gardening. Not only did media depictions minimize the work done by clubs; it stereotyped club membership to erase all traces of economically or ethnically diverse women, thus furthering misconceptions of clubdom as the realm of spoiled and frivolous white women.

8.   In the late nineteenth century, the Social Gospel Movement sought to further connections between the church and social reform. With the advance of urbanization and industrialization in the last decades of the century, leaders of many Protestant churches

increasingly saw themselves as part of an important fight for social justice. While Walter Rauschenbusch is perhaps the best-known proponent of the Social Gospel, Jane Addams was also influenced by this movement.

9. Suffrage organizations were not egalitarian efforts, and, while arguing for women to unite around their disenfranchised position, white suffragists often tried to distance themselves from their black "sisters." Suffrage leaders—primarily northern, upper- and middle-class women—devised racist strategies to bring more southern women into their organizations. One prominent strategy involved distancing suffrage work from black women because white suffragists feared they would lessen their chances of enfranchisement if they became too entangled with civil rights issues. As Jacqueline Jones explains, "White suffragists wanted to avoid 'tainting' their cause with the civil rights issue, and at the same time they sought to safeguard their racial and class prerogatives" (115). Other potential suffrage supporters disagreed over the tactics appropriate for suffrage work.

10. Settlement houses first appeared in American cities in the late 1880s and were modeled after London's Toynbee Hall, established in 1884 by the nonviolent Fabian Socialists. Settlements reached the height of their popularity, Trolander suggests, just before World War I, when the movement included approximately four hundred houses. Following this peak, work traditionally done in settlements was taken over by professional social service, social work, and governmental agencies.

11. According to Catt biographer Jacqueline Van Voris, the Sheppard-Towner Act of 1921 "provided a system of federal aid to the states for maternal and infant health programs. Passage of the bill was the first intensive lobbying activity of the new League of Women Voters" (191).

12. For more details on Gilman, see Gilman.

13. As Francille Wilson has argued, black social scientists in the early years of the twentieth century also regularly combined research and social activism. The group of black scholars Wilson has studied (including W. E. B. Dubois, R. R. Wright Jr., George E. Haynes, Carter Woodson, Charles Wesley, Charles E. Johnson, Abram Harris, Ira Reid, and Robert Weaver) "wrote over twenty monographs, scores of articles, and led major research projects for the Department of Labor and Commerce" (1–2). These social scientists also actively participated in the political battles affecting African Americans at the time. Several of these black social scientists, most notably George E. Haynes, agreed with the settlement house vision that research might serve as the basis for social planning (Wilson 233).

14. The scientific study of social problems and the use of extensive statistical reports as evidence in arguments for reform became common procedures in women's organizations during the final two decades of the nineteenth century and the first decade of the twentieth. As Ginzberg has compellingly suggested, much of women's increasing attraction to the scientific study and management of benevolent activity resulted from their experiences in responding to the Civil War. War relief work, Ginzberg explains, required extensive coordination and centralized planning, along with an aura of military discipline. Influenced by these experiences, many postbellum women's organizations "sought to bring order from the supposed chaos of benevolent enthusiasm" (141). The prominence given these more empirical approaches to social problems also reflects

the growth of the academic social sciences, a growth that reform women took part in. Of particular note is the work of the Chicago School of Civics and Philanthropy, incorporated in 1908 and led by reform-oriented women such as Julia Lathrop, Edith Abbott, and Sophonisba Breckenridge, all of whom knew each other from their work in lecturing and leadership at Hull House (Fitzpatrick 174–75). According to the school's charter, the institution was to "promote through instruction, training, investigation and publication, the efficiency of civic, philanthropic, and social work, and the improvement of living and working conditions" (qtd. in Fitzpatrick 175). Coursework at the school included instruction in methods of study and methods of reporting findings so that research might lead to social and civic betterment. As Fitzpatrick explains, the school's leaders

> encouraged their students to carefully study social sciences. They prodded them to pursue detailed investigations of contemporary social problems. They emphasized empirical study as a superior method of social research. And they helped students publish their findings as a way of advancing enlightened reform. (176)

2. The Women's International League for Peace and Freedom: Rhetorical Practices of a New Internationalism

1.   Earlier that year, Addams and Balch had convened a conference of thousands of representatives from U.S. women's organizations to discuss possibilities for peace. Out of this conference emerged the Woman's Peace Party (WPP), an organization that became the U.S. branch of the WILPF.

2.   For more perspectives on the link between women and motherhood, see Belenky, et al.; Chodorow; Gilligan; and Ruddick.

3.   Maternalist feminism, as described by Dietz, is influenced by the psychoanalytic object-relations theory of Carol Gilligan and Nancy Chodorow. In simplified terms, this theory suggests that

> striking contrasts exist between men and women and can be understood in terms of certain experiential differences in the early stages of their development. . . . In their work, "the male voice" is that of the liberal individualist who stands in opposition to the female, whose voice is that of the compassionate citizen as loving mother. (Dietz 388)

4.   The leadership of the organization even hinted that women should not taint their political work with the influence of men. Perhaps, Addams suggested, women should not ask for equal rights if that meant asking for the right to participate equally in a militaristic configuration of politics constructed by male statesmen: "I have become conscious of an unalterable cleavage between feminism and militarism," Addams explained:

> The militarists believe that government finally rests upon a basis of physical force. . . . It would be absurd for women even to suggest equal rights in a world governed solely by physical force, and feminism must necessarily assert the ultimate supremacy of moral agencies. ("War Times" 135)

5. According to a report of the Hague Congress, countries represented included

> The United States of America with 47 members; Sweden, which sent 12; Norway, 12; Netherlands, 1,000; Italy, 1; Hungary, 9; Germany, 28; Denmark, 6; Canada, 2; Belgium, 5; Austria, 6; and Great Britain, 3, although 180 others were prevented from sailing owing to the closing of the North Sea for military reasons. (Addams, Balch, and Hamilton 148–49)

6. For other critiques of the maternalist approach, see the works of Joan Scott; and Alcoff and Potter.

7. For an excellent discussion of the WILPF's struggle to embrace racial difference within the organization, see Plastas, who carefully analyzes the racial implications of the organization's gendered arguments and illustrates the ongoing conflicts between the organization's earnest desire to confront racism and the racist assumptions that often informed their arguments and policy decisions.

8. This strategy was similar to the arguments used by female reformers from the previous century. For example, the WCTU, Carol Mattingly explains,

> sought the protection of traditional cultural expectations for women at the same time that they insisted on changing them. They appealed to concepts of religion, home, and patriotism—in many ways acceptable venues for women's energies—but insisted on changes within each of those arenas. (*Well-Tempered* 57)

9. Addams and other leaders of the WILPF were clearly influenced by their settlement house interactions with the working class, and with numerous leaders of the working class, including communist/anarchist and intellectual Peter Kropotkin, who visited Hull House. Addams also admired the work of Leo Tolstoy and had visited him in Russia in 1896. While the organization did not embrace communism, a socialist spirit informed the organization's understanding of a just international structure.

10. Other WILPF leaders advocated the extensions of methods many of them had developed through their work in the settlement house movement as the panacea for troubled international relations. Several important skills necessary for organizing an international alliance based on cooperation were derived from the work women did in settlement houses, perhaps none more important than familiarity with rhetorical tactics that foster nonoppressive like-mindedness in the midst of diversity. In the settlement, Addams suggested, women learned numerous such tactics, including

> all those arts and devices which express kindly relation from man to man, from charitable effort to the most specialized social intercourse. . . . There is the historic statement, the literary presentation, the fellowship which comes when great questions are studied with the hope of modifying actual conditions, . . . so-called art exhibits, concerts, dramatic representations, every possible device to make operative on the life around it the concept of life which the settlement group holds. ("A Function" 326–27)

The methods of the skilled settlement worker, Addams asserted, should "produce a sense of infection which may ultimately result in identity of interest" accompanied by "a consciousness of participation and responsibility" ("A Function" 327). The rhetorical methods Addams identified for creating identity of interest within the settlement house stood in stark opposition to the ultimatums, secret treaties, and covert diplomacy that informed international relations in 1915.

11. Wales's plan had been officially endorsed by the Wisconsin legislature, and that body recommended it for the consideration of the U.S. Congress (Addams, Balch, and Hamilton 3).

12. Pethick-Lawrence's warnings about the end of the war were borne out in the Treaty of Versailles, the terms of which were bitterly disappointing to the WILPF. In their protest of the Treaty, the WILPF Congress assembled at Zurich in 1919 and "expresse[d] its deep regret that the terms of peace proposed at Versailles should so seriously violate the principles upon which alone a just and lasting peace can be secured, and which the democracies of the world had come to except." Particularly disturbing to the women was the settlement's seeming endorsement of secretive international communication:

> By guaranteeing the fruits of the secret treaties to the conquerors, the terms of peace tacitly sanction secret diplomacy, deny the principles of self determination, recognise the right of the victors to the spoils of war, and create all over Europe discord and animosities, which can only lead to future wars. (WILPF, *Report of the Second International Congress* 32)

Acting in accord with this unfortunately prophetic assessment of the terms of peace, the WILPF exerted much effort in the year following the end of the Great War protesting the terms of peace and advocating their revision.

The terms of peace were also disappointing because of how they structured the League of Nations. As initially formulated by President Wilson before the peace conference, the League of Nations seemed like it might be just the kind of international body of debate and conflict resolution the WILPF had been advocating. However, the actual charter of the League of Nations placed control of important international decisions in the hands of the Council—the administrative body structured to represent the interests of already large and powerful nations. Expressing the WILPF's disappointment, Catherine Marshall suggested to the 1921 Vienna Congress of the WILPF that, "To be frank, there is not much to be hoped from the Council. The people on the Council are the people who represent the old order of things, and most of them either want the League of Nations to do wrong things, or want it to do nothing" (*Report of the Third International Congress* 64). The WILPF advocated the relocation of primary power to the Assembly of the League of Nations, a secondary administrative body that included three representatives from each country, regardless of the country's size.

Most objectionable to the women of the WILPF was the fact that the treaty did not express a firm enough commitment to complete disarmament. Complete disarmament, the women argued, was a precondition for the establishment of truly international channels of discussion and conflict resolution. According to acting chair of the U.S. WILPF, Maude Richards, "No country can sincerely talk arbitration while at the same time maintaining a large military establishment. Under such circumstances a treaty might easily become 'a scrap of paper'" (qtd. in Pois 323). For agreements or treaties to have any rhetorical force, they had to be accompanied by acts of disarmament. Acting on this belief, the WILPF urged international leaders to replace a munitions-based balance of power with rhetorical machinery to negotiate conflicts.

13. Addams reports that even statesmen had become distressed by the slavish relationship between the government and the press:

> I remember a conversation with a mid-European statesman of large influence and service to the country, who bitterly resented the fact that at this time of stress his only knowledge of what was happening hung on the decision of a few men at the capital who practically decided what they wanted the people to know. ("Peace and the Press" 55)

14. Michael Sproule's substantial study of the pro-Allied and pro-war propaganda from the First World War illustrates the perilous and oppressive atmosphere in which the press served to advance the interests of the military. From the first days of the war, popular press reports of war activities were censored and distorted. One of the first acts belligerent Britain carried out was to sever cable connections between Germany and the U.S., forcing Americans to get their news of the European conflict almost exclusive through London and Paris (Sproule 6). When he led the nation into war in 1917, President Wilson also established a Committee on Public Information (CPI), composed of intellectuals and academics, to justify and promote the war effort. The CPI, under the leadership of journalist George Creel, sought to cultivate war support through all channels of mass media. With the blessing of the Wilson administration, the committee distributed an estimated fifty million pamphlets in which, Sproule notes, "scholarship compromised itself when devoted to promoting a national cause" as "CPI historians showered the reader with chauvinistic quotations plucked here and there from sundry German writers" (10). Not only did CPI-sponsored pamphlets enforce the militaristic spirit, the CPI devised numerous and seemingly omnipresent vehicles to promote the militaristic spirit:

> Under Creel's ministrations, Wilson's war pervasively enveloped Americans at every venue in their personal lives. For those traveling to work, there were trolley posters illustrating all manner of ways that the ordinary citizen personally could help win the war. Poster art, prepared by the CPI's Division of Pictorial Publicity, sparked many a campaign for the Treasury Department, War Department, Department of Agriculture, and Red Cross. Displayed in locales urban and rural, posters supplied some of the most evocative and best-remembered propaganda of the war in accordance with the belief of Division-chief Charles Dana Gibson . . . that wartime art needed to "appeal to the heart." (Sproule 10)

As Sproule details, the popular press also became a channel for the promotion of belligerent sentiments:

> Shedding congenital skepticism, America's journalists followed the lead of teachers, writers, and preachers by acquiescing in Creel's managed-news framework that forbade the press from roaming through federal agencies. . . . Creel's news office also prepared "a weekly digest of the official war news" that went to some 12,000 newspapers in galley form, ready for printing. (12–13)

Such were the powerful structures of mass media in the service of the war that the WILPF faced and fought.

3. "WE MUST MAKE ENORMOUS PROPAGANDA": THE WILPF AND PUBLIC OPINION FOR PEACE

1.　Envoys included Jane Addams, Frau Wollften Palthe, Alice Hamilton, Emily Balch, Chrystal MacMillan, Rosika Schwimmer, Madam Ramondt-Hirschman, Aletta Jacobs, and Julia Grace Wales.

2.　Detzer would later write an extensive autobiography, *Appointment on the Hill,* chronicling her groundbreaking work as a lobbyist.

3.　When campaigns were particularly urgent, such as when a critical bill came up for a vote, the WILPF opted for the speedier delivery available through the telegram. Throughout the U.S. section's archival materials, one finds urgent telegrams sent to the Senate clerk and to various congressmen protesting measures and urging them to vote a particular way. One of the earliest lobbying efforts on the part of the U.S. section involved convincing the public, Congress, and the president of the need for universal disarmament. Grace Odell, acting chairman of the U.S. branch at the time, sent "urgent word to all members that there [was] still need for constant and forceful expression of public opinion directed at the President, Secretary [of State] Hughes, and the press." In order to effect this expression, Odell continued, "there should be a steady flow of letters and telegrams expressing appreciation for what has already been done and urging that our country take the lead in working for complete and universal disarmament" (U.S. WILPF *Bulletin,* Nov. 1921). The WILPF also used immediate, positive reinforcement through telegrams, often sending telegrams to officials applauding their support of critical and controversial measures. In a telegram dated 20 December 1919, the U.S. WILPF praised then Secretary of the Treasury Carter Glass for his support of lifting the food blockade of Berlin:

> We rejoice that a high official of our government thus appeals to the humanity and good will of Congress and the people of the United States. As an organization we are doing our utmost to increase the volunteer aid to the starving and miserable people of Europe. But this is not sufficient to save the situation. We think we may assure you of the hearty support of American women for your just and generous proposal to secure a supply of food on government credit for the starving countries of Europe.

4.　Organizations participating in the disarmament campaign included the following: The International Alliance of Women for Suffrage and Equal Citizenship, World's Young Women's Christian Association, National Committee on the Causes and Cure of War, International Council of Women, European Federation of Soroptimist Clubs, International Federation of University Women, International Cooperative Women's Guild, League of Iberic and Spanish-American Women, League of Jewish Women, the WILPF, World Organization of Jewish Women, World Women's Christian Temperance Union, World Union of Women for International Concord, League of Mothers, and Educators for Peace (Pois 392).

5.　Common, inexpensive, easily circulated texts such as leaflets and pamphlets became essential for educating the broader public about peace. The number of such materials produced in the organization's first year reflects the intensity with which women produced these texts. In 1915 alone, the U.S. WILPF reported a total of 237,530 pamphlets and folders distributed through its national office (Thomas 47).

6.   At all levels of the organization, the WILPF provided publicity for pacifist playwrights, such as Norwegian playwright Minni Roll Anker, whose play *The Church* promoted maternalist attitudes toward pacifism. According to members of the WILPF, Anker's play "is a work of art of high value. . . . [Through] the deeds of its central figure, the woman and the mother, with her firm belief in love of humanity as the force to vanquish war, we feel throbbing the same note which brought women from belligerent countries together" (*Report of the Third International Congress* 239).

7.   The power of this form of public appeal is demonstrated by its adoption in 1917 by President Wilson's Committee on Public Information (CPI), an administrative arm that actively promoted the American war effort. The CPI trained and placed seventy-five thousand local speakers who "stood up during intermission time to address their captive audience on more than forty scheduled themes beginning with conscription and including the Liberty Loans, the income tax, the Red Cross, and food conservation" (Sproule 11).

4. Seeking Full Measure: The League of Women Voters and Partisan Political Communication

1.   Initially, the League had eight legislative committees, including committees on topics such as "Industry, Child Welfare, Citizenship, Elections, Social Morality, and Research" (Brown, Interview 958).

2.   For excellent analyses of the changing nature of partisanship in the late nineteenth and early twentieth centuries, see Michael McGerr, *The Decline of Popular Politics* and Michael Schudson, *The Good Citizen,* especially chapter 4.

3.   The LWV's archives contain numerous plays or descriptions of plays that offer strong critique of partisan politics in the 1920s. One such play, *Dearie Won't Do,* reveals the negative consequences of the patronage system that often accompanied party politics. According to the LWV's summary of this play, its plot is "taken from an actual instance where the young and ignorant daughter of a spoils politician was appointed to an important office she was absolutely unfitted to fill." The skit humorously portrays her inability while also illustrating how patronage corrupts politics (LWV, "Skits and Plays").

4.   When speaking within League publications, leaders suggested a more subversive goal for the Service. Writing in the newsletter of the national LWV, the chairman of the radio committee, Katherine Ludington, suggested that the Voters' Service was set up specifically to counter partisan rhetoric: "A wide public wants something better than the old time party spellbinding oratory" (Ludington, "Seven Months of the Voters' Service").

5.   Even Miller's seemingly unobjectionable proposal that the LWV focus on teaching governmental structures might have raised partisan hackles had the organization decided to follow it. As Black explains,

>   even the apparently innocuous goal of education of the citizenry was bound to have effects upon the power relations that depend upon citizens' not recognizing their

genuine interests. . . . Since elite retention of dominance depends on citizens being unaware of alternative options, inattention to the decision-making system and its outcomes is crucial to continuing control over citizens. Public education about government structure and policy is therefore political because it is a potential disruption of power. (295)

6.   While Catt was able to use narrow patriotic sentiments to her advantage on this occasion, those sentiments would come back to haunt the fledgling organization. Anxiety about foreigners and communists in 1919 fueled the Overman Congressional Committee and New York's Lusk Committee, both of which scrutinized the role of so-called political radicals, including many politically active women.

7.   Eighty-four women were elected to state legislatures in 1922, nearly double the number in 1920.

5. Rhetorical Education for Political Influence:
The LWV and Political Literacy

1.   Reflecting the substantial connection between the League and Deweyan educational theory, Sara Brumbaugh identifies Dewey's books *Democracy and Education* and *Experience and Education* as "Studies on the League of Women Voters" in her 1946 book about the League's first two decades of work (115–16). Indeed, the connection between Dewey and the work of women in voluntary associations is strong enough to suggest that the women influenced Dewey as much as Dewey influenced them. Dewey's notions of pragmatic education, in fact, may have originated from his observations of women's educational work at Hull House. Charlene Haddock Seigfried suggests that *Democracy and Education* is Dewey's formulation of the ideas he saw being practiced by female progressives like Addams, whom he came to know during his time at the University of Chicago (1894–1904).

2.   State and local Leagues also distributed study kits that functioned as informal correspondence courses for LWV members. Packaged as "convenient and compact envelopes," kits typically included informative pamphlets, plays, or other publications with references, tests, and questions for discussion ("New Kits").

3.   A 1928 St. Louis LWV questionnaire, for example, asked congressional candidates leading questions such as "What is your stand on measures promoting the more effective establishment and continuance in the state of work for maternity and infancy hygiene?" and "What is your stand on adequate appropriations for a Woman's Bureau in the U.S. Department of Labor?" (St. Louis County LWV). By inserting the descriptors "more effective" and "adequate" into these questions, the writers of the questionnaire conveyed the LWV's position on these measures.

4.   Another election play, *The Voting Machine,* relied on ethnic stereotypes to entertain while it educated. According to the national office's catalog of League plays and skits, "The characters and conversation are humorous as well as educational and include the traditional funny Irishwoman who wants to vote without having registered and claims that everyone knows her so she must be all right" (LWV, "Skits and Plays" 1). Presumably, the LWV did not have many traditional Irish women in its ranks.

5.   As Harvey explains, female divisions of political parties directly challenged the non-partisan educational efforts of the LWV throughout the 1920s by, among other things, sponsoring their own educational publications and training schools for female campaign speakers (see especially chapter 4, "The National Race to Mobilize Women, 1917–1932").

CONCLUSION: LEARNING FROM THE STRATEGIES
AND STRUGGLES OF THE LWV AND WILPF

1.   This is not to say that research has no part to play in the academy. As I hope this project reveals, I believe research can contribute a great deal to improving the communities in which we live.

2.   For examples of courses in the writing-*about*-the-community tradition, see Herzberg, "Community Service and Critical Teaching" and Brack and Hall, "Combining the Classroom and the Community."

3.   For a detailed example of a course in the writing-*for*-the-community tradition, see Cooper and Julier, "Democratic Conversations: Civic Literacy and Service Learning in the American Grains."

4.   Collaboration among rhetorical scholars in various disciplines may become more common thanks to the work of the Alliance of Rhetoric Societies (ARS), an organization begun in 2003 with the purpose of bringing together scholars of rhetoric from across the curriculum.

5.   Catherine Smith has proposed a model of how such interdisciplinary training for democratic participation might look. In this model, assignments across the curriculum would ask students to write and speak in "actual and simulated occasions for performing as writers (and speakers) in communication situations of practical democracy" (8). Within these assignments, students would assume roles (e.g., "private citizens; elected or appointed representatives; government staff; advocates for private or public interests; and members of the press" [8]) and practice genres (e.g., letters to representatives, laws and ordinances, press releases, fund raising documents, feature articles on community problems) common to democratic participation.

Works Cited

Adams, Katherine H. *Progressive Education and the Training of America's Persuaders.* Mahwah: Erlbaum, 1999.

Addams, Jane. Address. *Proceedings of the National Peace Congress, 1909.* Washington, DC: National Peace Congress, 1909. 252–54.

——. "Democracy and Education." *Chautauqua Assembly Herald* 26 Aug. 1900: 2.

——. "A Function of the Social Settlement." *Annals of the American Academy of Political and Social Science* 13 (1899): 323–45.

——. "New Ideals of Peace." *Proceedings of the National Arbitration and Peace Congress.* Washington, DC: National Arbitration and Peace Congress, 1907. 106–10.

——. *Peace and Bread in Time of War.* Silver Spring: National Association of Social Workers, 1922.

——. "Peace and Bread I: A Speculation on Bread-Labor and War-Slogans." *Survey* 31 Dec. 1921: 527–30.

——. "Peace and the Press." *Independent* 11 Oct. 1915: 55–56.

——. "Pragmatism in Politics." *Survey* 5 Oct. 1912: 1–2.

——. "War's Debasement of Women." Interview with Edward Marshall. *New York Times* 2 May 1919: Sec. 5, 3–4.

——. "War Times Challenge Woman's Tradition." *Survey* 5 Aug. 1916: 1–8. Rpt. in *Jane Addams on Peace, War, and International Understanding.* Ed. Allen F. Davis. New York: Garland, 1976. 127–39.

——. "Women's Clubs and Public Policies." *General Federation of Women's Clubs Twelfth Biennial Convention Report.* N.p.: GFWC, 1914. 24–30.

Addams, Jane, Emily G. Balch, and Alice Hamilton. *Women at the Hague: The International Congress of Women and Its Results.* New York: Macmillan, 1916.

Adler-Kassner, Linda, Robert Crooks, and Ann Watters, eds. *Writing in the Community.* Washington, DC: American Association for Higher Education, 1997.

Alcoff, Linda, and Elizabeth Potter, eds. *Feminist Epistemologies.* New York: Routledge, 1993.

Ames, Marie B. *Lessons for the Study of Citizenship.* Washington, DC: National LWV, n.d.

Andersen, Kristi. *After Suffrage: Women in Partisan and Electoral Politics Before the New Deal.* Chicago: U of Chicago P, 1996.

Avery, Helen M., and Frank W. Nye. *The Clubwoman's Book.* New York: Holt, 1954.

Aylesworth, M. H. *Voter's Campaign Information Service.* Boston: Massachusetts LWV, 1928.

Bagley, Grace H. *How Maggie MacTaggart Gained Her Citizenship.* Washington, DC: National LWV, 1921.

Baker, Paula. "The Domestication of Politics: Women and American Political Society, 1780–1920." *American Historical Review* 89 (1984): 601–22.

Bakhtin, Mikhail. *Speech Genres and Other Later Essays.* Ed. V. W. McGee. Trans. C. Emerson and M. Holquist. Austin: U of Texas P, 1986.

Balch, Emily. "The Hopes We Inherit." *Building International Goodwill.* Ed. World Alliance for Promoting International Friendship Through the Churches. New York: Macmillan, 1927: 3–18.

———. Letter to the *Boston Transcript.* 28 Mar. 1927. Records of the Women's International League for Peace and Freedom, U.S. Section. Swarthmore College Peace Collection. Swarthmore, PA.

Barton, David, and Mary Hamilton. "Literacy Practices." *Situated Literacies: Reading and Writing in Context.* Ed. David Barton, Mary Hamilton, and Roz Ivanic. New York: Routledge, 2000. 7–15.

Bazerman, Charles. "Systems of Genre and the Enactment of Social Intentions." *Rethinking Genre.* Ed. Aviva Freedman and Peter Medway. London: Taylor and Francis, 1994. 79–101.

Belenky, Mary Field, et al. *Women's Ways of Knowing: The Development of Self, Voice, and the Mind.* New York: Basic, 1986.

Berlin, James. "Revisionary Histories of Rhetoric: Politics, Power, and Plurality." *Writing Histories of Rhetoric.* Ed. Victor Vitanza. Carbondale: Southern Illinois UP, 1994. 112–27.

———. *Rhetorics, Poetics, and Cultures: Refiguring College English Studies.* Urbana: NCTE, 1996.

Biesecker, Barbara. "Coming to Terms with Recent Attempts to Write Women into the History of Rhetoric." *Philosophy and Rhetoric* 25 (1992): 140–61.

Bizzell, Patricia. "Feminist Methods of Research in the History of Rhetoric: What Differences Do they Make?" *Rhetoric Society Quarterly* 30 (2000): 5–18.

Black, Naomi. *Social Feminism.* Ithaca: Cornell UP, 1989.

Blair, Karen. *The Clubwoman as Feminist: True Womanhood Redefined, 1868–1914.* New York: Holmes, 1980.

Blake, Katherine. "Report of the Committee on Education at the National Conference in Chicago, April 29–May 1925." Records of the Women's International League for Peace and Freedom, U.S. Section. Swarthmore College Peace Collection. Swarthmore, PA.

Brack, Gay, and Leanna R. Hall. "Combining the Classroom and the Community: Service Learning in Composition at Arizona State University." Adler-Kassner, Crooks, and Watters 143–52.

Breines, Ingeborg. "A Gender Perspective on a Culture of Peace." *Towards a Women's Agenda for a Culture of Peace.* Ed. Ingeborg Breines, Dorota Gierycz, and Betty Reardon. Paris: UNESCO, 1999. 33–55.

Brereton, John, ed. *The Origins of Composition Studies in the American College, 1875–1925.* Pittsburgh: U of Pittsburgh P, 1995.

Brodkey, Linda. *Writing Permitted in Designated Areas Only.* Minneapolis: U of Minnesota P, 1996.

Brooks, Jane, and Carrie Chapman Catt. "The League of Women Voters." *Woman Citizen* 26 Apr. 1919: 1018+.

Brown, Mrs. Raymond. *The Voter and Political Parties.* Washington, DC: National LWV, 1922.

———. Interview. "What the League of Women Voters Is." *Woman Citizen* 12 Apr. 1919: 958+.

Brumbaugh, Sara. *Democratic Experience and Education in the National League of Women Voters.* New York: Teachers College P, 1946.

Bryan, Mary, Lynn McCree, and Allen F. Davis, eds. *One Hundred Years at Hull House.* Bloomington: Indiana UP, 1990.

———. Preface. Bryan, McCree, and Davis ix–xiii.

Bulkley, Mary. "Hopes and Fears of the League." *Woman Voter's Bulletin* 7 (Dec. 1927): 1+.

Burke, Kenneth. *A Rhetoric of Motives.* Berkeley: U of California P, 1969.

Bussey, Gertrude, and Margaret Tims. *Women's International League for Peace and Freedom, 1915–1965: A Record of Fifty Years' Work.* London: Allen and Unwin, 1965.

Cahier Committee. *The New International Order.* Geneva: WILPF International Office, 1924.

Campbell, JoAnn. "Afterword: Revealing the Ties that Bind." *Nineteenth-Century Women Learn to Write.* Ed. Catherine Hobbs. Charlottesville: UP of Virginia, 1995. 303–9.

Campbell, Karlyn Kohrs. "Consciousness-Raising: Linking Theory, Criticism, and Practice." *Rhetoric Society Quarterly* 32 (2002): 45–64.

———. *A Critical Study of Early Feminist Rhetoric, 1830–1925.* Vol. 1 of *Man Cannot Speak for Her.* Westport: Greenwood, 1989.

———. *Key Texts of Early Feminism, 1830–1925.* Vol. 2 of *Man Cannot Speak for Her.* Westport: Greenwood, 1989.

"Carrie Chapman Catt Course of Citizenship: The Primaries—Yours and Mine." *Woman Citizen* 3 Apr. 1920: 1086+.

Cathcart, Robert. "Defining Social Movements by Their Rhetorical Form." *Central States Speech Journal* 31 (1980): 267–73.

Catt, Carrie Chapman. Address. *Weekly News of the New York LWV* 4 Apr. 1920: 1–3.

———. *An Address to the Congress of the United States.* New York: National Woman Suffrage Publishing Company, 1917.

———. *A Nation Calls.* New York: National Woman Suffrage Publishing Company, 1919.

———. "Poison Propaganda." *Woman Citizen* 31 May 1924: 14+.

———. *Political Parties and Women Voters, An Address to the Congress of the League of Women Voters.* Washington, DC: LWV, 1920.

———. "Why Not Leave These Questions to the Political Parties?" *Woman Citizen* 3 May 1919: 1045.

Chodorow, Nancy. *The Reproduction of Mothering: Psychoanalysis and the Sociology of Gender.* Berkeley: U of California P, 1978.

Cincinnati League of Women Voters. *Know Cincinnati.* Cincinnati: Cincinnati LWV, 1928.

"A Citizenship School by Radio." *Woman Voter's Bulletin* 9 (Mar. 1929): 4.

"Civic Study." *Woman Citizen* 17 Jan. 1920: 740.

Clark, Gregory, and S. Michael Halloran, eds. *Oratorical Culture in Nineteenth-Century America: Transformations in the Theory and Practice of Rhetoric.* Carbondale: Southern Illinois UP, 1993.

Cleaveland, J. A. *A Woman's Hour at the Polls: A Voting Skit.* Mt. Clemens: Michigan LWV, 1928.

Cleveland League of Women Voters. *About Your Registration.* Cleveland: Cleveland LWV, 1921.

Code, Lorraine. *Rhetorical Spaces: Essays on Gendered Locations.* New York: Routledge, 1995.

Connecticut League of Women Voters. *Legislative Sketch.* Hartford: Connecticut LWV, 1925.

———. "Objection Overruled!" *Woman Voter's Bulletin* 7 (Jan. 1927): 1+.

———. "Why Do We Say, 'Join a Party'?" *Woman Voter's Bulletin* 6 (26 Apr. 1922): 1+.

Connecticut Woman Suffrage Association. "Press Release, Tuesday January 18, 1919." ts. Records of the League of Women Voters (U.S.). Library of Congress. Washington, DC.

Cooper, David, and Laura Julier. "Democratic Conversations: Civic Literacy and Service Learning in the American Grains." Adler-Kassner, Crooks, and Watters 79–94.

Coss, Clare. *Lillian D. Wald: Progressive Activist.* New York: Feminist, 2000.

Cott, Nancy. "Across the Great Divide: Women in Politics Before and After 1920." *Women, Politics, and Change.* Ed. Louise Tilly and Patricia Gurin. New York: Russell Sage Foundation, 1990. 153–76.

———. *The Grounding of Modern Feminism.* New Haven: Yale UP, 1987.

Cristy, Sarah. "Report of the Field Secretary, U.S. WILPF National Meeting, April 15–26." ts. Records of the Women's International League for Peace and Freedom, U.S. Section. Swarthmore College Peace Collection. Swarthmore, PA.

Crowley, Sharon. *Composition in the University: Historical and Polemical Essays.* Pittsburgh: U of Pittsburgh P, 1999.

Cushman, Ellen. "The Rhetorician as an Agent of Social Change." *CCC* 47 (1996): 7–28. Rpt. in *On Writing Research: The Braddock Essays 1975–1998.* Ed. Lisa Ede. Boston: Bedford/St. Martin's, 1999. 372–89.

Davis, Nira Yuval. *Gender and Nation.* London: Sage, 1997.

Deans, Thomas. *Writing Partnerships: Service Learning in Composition.* Urbana: NCTE, 2000.

Degen, Mary Louise. *The History of the Woman's Peace Party.* Baltimore: Johns Hopkins UP, 1939.

Detzer, Dorothy. *Appointment on the Hill.* New York: Holt, 1948.

———. Letter to leaders of women's organizations and peace groups. 30 July 1927. Records of the Women's International League for Peace and Freedom, U.S. Section. Swarthmore College Peace Collection. Swarthmore, PA.

———. *Peace Pressure Primer, 1936.* ts. Records of the Women's International League for Peace and Freedom, U.S. Section. Swarthmore College Peace Collection. Swarthmore, PA.

Deutsch, Sarah. "Learning to Talk More Like a Man: Boston Women's Class-Bridging Organizations, 1870–1940." *American Historical Review* 97 (1992): 379–404.

Dewey, John. *Democracy and Education.* New York: Free, 1916.

———. Introduction. *Peace and Bread in Time of War.* By Jane Addams. Boston: Hall, 1945. ix–xx.

———. *The Public and Its Problems.* Denver: Allen Swallow, 1927.

———. "The School as Social Center." Bryan and Davis 103–8.

Dietz, Mary G. "Context Is All: Feminism and Theories of Citizenship." *Daedalus* 116

(1987). Rpt. in *Feminism and Politics.* Ed. Anne Phillips. New York: Oxford UP, 1998. 378–400.

Donawerth, Jane, ed. *Rhetorical Theory by Women Before 1900: An Anthology.* Lanham: Rowman, 2002.

Edwards, Marie. "Excerpts from Report of Mrs. Richard Edwards, First Vice President, National League of Women Voters." ts. Records of the League of Women Voters (U.S.). Library of Congress. Washington, DC.

———. "The Question of the Questionnaire." *Woman Voter.* Supplement to *Woman Citizen* 9 Sept. 1922: 19.

Enos, Richard Leo. "The Archaeology of Women in Rhetoric: Rhetorical Sequencing as a Research Method for Historical Scholarship." *Rhetoric Society Quarterly* 32 (2002): 65–79.

Ervin, Elizabeth. "Encouraging Civic Participation among First-Year Writing Students; or, Why Composition Class Should Be More Like a Bowling Team." *Rhetoric Review* 15 (1997): 382–99.

Finnegan, Margaret. *Selling Suffrage: Consumer Culture and Votes for Women.* New York: Columbia UP, 1999.

Fishman, Stephen, and Lucille McCarthy. *John Dewey and the Challenge of Classroom Practice.* Urbana: NCTE, 1998.

Fitzpatrick, Ellen. *Endless Crusade: Women Social Scientists and Progressive Reform.* New York: Oxford UP, 1990.

Fletty, Valborg. *Public Services of Women's Organizations.* New York: George Banta, 1951.

Foss, Sonja K., and Cindy L. Griffin. "Beyond Persuasion: A Proposal for an Invitational Rhetoric." Speech Communication Association Convention, Miami. Nov. 1993. <http://www.msubillings.edu/commtheatre/ddg>.

Foster, Carrie A. *The Women and the Warriors: The U.S. Section of the Women's International League for Peace and Freedom, 1915–1946.* Syracuse: Syracuse UP, 1995.

Fraser, Nancy. "Rethinking the Public Sphere: A Contribution to the Critique of Actually Existing Democracy." *Social Text* 25/26 (1990): 56–80.

———. *Unruly Practices: Power, Discourse, and Gender in Contemporary Social Theory.* Minneapolis: U of Minnesota P, 1989.

Freedman, Estelle B. "Separation as Strategy: Female Institution Building and American Feminism 1870–1930." *Feminist Studies* 5 (1979): 512–29.

Freire, Paulo. Introduction. *Teachers as Intellectuals: Toward a Critical Pedagogy of Learning.* By Henry A. Giroux. South Hadley: Bergin, 1988. ii–xxi.

———. *Pedagogy of the Oppressed.* Trans. Myra Bergman Ramos. New York: Continuum, 1988.

The Garland School Catalogue, 1925–26. Boston: The Garland School for Homemaking, 1925.

Gaulke, Ruth. "On the Organization of College Leagues, April 10, 1928." ts. Records of the League of Women Voters (U.S.). Library of Congress. Washington, DC.

Gere, Anne Ruggles. *Intimate Practices: Literacy and Cultural Work in U.S. Women's Clubs, 1880–1920.* Chicago: U of Illinois P, 1997.

Gere, Anne Ruggles, and Sarah R. Robbins. "Gendered Literacy in Black and White: Turn-of-the-Century African-American and European-American Club Women's Printed Texts." *Signs* 21 (1996): 643–78.

Get Out the Vote: Why, When, How. Washington, DC: National LWV, 1924.

Gilligan, Carol. *In a Different Voice: Psychological Theory and Women's Development.* Cambridge: Harvard UP, 1993.

Gilman, Elizabeth. "Catheryne Cooke Gilman, Social Worker." *Women of Minnesota: Selected Biographical Essays.* Ed. Barbara Stuhler and Gretchen Kreuter. St. Paul: Minnesota Historical Society, 1977: 206.

Ginzberg, Lori D. *Women and the Work of Benevolence: Morality, Politics, and Class in the Nineteenth-Century United States.* New Haven: Yale UP, 1990.

Giroux, Henry. "Beyond the Ivory Tower: Public Intellectuals and the Crisis of Higher Education." *Higher Education Under Fire: Politics, Economics, and the Crisis in the Humanities.* Ed. Michael Berube and Cary Nelson. New York: Routledge, 1995.

———. *Schooling and the Struggle for Public Life.* Minneapolis: U of Minnesota P, 1988.

Glenn, Cheryl. *Rhetoric Retold: Regendering the Tradition from Antiquity Through the Renaissance.* Carbondale: Southern Illinois UP, 1997.

Greer, Jane. "'No Smiling Madonna': Marion Wharton and the Struggle to Construct a Critical Pedagogy for the Working Class, 1914–1917." *CCC* 51 (1999): 248–71.

Haarsager, Sandra. *Organized Womanhood: Cultural Politics in the Pacific Northwest, 1840–1920.* Normal: U of Oklahoma P, 1997.

Habermas, Jürgen. *The Structural Transformation of the Public Sphere: An Inquiry into a Category of Bourgeois Society.* Cambridge: MIT P, 1989.

Handbook on State League Conventions. ts. n.d. Records of the League of Women Voters (U.S.). Library of Congress. Washington, DC.

Hartford League of Women Voters. *A Smock Election.* Hartford: Connecticut LWV, 1926.

Hartsock, Nancy. *Money, Sex, and Power: Toward a Feminist Historical Materialism.* Boston: Northeastern UP, 1983.

Harvey, Anna L. *Votes Without Leverage: Women in American Electoral Politics, 1920–1970.* New York: Cambridge UP, 1998.

Hauser, Elizabeth. "Our Own Four Pages." *Woman Voter.* Supplement in *Woman Citizen* 9 Sept. 1922: 18.

Herzberg, Bruce. "Community Service and Critical Teaching." Adler-Kassner, Crooks, and Watters 57–70.

Hewitt, Nancy A. *Women's Activism and Social Change, Rochester, New York, 1822–1872.* Ithaca: Cornell UP, 1984.

Heymann, Lida Gustava. *Survey of the Nine Years' History of the Women's International League for Peace and Freedom.* Geneva: WILPF, 1925.

Higginbotham, Evelyn Brooks. *Righteous Discontent: The Women's Movement in the Black Baptist Church, 1880–1920.* Cambridge: Harvard UP, 1993.

Himley, Margaret. "Writing Programs and Pedagogies in a Globalized Landscape" *WPA* 26 (2003): 49–66.

Hobbs, Catherine, ed. *Nineteenth-Century Women Learn to Write.* Charlottesville: UP of Virginia, 1995.

Hobhouse, Emily. Preface. *Report of the International Congress of Women, the Hague, 1915, April 28–May 1.* London: British Section WILPF, 1915. iii–xii.

Hochstein, Irma. "Wisconsin Legislation Against Militarism, Session 1923." *Pax* Sept.–Oct. 1923: 4.

hooks, bell. *Teaching to Transgress: Education and the Practice of Freedom.* New York: Routledge, 1994.

Horner, Bruce. "Resisting Academics." *Insurrections: Approaches to Resistance in Composition Studies.* Ed. Andrea Greenbaum. Albany: State U of New York P, 2001. 169–84.

Horner, Bruce, and John Trimbur. "English Only and U.S. College Composition." *CCC* 53 (2002): 594–630.

How Not to Do It: A Non–Money Raising Interview. ts. 1929. Records of the League of Women Voters (U.S.). Library of Congress. Washington, DC.

Huxman, Susan Schultz. "*The Woman's Journal,* 1870–1890: The Torchbearer for Suffrage." Solomon, *Voice* 87–109.

"In Boston." *Woman Citizen* 1 May 1920: 1214.

Indianapolis League of Women Voters. *An Americanization Pageant.* Indianapolis: Indiana LWV, 1921.

"In Missouri." *Woman Citizen* 8 May 1920: 1125.

"Institute of Government and Politics Conducted by the National League of Women Voters in Co-Operation with Columbia University, July 16–27." *Woman Voter's Bulletin* 3 (9 June 1923): 1+.

"In the South." *Woman Citizen* 15 May 1920: 1276.

Iowa League of Women Voters. *You Are Democracy.* Des Moines: Iowa LWV, [1920?].

Jarratt, Susan, and Lynn Worsham, eds. *Feminism and Composition Studies: In Other Words.* New York: MLA, 1998.

Jerry, E. Clair. "The Role of Newspapers in the Nineteenth-Century Woman's Movement." Solomon, *Voice* 17–29.

Johnson, Elizabeth. "Report of the National Art Committee, United States Section, Women's International League for Peace and Freedom, May, 1924." Records of the Women's International League for Peace and Freedom, U.S. Section. Swarthmore College Peace Collection. Swarthmore, PA.

Johnson, Grace A. "English 7: Extemporaneous Speaking Course Syllabus." ts. Grace Allen Johnson Papers (Woman's Rights Collection), Schlesinger Library, Radcliffe Institute, Harvard University, Cambridge, MA.

———. "Lecture Notes." ms. Grace Allen Johnson Papers.

Jones, Jacqueline. "The Political Implications of Black and White Women's Work in the South, 1890–1965." *Women, Politics, and Change.* Ed. Louise Tilly and Patricia Gurin. New York: Russell Sage Foundation, 1990. 108–30.

Jones, Kathleen B. "What Is Authority's Gender?" *Revisioning the Political.* Ed. Nancy J. Hirschmann and Christine Di Stefano. Boulder: Westview, 1996. 75–94.

Judd, Dorothy. Letter to Gladys Harrison. 8 Oct. 1929. Records of the League of Women Voters (U.S.). Library of Congress, Washington, DC.

"Judges, Juries, Courts, and People." *Woman Voter's Bulletin* 7 (6 May 1927): 3.

Junior International Leagues Department. "Peace Projects, 1923." Records of the Women's International League for Peace and Freedom, U.S. Section. Swarthmore College Peace Collection. Swarthmore, PA.

Kates, Susan. *Activist Rhetorics and American Higher Education, 1885–1937.* Carbondale: Southern Illinois UP, 2001.

Kelley, Florence. "Florence Kelley Comes to Stay." Bryan, McCree, and Davis 23–28.

Kellogg, Paul. "Twice Twenty Years at Hull-House." Bryan, McCree, and Davis 189–94.

Kenney, Mary. "Mary Kenney Is Invited In." Bryan, McCree, and Davis 21–23.

Kentucky League of Women Voters. *Kentucky Election Laws in Brief.* Louisville: Kentucky LWV, 1921.

Kirschner, Don S. *The Paradox of Professionalism: Reform and Public Service in Urban America, 1900–1940.* New York: Greenwood, 1986.

Kitchelt, Florence. "Newspapers and the Getting of News." ts. Florence Ledyard Kitchelt Papers. Schlesinger Library, Radcliffe Institute, Harvard University, Cambridge, MA.

"Know Your Party: A Test of Twenty Questions." ts. n.d. Records of the League of Women Voters (U.S.). Library of Congress, Washington, DC.

Lawrence, David. "Women Voters' Meeting Like University Extension Course." *St. Louis Post-Dispatch* 16 Apr. 1926: N. pag.

"League of Women Voters." *Woman Citizen* 5 Apr. 1919: 1+.

League of Women Voters. "Advanced Announcement." ts. n.d. Records of the League of Women Voters (U.S.). Library of Congress, Washington, DC.

———. *Ballot Box Review* 15 Apr. 1926.

———. *A Brief Reading List on Government and Politics.* Washington, DC: National LWV, 1921.

———. "Educational Methods, 1920–1930." ts. n.d. Records of the League of Women Voters (U.S.). Library of Congress, Washington, DC.

———. *Get Out the Vote: A Handbook of Pre-Election Activities.* Washington, DC: National LWV, 1928.

———. *Guide to the Services of the National League of Women Voters.* Washington, DC: National LWV, 1927.

———. *Handbook for League Workers.* Washington, DC: National LWV, [1929?].

———. "The League as Publisher, 1920–1930." ts. [c. 1930.] Records of the League of Women Voters (U.S.). Library of Congress, Washington, DC.

———. "League's Efficiency in Government Department, 1920." ts. n.d. Records of the League of Women Voters (U.S.). Library of Congress, Washington, DC.

———. "League Will Train Women in Politics." ts. [c. 1920] Records of the League of Women Voters (U.S.). Library of Congress, Washington, DC.

———. *Practical Suggestions for a Voter's First Birthday Party.* Washington, DC: National LWV, 1923.

———. "Press Release April 19, 1922." ts. Records of the League of Women Voters (U.S.). Library of Congress, Washington, DC.

———. *Principles and Policies of the League of Women Voters.* Washington, DC: National LWV, 1920.

———. "Procedure for the Preparation of Manuscripts." ts. n.d. Records of the League of Women Voters (U.S.). Library of Congress, Washington, DC.

———. "Purpose of the League of Women Voters" ts. [c. 1920]. Records of the League of Women Voters (U.S.). Library of Congress, Washington, DC.

———. "School of Politics: Foreign Affairs, Radcliffe College, January 8, 9, and 10, 1924" ts. Records of the League of Women Voters (U.S.). Library of Congress, Washington, DC.

———. "School of Politics: Growth of Popular Control under Law, Radcliffe College,

October 18, 19, and 20, 1922" ts. Records of the League of Women Voters (U.S.). Library of Congress, Washington, DC.

——. "Skits and Plays, Compiled July 1928." ts. Records of the League of Women Voters (U.S.). Library of Congress, Washington, DC.

——. "Speakers in the Voter's Service." ts. n.d. Records of the League of Women Voters (U.S.). Library of Congress, Washington, DC.

——. "Summary of Interviews with the Presidential Candidates, 1920" ts. Records of the League of Women Voters (U.S.). Library of Congress, Washington, DC.

——. *What Every League Should Know: An Organization Play.* ts. 1926. Records of the League of Women Voters (U.S.). Library of Congress, Washington, DC.

——. "Women in the Political Parties." ts. [c. 1920] Records of the League of Women Voters (U.S.). Library of Congress, Washington, DC.

"Leagues in Journalism." *Woman Voter.* Supplement to *Woman Citizen* 18 Nov. 1922: 18–19.

Lister, Ruth. *Citizenship: Feminist Perspectives.* New York: Macmillan, 1998.

Logan, Shirley Wilson, "'To Get an Education and Teach My People': Rhetoric for Social Change." Rhetorical Education in America. The Penn State Conference on Rhetoric and Composition. Nittany Lion Inn, University Park, PA. 5 July 1999.

——. *"We Are Coming": The Persuasive Discourse of Nineteenth-Century Black Women.* Carbondale: Southern Illinois UP, 1999.

Ludington, Katherine. "Citizenship School by Radio on Citizen's Relation to Government, March 4, 1930." ts. Records of the League of Women Voters (U.S.). Library of Congress, Washington, DC.

——. "A New Tool for Democracy, 1928." ts. Records of the League of Women Voters (U.S.). Library of Congress, Washington, DC.

——. "Report of the Radio Committee Chair: Press Release, 30 April." ts. Records of the League of Women Voters (U.S.). Library of Congress, Washington, DC.

——. "Seven Months of the Voters' Service." *Woman Voter's Bulletin* 8.9 (Sept. 1928): 5.

——. "Something New in Broadcasting." ts. n.d. Records of the League of Women Voters (U.S.). Library of Congress, Washington, DC.

Lunsford, Andrea A., ed. *Reclaiming Rhetorica: Women in the Rhetorical Tradition.* Pittsburgh: U of Pittsburgh P, 1995.

Mabie, Janet. "League of Women Voters Helps Citizens Pursue Continuous Self-Education in Politics." *Christian Science Monitor* n.d.: N. pag. Clipping in Belle Sherwin Papers. Schlesinger Library, Radcliffe Institute, Harvard University, Cambridge, MA.

Mailloux, Steven. "Practices, Theories, and Traditions: Further Thoughts on the Disciplinary Identities of English and Communication Studies." *Rhetoric Society Quarterly* 33 (2003): 129–38.

Mansbridge, Jane. "Reconstructing Democracy." *Revisioning the Political: Feminist Reconstructions of Traditional Western Political Theory.* Ed. Nancy J. Hirschmann and Christine Di Stefano. Boulder: Westview, 1996. 117–38.

Marks, Nora, and Ellen Gates Starr. "Two Women's Work, Tenements, and a Name." Bryan, McCree, and Davis 15–20.

Marsh, Beatrice. "A Mock Election." *Woman Voter's Bulletin* 6.41 (Apr. 1926): 1.

Martin, Anne. "Feminists and Future Political Action." *Nation* 18 Feb. 1925: 185–86.

Martin, Theodora Penny. *The Sound of Our Own Voices: Women's Study Clubs.* Boston: Beacon, 1987.

Martyn, Marguerite. "League Grows More Conservative and Less Democratic." *St. Louis Post-Dispatch* 23 Apr. 1926: N. pag.

Massachusetts League of Women Voters. *Election Day.* Boston: Massachusetts LWV, 1921.

———. *Registration Day.* Boston: Massachusetts LWV, 1921.

"Mass Meeting at Poli's Theater." *Report of the First Annual Meeting of the Woman's Peace Party.* Chicago: Woman's Peace Party, 1915. 14–26.

Mattingly, Carol. "Telling Evidence: Rethinking What Counts in Rhetoric." *Rhetoric Society Quarterly* 32 (2002): 99–108.

———, ed. *Water Drops from Women Writers: A Temperance Reader.* Carbondale: Southern Illinois UP, 2001.

———. *Well-Tempered Women: Nineteenth-Century Temperance Rhetoric.* Carbondale: Southern Illinois UP, 1998.

McCulloch, Catherine Waugh. "Political Independence for Voting Women." ts. Catherine Waugh McCulloch Papers (Dillon Collection). Schlesinger Library, Radcliffe Institute, Harvard University, Cambridge, MA.

McGerr, Michael. *The Decline of Popular Politics.* New York: Oxford UP, 1986.

McGuire, A. J. *The Voter's Dream.* Minneapolis: Minnesota LWV, 1926.

Mead, Lucia Ames. "National Secretary's Report." *Yearbook of the Woman's Peace Party, 1916.* Washington, DC: Woman's Peace Party, 1916.

Miller, Christine. "New York." *Pax* Sept.–Oct. 1923: 2.

Miller, Diane Helene. "From One Voice a Chorus: Elizabeth Cady Stanton's 1860 Address to the New York State Legislature." *Women's Studies in Communication* 22 (1999): 152–89.

Miller, Thomas. *The Formation of College English: Rhetoric and Belles Lettres in the British Cultural Provinces.* Pittsburgh: U of Pittsburgh P, 1997.

———. "Reinventing Rhetorical Traditions." *Learning from the Histories of Rhetoric.* Ed. Theresa Enos. Carbondale: Southern Illinois UP, 1993. 26–41.

Miller, Thomas, and Melody Bowdon. "Archivists with an Attitude: A Rhetorical Stance on the Archives of Civic Action." *CCC* 61 (1999): 591–98.

"The Mission of the League." *Woman Voter.* Supplement to *Woman Citizen* 4 Nov. 1922: 19.

"Miss Sherwin Back from Paris Victory." Newspaper clipping dated June 22, 1926. Belle Sherwin Papers. Schlesinger Library, Radcliffe Institute, Harvard University, Cambridge, MA.

Moley, Raymond. *League of Women Voters Efficiency in Government Studies No. 1: The Contribution of the Average Citizen to Local Surveys.* Washington, DC: National LWV, 1923.

Mortensen, Peter. "Going Public." *CCC* 50 (1998): 182–205.

"Mrs. Catt's Address." *Weekly News of the New York LWV.* 4 Apr. 1930: 1–3.

Muncy, Robyn. *Creating a Female Dominion in American Reform, 1880–1935.* New York: Oxford UP, 1991.

"New Kits." *Woman Voter's Bulletin* 8 (Nov. 1928): 5.

New York League of Women Voters. *Handbook for New York Voters.* New York: New York LWV, 1926.

Oliver, Mrs. Robert. "Public Forums." ts. n.d. Records of the League of Women Voters (U.S.). Library of Congress, Washington, DC.

Olson, Lester C. "Liabilities of Language: Audre Lorde Reclaiming Difference." *Quarterly Journal of Speech* 84 (1998): 448–70.

Park, Maud Wood. "After Seven Years of the League of Women Voters." ts. [c. 1927]. Records of the League of Women Voters (U.S.). Library of Congress, Washington, DC.

———. *Organized Women and Their Legislative Program.* Washington, DC: Women's Joint Congressional Committee, 1925.

Peaden, Catherine. "Jane Addams and the Social Rhetoric of Democracy." Clark and Halloran 184–207.

Peck, Mary Gray. *How We Make Them Love Us, or Pitfalls in Politics: A Punch and Judy Show.* New York: New York LWV, 1923.

Peck, Wayne, Linda Flower, and Lorraine Higgins. "Community Literacy." *CCC* 46 (1995): 199–222.

Pethick-Lawrence, Emmeline. "Appendix 1: Opinions of the Congress." WILPF, *Report of the International Congress,* 142–43.

Plastas, Melinda Ann. "'A Band of Noble Women': The WILPF and the Politics and Consciousness of Race in the Women's Peace Movement, 1915–1945." Diss. SUNY-Buffalo, 2001.

Pois, Anne Marie. "The Politics and Process of Organizing for Peace: The United States Section of the Women's International League for Peace and Freedom, 1919–1939." Diss. U of Colorado, 1988.

Pringle, Rosemary, and Sophie Watson. "'Women's Interests' and the Poststructuralist State." *Destabilizing Theory: Contemporary Feminist Debates.* Ed. M. Barrett and A. Phillips. New York: Polity, 1992. 57–73. Rpt. in *Feminism and Politics.* Ed. Anne Phillips. New York: Oxford UP, 1998. 203–23.

Radio Committee of the National League of Women Voters. "Something New in Broadcasting." ts. n.d. Records of the League of Women Voters (U.S.). Library of Congress, Washington, DC.

Ratcliffe, Krista. *Anglo-American Feminist Challenges to the Rhetorical Tradition(s): Virginia Woolf, Mary Daly, Adrienne Rich.* Carbondale: Southern Illinois UP, 1994.

Readings, Bill. Foreword. *Political Writings.* By Jean-François Lyotard. Trans. Bill Readings and Kevin Paul Geiman. Minneapolis: U of Minnesota P, 1993. xiii–xxvi.

Reynolds, Nedra. "Interrupting Our Way to Agency: Feminist Cultural Studies and Composition." Jarratt and Worsham 58–73.

Ricks, Vickie. "'In an Atmosphere of Peril': College Women and Their Writing." Hobbs 59–83.

Riley, Denise. *Am I That Name? Feminism and the Category of "Women" in History.* Minneapolis: U of Minnesota P, 1988.

Ritchie, Joy, and Kate Ronald, eds. *Available Means: An Anthology of Women's Rhetoric.* Pittsburgh: U of Pittsburgh P, 2001.

———. "Riding Long Coattails, Subverting Tradition: The Tricky Business of Feminists Teaching Rhetoric(s)." Jarratt and Worsham 217–38.

Rogow, Faith. *Gone to Another Meeting: The National Council of Jewish Women, 1883–1993*. Tuscaloosa: U of Alabama P, 1993.

Ross, Dorothy. *The Origins of American Social Science*. New York: Cambridge UP, 1991.

Royster, Jacqueline Jones. *Traces of a Stream: Literacy and Social Change among African American Women*. Pittsburgh: U of Pittsburgh P, 2000.

Ruddick, Sara. *Maternal Thinking: Toward a Politics of Peace*. Boston: Beacon, 1989.

Ryan, Mary. *Women in Public: Between Banners and Ballots, 1825–1880*. Baltimore: Johns Hopkins UP, 1990.

Schott, Linda K. *Reconstructing Women's Thoughts: The Women's International League for Peace and Freedom Before World War II*. Stanford: Stanford UP, 1997.

Schudson, Michael. *The Good Citizen: A History of American Civic Life*. Cambridge: Harvard UP, 1998.

Scott, Anne Firor. *Natural Allies: Women's Associations in American History*. Chicago: U of Illinois P, 1991.

Scott, Joan Wallach. "Gender: A Useful Category of Historical Analysis?" *American Historical Review* 91 (1986): 1023–75.

———. *Gender and the Politics of History*. New York: Columbia UP, 1988.

Seigfried, Charlene Haddock. *Feminism and Pragmatism: Reweaving the Social Fabric*. Chicago: U of Chicago P, 1996.

Sherwin, Belle. "Information for the Convenience of Speakers." ts. nd. Records of the League of Women Voters (U.S.). Library of Congress, Washington, DC.

———. "Radio Address, January 3, 1928." ts. Records of the League of Women Voters (U.S.). Library of Congress, Washington, DC.

Silverberg, Helene, ed. *Gender and American Social Science*. Princeton: Princeton UP, 1998.

Simmons, Sue Carter. "Radcliffe Responds to Harvard Rhetoric: 'An Absurdly Stiff Way of Thinking.'" Hobbs 264–92.

Sklar, Katherine Kish. "The 'Quickened Conscience': Women's Volunteerism and the State, 1890–1920." *Report from the Institute for Philosophy and Public Policy* 18 (1998): 27.

Skocpol, Theda. *Protecting Soldiers and Mothers: The Political Origins of Social Policy in the United States*. Cambridge: Harvard UP, 1992.

Smith, Catherine. "Learning Democracy by Writing Across the Curriculum." Unpublished essay, 2003.

Smith, Ethel. "The Women's Industrial Conference." *Woman Citizen* 1 Feb. 1926: 1120+.

Smith, Gertrude D. "Thinking Party Membership." *Newsletter of the Connecticut League of Women Voters* 4.11 (Dec. 1924): 1+.

Smith-Rosenberg, Carroll. *Disorderly Conduct: Visions of Gender in Victorian America*. New York: Knopf, 1985.

Solomon, Martha. "The Role of the Suffrage Press in the Woman's Rights Movement." Solomon, *Voice* 1–16.

———, ed. *A Voice of Their Own: The Woman Suffrage Press, 1840–1910*. Tuscaloosa: U of Alabama P, 1991.

"Speeding Up the Schools." *Woman Citizen* 17 Apr. 1920: 1150+.

Spencer, Anna Garlin. "Educational Aspects of the Army Reorganization Act." *Proceedings of the National Conference of Social Work*. Washington, DC: NCSW, 1923. N.pag.

Spivak, Gayatri. *The Post-Colonial Critic: Interviews, Strategies, Dialogues.* New York: Routledge, 1990.

Sproule, Michael. *Propaganda and Democracy: The American Experience of Media and Mass Persuasion.* New York: Cambridge UP, 1997.

"State Leagues Pushing Citizenship." *Woman Citizen* 1 May 1920: 1213.

Stewart, Charles J., Craig Allen Smith, and Robert E. Denton Jr. *Persuasion and Social Movements.* 3d ed. Prospect Heights: Waveland, 1994.

St. Louis County League of Women Voters. *The Voter's Guide.* St. Louis: St. Louis County LWV, 1928.

Stockwell, Maude C. "Minnesota." *Pax* Sept.–Oct. 1923: 2.

"Store School of Providence, R.I." *Woman Citizen* 26 Mar. 1921: 1109.

"Survey of Citizenship School Work." *Woman Citizen* 29 May 1920: 1339+.

Swanick, Helena M. "International Summer School." WILPF, *Report of the Second International Congress* 187–88.

Thomas, Harriet. "Annual Report of the Executive Secretary." *Report of the First Annual Meeting of the Woman's Peace Party.* Chicago: Woman's Peace Party, 1915. 46–48.

Tickner, J. Ann. *Gendering World Politics.* New York: Columbia UP, 2001.

"Trinity College Offers Citizenship Course to Women." *Woman Voter's Bulletin* 2.3 (Mar. 1922): 1+.

Trolander, Judith. *Professionalism and Social Change.* New York: Columbia UP, 1987.

"Tune-in Tuesdays." *Woman Voter's Bulletin.* 9 (Feb. 1928): 5.

Tylee, Claire M., Elaine Turner, and Agnes Cardinal, eds. *War Plays by Women.* New York: Routledge: 1999.

U.S. Section, Women's International League for Peace and Freedom. "Art Gives Her Strength for Peace." *Pax* Mar. 1923: 5.

——. *Bulletin* Aug. 1920.

——. *Bulletin* Nov. 1921.

——. "A Call to Club Women for Reconstructive Work." Washington, DC: U.S. WILPF 1921.

——. *Education for World Mindedness: Woodbury High School, Woodbury, New Jersey.* Newark: Women's International League for Peace and Freedom, 1926.

——. "Envoys." *Pax* Mar. 1923: 5.

——. "Minutes of the Annual Meeting, 1923, Washington, DC." ts. Records of the Women's International League for Peace and Freedom, U.S. Section. Swarthmore College Peace Collection. Swarthmore, PA.

——. "Pennsylvania." *Pax* Sept.–Oct. 1923: 1.

——. "Plans for 1924–5." *Pax* Oct. 1924: 1.

——. *A Program for Women's Clubs: A Year's Work in Interracial Understanding and International Peace, Prepared Especially for the Clubs in the National Association of Colored Women.* N.p.: WILPF, n.d. Records of the Women's International League for Peace and Freedom, U.S. Section. Swarthmore College Peace Collection. Swarthmore, PA.

——. "Report of Executive Secretary, 1921." Records of the Women's International League for Peace and Freedom, U.S. Section. Swarthmore College Peace Collection. Swarthmore, PA.

——. "Report of the Literature Committee, 1927." Records of the Women's International League for Peace and Freedom, U.S. Section. Swarthmore College Peace Collection. Swarthmore, PA.

——. "Suggestions for Good Will Day, May 18, 1926." Records of the Women's International League for Peace and Freedom, U.S. Section. Swarthmore College Peace Collection. Swarthmore, PA.

——. Telegram to Carter Glass. 20 Dec. 1919. Records of the Women's International League for Peace and Freedom, U.S. Section. Swarthmore College Peace Collection. Swarthmore, PA.

——. "The Work of 1923." *Pax* 7 Sept.–Oct. 1923: 1–4.

Vanderford, Marsha L. "*The Woman's Column:* Extending the Suffrage Community, 1888–1904." Solomon 129–52.

Van Voris, Jacqueline. *Carrie Chapman Catt: A Public Life.* New York: Feminist, 1987.

Virginia League of Women Voters and Elizabeth Jeffries Heinrich. *Ten Practical Lessons for Virginia Citizens.* Richmond: Virginia LWV, 1929.

Voet, Rian. *Feminism and Citizenship.* Thousand Oaks: Sage, 1998.

Volosinov, V. N. *Marxism and the Philosophy of Language.* Trans. Ladislav Matejka and I. R. Titunik. Cambridge: Harvard UP, 1986.

"The Voter, the Press, and the Radio." ts. Belle Sherwin Papers. Schlesinger Library, Radcliffe Institute, Harvard University, Cambridge, MA.

Wales, Julia Grace. "Appendix A: International Plan for Continuous Mediation Without Armistice." Addams, Balch, and Hamilton 167–71.

——. *Continuous Mediation Without Armistice.* Geneva: WILPF International Office, 1916.

Ware, Susan. *Beyond Suffrage: Women and the New Deal.* Cambridge: Harvard UP, 1987.

——. *Holding Their Own: American Women in the 1930s.* Boston: Twayne, 1982.

Washburn, Marion Foster. "A Labor Museum." Bryan, McCree, and Davis 74–83.

"We Are Coming Hundreds of Thousands Strong." *Woman Citizen* 9 Apr. 1921: 1158+.

Weil, Elsie F. "The Hull-House Players." Bryan, McCree, and Davis 92–95.

Weisser, Christian R. *Moving Beyond Academic Discourse: Composition Studies and the Public Sphere.* Carbondale: Southern Illinois UP, 2002.

Welch, Kathleen. "Dialectic/Rhetoric/Writing." *Learning from the Histories of Rhetoric.* Ed. Theresa Enos. Carbondale: Southern Illinois UP, 1993. 133–43.

Wells, Marguerite. *Some Effects of Woman Suffrage.* Washington, DC: National LWV, 1929.

Wells, Susan. "Rogue Cops and Health Care: What Do We Want from Public Writing?" *CCC* 43 (1996): 325–41.

Wentworth, Marion Craig. *War Brides.* Tylee, Turner, and Cardinal 13–26.

Wertheimer, Molly, ed. *Listening to Their Voices: The Rhetorical Activities of Historical Women.* Columbia: U of South Carolina P, 1997.

Wheelock College Course Catalogue, 1931–32. Boston: Wheelock College, 1931.

"Where Citizenship Has Been Taught." *Woman Voter.* Supplement to *Woman Citizen* 4 Nov. 1922: 18+.

White, Martha E. D. *Massachusetts Primer of Citizenship and Government.* Boston: Massachusetts LWV, 1920.

White, True Worthy. *My Lady's Stockings: A Legislative Sketch.* Boston: Massachusetts LWV, 1929.

Whitney, R. M. *Peace at Any Old Price.* New York: Beckwith, 1923.

Wilkinson, Charles A. "A Rhetorical Definition of Movements." *Central States Speech Journal* 27 (1976): 88–94.

Wilson, Francille R. "The Segregated Scholars: Black Labor Historians, 1895–1950." Diss. U of Pennsylvania, 1990.

Woman's Peace Party. *Preamble and Platform Adopted at Washington, January 10, 1915.* Washington, DC: Woman's Peace Party, 1915.

———. *Report of the First Annual Meeting, Washington DC, January 8–10, 1916.* Washington DC: Woman's Peace Party, 1916.

Women's International League for Peace and Freedom. "Minutes of the Annual Meeting, December 1922, the Hague." Records of the Women's International League for Peace and Freedom, U.S. Section. Swarthmore College Peace Collection. Swarthmore, PA.

———. *Proposals as to Policy.* Geneva: International Office WILPF, 1927.

———. *Report of the Fourth Congress of the Women's International League for Peace and Freedom, Washington, May 1 to 7, 1924.* Washington, DC: U.S. Section WILPF, 1924.

———. *Report of the International Congress of Women, the Hague, 1915, April 28–May 1.* London: British Section WILPF, 1915.

———. *Report of the Second International Congress of Women, Zurich, May 12–17, 1919.* London: British Section of the WILPF, 1919.

———. *Report of the Sixth Congress of the Women's International League for Peace and Freedom, Prague, August 24 to 28.* Geneva: International Office WILPF, 1929.

———. *Report of the Third International Congress of Women, Vienna, July 10–17, 1921.* Geneva: International Office WILPF, 1921.

Women's Joint Congressional Committee. "Meeting Minutes, 17 April 1924." ts. Women's Joint Congressional Committee Papers. Library of Congress, Washington, DC.

———. "Press Notice for 1921." ts. Women's Joint Congressional Committee Papers. Library of Congress, Washington, DC.

Woods, Amy. "Minutes of Annual Meeting, U.S. WILPF, Washington, DC. 8 May 1924." Records of the Women's International League for Peace and Freedom, U.S. Section. Swarthmore College Peace Collection. Swarthmore, PA.

———. "Suggestions to State and Local Branches: National Defense Questionnaire." *Pax* Apr. 1923: 8.

Wood-Simons, May. *Wisconsin Citizen's Handbook.* N.p.: Wisconsin LWV, 1920.

Y-Dames of Bethlehem, Pennsylvania. *Volunteer Training Program.* Bethlehem, PA: YWCA, 1956.

Young, Iris Marion. "Polity and Group Difference: A Critique of the Ideal of Universal Citizenship." *Ethics* 8 (1989): 250–74. Rpt. in *Feminism and Politics.* Ed. Anne Phillips. New York: Oxford UP, 1998. 401–29.

Young, Louise M. *In the Public Interest: The League of Women Voters, 1920–1970.* New York: Greenwood, 1989.

"Your Vote and How to Use It." *Woman Citizen* 24 May 1919: 1134.

Index

Abbott, Grace, 77
abolitionist organizations, 16–20, 184n6
academic essay, 173–74
Activist Rhetorics and American Higher Education, 1885–1937 (Kates), 160
Adams, Katherine, 164, 176
Addams, Jane, 4, 35, 38, 42, 57, 64, 186n4, 187n9; on patriotic slogans, 62; on press, 55, 57–58, 189n13; on reason, 46; on rhetorical methods, 187–88n9; settlement house movement and, 29, 31, 32; on traditional diplomatic communication, 65–66; on universities, 170; on Wales Plan, 50; on Wilson, 87–88; on women's clubs practices, 21, 23; *Works: Newer Ideals of Peace,* 87; *Peace and Bread in Time of War,* 65, 90; "Peace and the Press," 178; *Twenty Years at Hull House,* 32
advocacy, lessons in, 145–49
aesthetics, 72–73, 77–78
African Americans, 21, 22, 24, 109, 184n6, 185n13
Allen, Florence, 29
Ames, Marie, 144
Andersen, Kristi, 93
Andrews, Fannie Fern, 79
Anti-Slavery Convention of American Women, 19
argumentative briefs, 139
Armistice Week, 78
art, as argument for peace, 72–78, 81
articulatory practices, 165
Atwood, Charlotte, 71
audience, 6, 9, 14, 43, 138–39, 149, 175
authority, 26–27, 44–45
Aylesworth, M. H., 114

Bagley, Grace, 149–50, 152–53
Baker, Paula, 8, 34
Bakhtin, Mikhail, 12–13, 178
Balch, Emily Greene, 35, 44, 57, 71, 176
Ballot Box Review (LWV), 108–9
Bazerman, Charles, 68
Beecher, Henry Ward, 139
benevolent societies, 15, 16–20, 41
Berlin, James, 77, 162

Biesecker, Barbara, 6
Bizzell, Patricia, 2
Black, Naomi, 33–34, 160, 191–92n5
Blair, Emily Newell, 94
Blatch, Harriet Stanton, 85
Bourdieu, Pierre, 77
Bowdon, Melody, 162
Brandegee, Frank, 117
Breckenridge, Sophonisba, 77
Breines, Ingeborg, 166–67
Brereton, John, 6
Brewer, Minnie, 111
Brodkey, Linda, 10
Brooks, Jane, 94
Brumbaugh, Sara, 192n1
Bulkley, Mary, 129
Burke, Kenneth, 27

Campbell, Jo Ann, 2
Campbell, Karlyn Kohrs, 18
candidates: LWV stance on, 117–18, 158; questionnaires for, 111–12, 147–48, 192n3; women as, 125
capitalism, 88, 90
caring labor, 37–38
Cary, Mary Ann Shad, 184n6
Cathcart, Robert, 11
Catt, Carrie Chapman, 4, 25, 34, 132, 139, 157; address to LWV, 1920, 97–102; critique of partisan methods, 91, 94, 96, 98, 101; literacy crisis address, 119, 120–23, 192n6; male membership in LWV and, 125–26
Chicago School of Civics and Philanthropy, 186n14
Child Labor Amendment, 111, 153, 156
Child Labor Morality Play (Washington LWV), 153
church, 24, 141, 184–85n8
citizenship, 3, 8, 117; decision-making positions and, 166–67; feminist reinterpretations of, 167–68; gendered male, 46, 167; linked to status of husband, 152–53; regional understandings of, 7–8
Citizenship Day, 132–33
citizenship schools, 25, 132–33, 141–42

Pethick-Lawrence, Emmeline, 40, 53, 188n12
physical education, 81–82
Pois, Anne Marie, 89
political influence, 15, 17–18, 32, 63–64, 134; art as, 72–74; legislative testimony, 152–53. *See also individual women's organizations;* public opinion
political literacy, 9, 14; as interdisciplinary concern, 176–77; promotion of, 127–31; texts, 142–49. *See also* literacy; literate practices
political participation, 3; accessible language and, 112–14, 144; decision-making positions, 93, 166–67; in local politics, 143; post-Nineteenth Amendment, 33–34; women candidates, 125
political sphere, 17–18
power relations, 8, 42, 94, 191–92n5; counterpublics and, 11–12; in international relations, 86–88
present, understanding of, 166–68
press, 19, 109; bias of, 26, 55–59, 97, 106, 184n7; critical analysis of, 107–8, 175; international relations and, 55–62; pacifism and, 55–57; peace press service, 70–71; propaganda of, 139–40, 189n14; public opinion and, 58–59, 106–7; role in prolonging hostilities, 58–59; stereotypes of women, 108–9; war propaganda, 57–62, 69–70, 189n14; WILPF and, 84, 88–89
pre-suffrage women's organizations, 15–16; benevolent societies and abolitionist organizations, 16–20; mission societies and temperance work, 24–27; settlement house movement, 29–33; suffrage organizations, 27–29; women's clubs, 20–23. *See also individual organizations;* women's organizations
Pringle, Rosemary, 164
professional values, elite, 168–69
professional women, 30, 32
propaganda, 139–40; analysis, 59–60; war, 57–62, 69–70, 189n14
prostitution, 17, 18
Provincial Freeman, 184n6
Public and Its Problems, The (Dewey), 108
publications: of abolitionist organizations, 20; African American, 109, 184n6; circulation of, 21–22; collections of pacifist reading material, 71–72; educational, 68–72; League of Women Voters, 108–14; national, state, and local, 110–11; reader involvement in, 110; settlement house movement, 32; suffrage organizations, 28–29; voter turn-out and, 145–46; WCTU, 26; women's clubs, 20, 21–22, 184n7. *See also* genre
public forums, 147
publicity, 18, 52; genres of, 68–69; lessons in, 134, 145–49; limitations of, 86–90
public opinion, 15, 17, 23, 32, 46; press and, 58–59, 106–7; rhetorical strategies and, 63–64; Wales Plan and, 52–53; weak publics and, 86, 156. *See also* political influence
public opinion formation: benevolent and abolitionist organizations, 17; women's clubs and, 23

questionnaires, 111–12, 147–48, 192n3
"Question of the Questionnaire, The" (Edwards), 148

Rachel (Grimes), 31–32
racism, in suffrage movement, 40–41, 185n9
Radcliffe College, 133–34, 136
radio broadcasts, 114–16, 118, 141–42, 191n4
Ragaz, Clara, 55
Rankin, Jeanette, 66
Readings, Bill, 165
reason/rationality, 46, 49, 54
Registration Day (Massachusetts LWV), 150
Republican Party, Women's Division, 124
research: pre-suffrage era, 18–19, 22, 23; settlement house movement and, 32–33; statistical studies, 32–33, 185n14
Reynolds, Nedra, 169
rhetor, character of, 43
rhetorical education, 9, 192n2; alternative classrooms, 140–42; citizenship schools, 25, 132–33, 141–42; in critical media analysis, 107–8; dramatic productions, 149–54; higher education for citizenship, 135–40; institutes of government and politics, 133–35; institutions for peace, 83–85; in international relations, 78–85; language use, 79–80, 112–13, 144; meeting techniques, 25–27; nonpartisan, as political strategy, 154–61; pedagogical implications, 168–79; political literacy texts, 142–49; publicity and advocacy, 145–49; question-and-answer format, 145; roundtable discussions, 134, 135; of speakers, 84–85, 134, 137–39; summer schools, 25, 83–85. *See also* education; League of Women Voters
rhetorical sequencing, 10
rhetorical space, 162–63
rhetorical strategies, 12, 14; domestic sphere as,

Voter's Guide (St. Louis LWV), 143
voter's prayer, 131
voters' schools, 132–33
Voters' Service (radio programming), 114–16, 118, 191n4
voter turnout, 130; 1920s, 33–34; publications, 145–46
Voting Machine, The (Grand Rapids LWV), 150, 192n4

Wadsworth, James W., 117
Wales, Julia Grace, 48–55, 86, 175
Wales Plan, 48–55, 66, 86, 87, 188n11; continuous mediation, 51–53; as counter to militarism, 52–53; discursive mechanisms, 49–50
war, 37, 122; amendment proposal, 67; propaganda, 57–62, 69–70, 189n14
War Brides (Wentworth), 74–78
Waterworth, Edith, 39
Watson, Sophie, 164
wave model, 3, 4, 7
weak publics, 86, 156
"We Are Coming Hundreds of Thousands Strong" (LWV), 109–10
Weeks, John, 57
Weisser, Christian, 6, 169
Welch, Kathleen, 168–69
Wells, Marguerite, 129
Wells, Susan, 138, 175
Wentworth, Marion Craig, 74–78
Wharton, Marian, 13
Whitney, R. M., 57
Willard, Francis, 24–25
Willing, Jennie, 24
Wilson, Francille, 185n13
Wilson, Woodrow, 79, 87–88, 188n12, 189n14, 191n7
Wisconsin Citizens' Handbook, 143
Woman Citizen, 28, 109–10, 118–19, 132, 159
Woman's Journal, 28
Woman's Peace Party (WPP), 73, 186n1
Woman Voter, 110, 148
Women's Bureau, 159
Women's Christian Temperance Union (WCTU), 24, 26, 187n8
women's clubs, 20–23, 69–70, 184n7
Women's International League for Peace and Freedom (WILPF), 4, 8, 183n2, 187n7; annual meetings, 85; archival materials, 9–11; art as argument for peace, 72–78; "A Call to Club Women for Reconstructive Work,"

69; challenges to wartime propaganda, 57–62; class issues, 41–42; critique of traditional diplomacy, 48–49; curricula proposals, 80–81; discussion method, 49–50, 54; educational institutions for peace, 83–85; educational programs, 25, 78–85; educational publications, 68–72; language differences and, 46–47; Law-Not-War day, 69; League of Women Voters and, 69; legislative activity, 31, 66; libraries and, 71–72; limitations of, 86–90; literature committee, 71; military training, view of, 82–83; as model for League of Nations, 54–55; national boundaries, view of, 44, 47; New International Order proposal, 88–89; patriotic symbols, critique of, 60–62, 78; peaceful rhetorical model, 45–46; peace press service, 70–71; "Plans for 1924–5," 67; power relations and, 86–88; predecessors, 25, 27–28, 73; press and, 84, 88–89; propaganda analysis, 59–60; strategic positioning, 65–67; structure, 27–28, 69; summer schools, 25, 83–85; systemic change as goal of, 88–89; Wales Plan, 48–55, 175; "What Is This League?", 68; women's clubs and, 69–70. *See also* international relations
Women's Joint Congressional Committee (WJCC), 104
women's organizations, 4, 6, 8, 183n1; auxiliaries, 27; disagreements over policy questions, 158–59, 165; elitist attitudes, 163–64; gender issues, 164–65; networks, 69, 104, 109–10, 184n2; research by, 18–19, 22–23, 32–33, 185n14; text circulation, 21–22. *See also* League of Women Voters; pre-suffrage women's organizations; Women's International League for Peace and Freedom
Women's Trade Union League, 31
Woods, Amy, 56
World Anti-Slavery Convention, 19
World War I context, 48, 53. *See also* Wales Plan
writing about, for, and with the community, 171–72

Y-Dames club, 1, 2
You Are Democracy (Iowa LWV), 142, 143
Youmans, Mrs. Henry, 112
Young, Iris Marion, 163–64
Young, Louise M., 17, 19–20, 25, 91, 125–26
"Your Vote and How to Use It" (LWV), 113

Wendy B. Sharer is an assistant professor of English at East Carolina University, where she also serves as Associate Director of Composition. She received the 2002 James Berlin Memorial Outstanding Dissertation Award from the Conference on College Composition and Communication. Her work has appeared in *Rhetoric Review* and *Rhetoric Society Quarterly.*

Studies in Rhetorics and Feminisms

S tudies in Rhetorics and Feminisms seeks to address the interdisciplinarity that rhetorics and feminisms represent. Rhetorical and feminist scholars want to connect rhetorical inquiry with contemporary academic and social concerns, exploring rhetoric's relevance to current issues of opportunity and diversity. This interdisciplinarity has already begun to transform the rhetorical tradition as we have known it (upper-class, agonistic, public, and male) into regendered, inclusionary rhetorics (democratic, dialogic, collaborative, cultural, and private). Our intellectual advancements depend on such ongoing transformation.

Rhetoric, whether ancient, contemporary, or futuristic, always inscribes the relation of language and power at a particular moment, indicating who may speak, who may listen, and what can be said. The only way we can displace the traditional rhetoric of masculine-only, public performance is to replace it with rhetorics that are recognized as being better suited to our present needs. We must understand more fully the rhetorics of the non-Western tradition, of women, of a variety of cultural and ethnic groups. Therefore, Studies in Rhetorics and Feminisms espouses a theoretical position of openness and expansion, a place for rhetorics to grow and thrive in a symbiotic relationship with all that feminisms have to offer, particularly when these two fields intersect with philosophical, sociological, religious, psychological, pedagogical, and literary issues.

The series seeks scholarly works that both examine and extend rhetoric, works that span the sexes, disciplines, cultures, ethnicities, and sociocultural practices as they intersect with the rhetorical tradition. After all, the recent resurgence of rhetorical studies has not so much been a discovery of new rhetorics; it has been more a recognition of existing rhetorical activities and practices, of our newfound ability and willingness to listen to previously untold stories.

The series editors seek both high-quality traditional and cutting-edge scholarly work that extends the significant relationship between rhetoric and feminism within various genres, cultural contexts, historical periods, methodologies, theoretical positions, and methods of delivery (e.g., film and hypertext to elocution and preaching).

Queries and submissions:
Professor Cheryl Glenn, Editor
   E-mail: cjg6@psu.edu
Professor Shirley Wilson Logan, Editor
   E-mail: Shirley_W_Logan@umail.umd.edu

Studies in Rhetorics and Feminisms
Department of English
142 South Burrowes Bldg
Penn State University
University Park, PA 16802-6200